Better Homes and Gardens®

Quick & Easy

Comfort Cooking

BETTER HOMES AND GARDENS® BOOKS

DES MOINES, IOWA

Better Homes and Gardens® Books
An imprint of Meredith® Books

Quick & Easy Comfort Cooking
Editor: Chuck Smothermon
Senior Associate Design Director: John Eric Seid
Copy Chief: Terri Fredrickson
Copy and Production Editor: Victoria Forlini
Editorial Operations Manager: Karen Schirm
Managers, Book Production: Pam Kvitne, Marjorie J. Schenkelberg
Contributing Copy Editor: Donna Segal
Contributing Proofreaders: Maria Duryée, Susan J. Kling, Elise Marton
Indexer: Elizabeth Parson
Electronic Production Coordinator: Paula Forest
Editorial and Design Assistants: Karen McFadden, Mary Lee Gavin
Test Kitchen Director: Lynn Blanchard
Test Kitchen Product Supervisor: Marilyn Cornelius

Meredith® Books
Publisher and Editor in Chief: James D. Blume
Design Director: Matt Strelecki
Managing Editor: Gregory H. Kayko
Executive Editor, Food and Crafts: Jennifer Dorland Darling

Director, Operations: George A. Susral
Director, Production: Douglas M. Johnston

Vice President and General Manager: Douglas J. Guendel

Better Homes and Gardens® Magazine
Editor in Chief: Karol DeWulf Nickell
Deputy Editor, Food and Entertaining: Nancy Hopkins

Meredith Publishing Group
President, Publishing Group: Stephen M. Lacy
Vice President-Publishing Director: Bob Mate

Meredith Corporation
Chairman and Chief Executive Officer: William T. Kerr

Chairman of the Executive Committee: E. T. Meredith III

All of us at Better Homes and Gardens® Books are dedicated to providing you with the information and ideas you need to create delicious foods. We welcome your comments and suggestions. Write to us at: Better Homes and Gardens Books, Cookbook Editorial Department, 1716 Locust St., Des Moines, IA 50309-3023.

If you would like to purchase any of our cooking, crafts, gardening, home improvement, or home decorating and design books, check wherever quality books are sold. Or visit us at: bhgbooks.com

For more recipes, visit our Recipe Center at bhg.com/bhg/recipe

Pictured on front cover: Maryland Fried Chicken (see recipe, page 140)

TABLE OF CONTENTS

INTRODUCTION

Easy, comforting foods your friends and family will love

When you sit down to plan meals, aren't easy, comforting foods what you're usually looking for? Something simple, yet satisfying—recipes that nourish the body, warm the soul, and make everyone remember why gathering around the table is such a meaningful part of the day.

Can a recipe do all that? Yes, when it comes from the recipe files of Better Homes and Gardens® Books, the experts in great home cooking. For more than 70 years, we've been helping families bring wholesome, comforting recipes to the table, and collected here are more than 220 of our all-time-best family-pleasing favorites.

You're sure to find the perfect recipe for any occasion—whether you're in the mood for such home-style American classics as Chicken 'n' Dumpling Soup, Oven-Barbecued Ribs, and Flaky Biscuits or something globally inspired, such as Greek-Style Chicken or Pork and Green Chile Bake.

Sound good? They are good, because each and every recipe has been tested to perfection in the Better Homes and Gardens® Test Kitchen. If a recipe doesn't yield delicious, high-quality results, it's not in this book.

Go ahead! Dig into this collection of comfort-food favorites.
Many are sure to become the most often requested recipes you make.

Chapter One
Starters

Asparagus with Raspberry-Dijon Dipping Sauce, p. 14

Olive Cheese Ball

This time-tested combo of cream cheese, blue cheese, ripe olives, and walnuts still makes a terrific nibble for modern-day parties.

PREP: 35 minutes CHILL: 4 to 24 hours STAND: 15 minutes MAKES: 48 (1 tablespoon) servings

1   8-ounce package cream cheese

2   cups crumbled blue cheese (8 ounces)

¼   cup butter or margarine

1   4½-ounce can chopped pitted ripe olives, well drained

2   tablespoons snipped fresh chives

⅓   cup coarsely chopped walnuts or almonds, toasted

Fresh parsley (optional)

Assorted crackers or apple slices

1 In a large mixing bowl place cream cheese, blue cheese, and butter; let stand until room temperature. Beat cheeses and butter with electric mixer on low speed until smooth. Stir in olives and chives. Cover and chill for at least 4 hours or up to 24 hours.

2 Shape mixture into a ball; cover and chill until serving time. Before serving, roll in walnuts. Let stand for 15 minutes. If desired, garnish with parsley. Serve with assorted crackers or apple slices.

NUTRITION FACTS PER SERVING: 50 cal., 5 g total fat (3 g sat. fat), 11 mg chol., 106 mg sodium, 1 g carbo., 0 g fiber, 2 g pro. DAILY VALUES: 3% calcium, 1% iron

CHEESE BALLS CATCH ON Nobody knows exactly when the first cheese ball appeared at a party, but miniature morsels of cheese have been part of ladies' luncheons since the turn of the 20th century. In the 1940s, bite-size balls of cheese coated in nuts, parsley, or chipped beef were common fare at cocktail parties. By the 1950s, the full-size version was popular. Early cheese balls often were based on processed cheese spreads spiked with Worcestershire sauce or bottled hot pepper sauce and rolled in pecans or walnuts for crunch. As the decade passed, cooks varied the cheese ball theme and came up with unique combinations, such as Olive Cheese Ball, above.

Curry-Chutney Dip

A little bit nutty, a little bit spicy, this Indian-inspired recipe journeys off the well-beaten chip-and-dip path. Choose a chutney to suit your taste—some are sweeter, others are hot.

PREP: 10 minutes CHILL: 2 to 48 hours MAKES: 10 (2 tablespoon) servings

¼   cup mango chutney

½   of an 8-ounce package reduced-fat cream cheese (Neufchâtel), softened

⅔   cup light dairy sour cream

1   teaspoon curry powder

¼   cup chopped dry roasted or honey roasted cashews

Crisp breadsticks and/or assorted vegetable dippers

1 Snip any large pieces of fruit in chutney; set aside. In a small bowl stir together cream cheese, sour cream, and curry powder. Stir in chutney. Cover and chill for 2 to 48 hours.

2 Before serving, sprinkle dip with cashews. Serve with breadsticks and/or vegetable dippers.

NUTRITION FACTS PER SERVING: 92 cal., 6 g total fat (3 g sat. fat), 14 mg chol., 84 mg sodium, 8 g carbo., 0 g fiber, 3 g pro. DAILY VALUES: 10% vit. A, 5% vit. C, 4% calcium, 2% iron

CHOOSE A CHUTNEY A condiment for Indian curries, sweet-tart chutney (Hindi for strongly spiced) also sparks simple poultry dishes, salads, and sandwiches. Pick a favorite among these rich jams concocted of chopped fruit, vegetables, and spices enlivened with hot peppers, fresh ginger, or vinegar, and keep a jar on hand for a quick mealtime fix.

Dried Tomato and White Bean Dip

If there's extra, spread this hummus-style dip on a toasted bagel.

START TO FINISH: 25 minutes OVEN: 350° MAKES: 16 appetizer servings

2	15-ounce cans white kidney (cannellini) beans, rinsed and drained	1	tablespoon snipped fresh oregano or ½ teaspoon dried oregano, crushed
4	teaspoons lemon juice	½	teaspoon ground cumin
1	cup sliced green onions (8)	¼	teaspoon salt
3	cloves garlic, minced		Several dashes bottled hot pepper sauce
1	tablespoon olive oil	1	recipe Pita Crisps
¼	cup oil-packed dried tomatoes, drained and finely chopped		

1 In a food processor bowl or blender container combine half of the drained beans and the lemon juice. Cover and process or blend until nearly smooth; set aside.

2 In a large skillet cook green onions and garlic in oil just until tender. Stir in processed beans, whole beans, dried tomatoes, oregano, cumin, salt, and hot pepper sauce. Heat through. Serve warm with Pita Crisps.

Pita Crisps: Split 3 large pita bread rounds in half horizontally, separating into two rounds. Cut each round into eight wedges (48 total). Stir together 2 tablespoons olive oil, ½ teaspoon chili powder, and ¼ teaspoon garlic salt. Brush mixture lightly over rough surfaces of pita wedges. Arrange wedges, brushed side up, in a single layer on ungreased baking sheets. Bake in a 350° oven for 10 to 12 minutes or until crisp; cool. Store in an airtight container at room temperature for up to 1 week.

NUTRITION FACTS PER SERVING: 90 cal., 3 g total fat (0 g sat. fat), 0 mg chol., 214 mg sodium, 14 g carbo., 3 g fiber, 4 g pro. DAILY VALUES: 6% vit. C, 2% calcium, 7% iron

Fresh Onion Dip

Go wild with dippers! Start with chips: potato, sweet potato, beet, and corn; pile on home-baked tortilla chips; add vegetables, such as wax beans, daikon, and carrots.

PREP: 20 minutes CHILL: 1 to 24 hours MAKES: 12 (2 tablespoon) servings

1½	cups chopped sweet onion (such as Vidalia or Walla Walla)
2	tablespoons butter or margarine
1	8-ounce carton dairy sour cream
¼	teaspoon salt
¼	teaspoon coarsely ground black pepper

⅛	teaspoon ground red pepper
4	teaspoons snipped fresh chives
	Milk (optional)
	Dippers such as assorted chips and/or vegetables

1 In a medium skillet cook onion in hot butter until tender but not brown. Cool.

2 In a blender container or food processor bowl combine cooked onion, sour cream, salt, black pepper, and red pepper. Cover and blend or process until nearly smooth. Transfer to a small bowl. Stir in chives. Cover and chill for 1 to 24 hours.

3 Before serving, stir in milk, a teaspoon at a time, if necessary, to make a dipping consistency. Serve with a variety of dippers.

NUTRITION FACTS PER SERVING: 66 cal., 6 g total fat (4 g sat. fat), 14 mg chol., 80 mg sodium, 3 g carbo., 0 g fiber, 1 g pro. DAILY VALUES: 2% vit. C, 3% calcium

Hot Artichoke and Roasted Pepper Dip

Leftovers make an excellent sandwich filling for pita bread.

PREP: 15 minutes BAKE: 20 minutes OVEN: 350° MAKES: 26 (2 tablespoon) servings

1 medium leek, quartered lengthwise and thinly sliced, or ⅓ cup sliced green onions

2 teaspoons butter or margarine

1 14-ounce can artichoke hearts, drained and coarsely chopped

1 cup grated Parmesan cheese

1 7-ounce jar roasted red sweet peppers, drained and coarsely chopped

1 cup mayonnaise, salad dressing, or light mayonnaise dressing*

⅛ teaspoon ground black pepper

1 tablespoon snipped fresh parsley

2 tablespoons grated Parmesan cheese or Romano cheese

Assorted vegetable dippers, flatbreads, or crackers

1 In a medium skillet cook sliced leek in hot butter until tender but not brown. Remove from heat. Stir in artichoke hearts, the 1 cup Parmesan cheese, roasted sweet peppers, mayonnaise, and black pepper. Transfer mixture to an 8-inch quiche dish or 9-inch pie plate, spreading evenly. Sprinkle with parsley and the 2 tablespoons Parmesan cheese.

2 Bake, uncovered, in a 350° oven about 20 minutes or until heated through. Or microwave on 75% power (medium-high) power for 6 to 8 minutes or until heated through, turning dish halfway through cooking time. Serve with assorted cut-up raw vegetables, flatbreads, or crackers.

NUTRITION FACTS PER SERVING: 91 cal., 8 g total fat (2 g sat. fat), 9 mg chol., 182 mg sodium, 2 g carbo., 1 g fiber, 2 g pro. DAILY VALUES: 24% vit. C, 3% calcium, 3% iron

*__Note:__ Do not make with fat-free mayonnaise dressing or salad dressing. Dip will not set.

TO MAKE AHEAD: Prepare dip as directed; do not bake. Cover and chill for up to 24 hours. Bake as directed.

Spinach and Chicken Spread

Anticipating a flurried countdown to party time? Stay collected with this make-ahead treat. It needs to chill at least 6 hours in advance—one more recipe you can check off your to-do list early.

PREP: 25 minutes CHILL: 6 hours MAKES: 20 appetizer servings

1	8-ounce package reduced-fat cream cheese (Neufchâtel), softened
1/4	teaspoon lemon-pepper seasoning
1/4	teaspoon dried tarragon or thyme, crushed
1/2	of a 10-ounce package frozen chopped spinach, thawed and well drained
1/4	cup chopped onion
2	tablespoons finely chopped roasted red sweet pepper

1/2 of a 9-ounce package frozen chopped, cooked chicken breast, thawed (1 cup)

1 5-ounce container semisoft cheese with garlic and herbs

Flowering kale (optional)

Roasted red sweet pepper strips (optional)

Assorted bread or crackers

1 Line bottom and sides of a 3-cup mold, bowl, or a 7¹/₂×3¹/₂×2¹/₂-inch loaf pan with clear plastic wrap; set aside. In a medium bowl stir together cream cheese, lemon-pepper seasoning, and tarragon. Stir in spinach, onion, and the 2 tablespoons roasted red sweet pepper. Spread half of the mixture evenly in the bottom of the prepared mold.

2 In a food processor bowl combine chicken and semisoft cheese. Cover and process until smooth. Spread chicken-cheese mixture over spinach mixture in the mold. Drop remaining spinach mixture by spoonfuls onto the chicken-cheese mixture; spread. Cover and chill for at least 6 hours.

3 To serve, invert mold onto a serving platter; remove plastic wrap. If desired, garnish with flowering kale and roasted red pepper strips. Serve with assorted bread or crackers.

NUTRITION FACTS PER SERVING: 134 cal., 6 g total fat (3 g sat. fat), 11 mg chol., 284 mg sodium, 13 g carbo., 1 g fiber, 5 g pro. DAILY VALUES: 23% vit. A, 5% vit. C, 3% calcium, 4% iron

Guacamole

For optimum results, select avocados with shiny skins that yield slightly to pressure; unripe ones require three to four days to ripen in a cool, dry, shaded area of the kitchen.

START TO FINISH: 15 minutes MAKES: About 11 (2 tablespoon) servings

2	medium avocados, seeded, peeled, and cut up	1	to 2 tablespoons chopped fresh jalapeño or serrano chile peppers*
1	tablespoon lime juice	¼	teaspoon salt
½	cup chopped purchased roasted red sweet peppers	¼	teaspoon ground black pepper
6	tablespoons finely chopped green onions (3)	⅛	teaspoon ground red pepper
			Tortilla chips

1 In a medium bowl combine avocados and lime juice. Using a potato masher, coarsely mash avocado mixture (mixture should be slightly lumpy).

2 Stir roasted sweet peppers, green onions, chile peppers, salt, black pepper, and ground red pepper into avocado mixture. Cover and chill until serving time. Serve with tortilla chips.

***Note:** Because chile peppers contain volatile oils that can burn your skin and eyes, avoid direct contact with them as much as possible. When working with chile peppers, wear plastic or rubber gloves. If your bare hands do touch the chile peppers, wash your hands well with soap and water.

NUTRITION FACTS PER SERVING: 58 cal., 5 g total fat (1 g sat. fat), 0 mg chol., 57 mg sodium, 3 g carbo., 2 g fiber, 1 g pro. DAILY VALUES: 37% vit. C, 1% calcium, 3% iron

TIMESAVING TIPS Choose a few star recipes, then round out your food table with purchased items, such as trays of cheeses, meats, fresh vegetable crudités, and fruit pieces. Accompany these with baskets of crackers, baguette slices, and chips.

❶ Plan your menu and grocery list one to two weeks in advance and include make-ahead recipes.

❷ If you love to entertain but have no time to cook, consider hiring a caterer or a friend who cooks to help with food preparations. Often caterers will let you supply the recipes, if desired.

❸ Hire someone to help pour beverages and keep food trays replenished so you can enjoy your own party.

Tropical Fruit-Black Bean Salsa

Add the kiwifruit just before serving so the salsa doesn't become too juicy.

PREP: 10 minutes CHILL: 4 to 24 hours MAKES: 28 (2 tablespoon) servings

1 cup rinsed and drained canned black beans

1 small papaya or mango, peeled, seeded, and chopped (¾ cup)

½ cup finely chopped fresh pineapple or one 8-ounce can crushed pineapple (juice-packed), drained

1 medium orange, peeled, sectioned, and finely chopped (⅓ cup)

¼ cup thinly sliced green onions (2)

¼ cup finely chopped red sweet pepper

2 tablespoons snipped fresh cilantro

1 tablespoon lime juice or lemon juice

3 small kiwifruit, peeled and finely chopped (⅔ cup)

Tortilla chips

1 In a medium bowl stir together black beans, papaya, pineapple, orange, green onions, sweet pepper, cilantro, and lime juice. Cover and chill for 4 to 24 hours.

2 Just before serving, stir kiwifruit into salsa. Using a slotted spoon, transfer salsa to a serving dish. Serve with tortilla chips.

NUTRITION FACTS PER SERVING: 18 cal., 0 g total fat (0 g sat. fat), 0 mg chol., 34 mg sodium, 4 g carbo., 1 g fiber, 1 g pro. DAILY VALUES: 25% vit. C, 1% calcium, 1% iron

Asparagus with Raspberry-Dijon Dipping Sauce

*Asparagus stars as a fresh and light starter with a fruity dipping sauce.
If you like, prepare the sauce ahead and refrigerate it for up to 4 hours before serving.
(See photo, page 5.)*

START TO FINISH: 25 minutes MAKES: 12 appetizer servings

1	pound medium asparagus spears		Dash salt
8	ounces sugar snap peas	¼	cup cooking oil
3	tablespoons raspberry vinegar	¼	cup olive oil
1	tablespoon honey mustard		Shredded red cabbage (optional)
¼	teaspoon freshly ground black pepper		Fresh raspberries (optional)

1 Snap off and discard woody bases from asparagus. If desired, remove tips and strings from sugar snap peas. In a large, deep skillet bring 1 inch of salted water to boiling. Add asparagus; reduce heat. Simmer, uncovered, about 4 minutes or until crisp-tender. Using tongs, transfer asparagus to a large bowl of ice water to cool quickly. Add sugar snap peas to simmering water and cook about 2 minutes or until crisp-tender. Drain and transfer to a bowl of ice water.

2 Meanwhile, for dipping sauce, in a blender container or food processor bowl combine vinegar, honey mustard, pepper, and salt. Cover and blend or process until combined. With the blender or processor running, slowly add the oils in a thin, steady stream. Continue blending or processing until mixture is thick.

3 If desired, line a serving platter with shredded red cabbage. Arrange asparagus and sugar snap peas on top of the cabbage. Serve with dipping sauce. If desired, garnish with raspberries.

NUTRITION FACTS PER SERVING: 96 cal., 9 g total fat (1 g sat. fat), 0 mg chol., 14 mg sodium, 3 g carbo., 1 g fiber, 1 g pro. DAILY VALUES: 26% vit. C, 1% calcium, 3% iron

DON'T CONFUSE THE PEAS, PLEASE! Sugar snap peas (also called sugar peas) are sometimes confused with snow peas. While both have edible pods, the peas inside the snow pea are tiny, and the pod is almost translucent. The peas inside the sugar snap pea are larger. Each legume yields different flavors and textures.

Monterey Jack fondue

Monterey Jack cheese was hip in the '60s; fondue, hot in the '70s.
Together they're forever cool. Dip in!

START TO FINISH: 15 minutes MAKES: 6 (1/4 cup) servings

3	tablespoons butter or margarine	1	5-ounce can (2/3 cup) evaporated milk
3	tablespoons all-purpose flour	1/2	cup chicken broth
1	teaspoon dried minced onion	1 1/4	cups shredded Monterey Jack cheese (5 ounces)
1/8	teaspoon garlic powder		French bread cubes
1/8	teaspoon ground red pepper		

1 In a small saucepan melt butter. Stir in flour, onion, garlic powder, and red pepper. Stir in evaporated milk and chicken broth all at once. Cook and stir over medium heat until thickened and bubbly. Gradually add Monterey Jack cheese, stirring until cheese is melted.

2 Transfer cheese mixture to a fondue pot and place over fondue burner. Serve with bread cubes. (Add additional chicken broth, as necessary, for desired consistency.)

NUTRITION FACTS PER SERVING: 249 cal., 16 g total fat (9 g sat. fat), 43 mg chol., 418 mg sodium, 18 g carbo., 0 g fiber, 9 g pro. DAILY VALUES: 1% vit. C, 24% calcium, 2% iron

Greek-Style Party Pizzas

Be adventurous and serve these feta-and-hummus-topped
mini pizzas at your next gathering.

PREP: 15 minutes BAKE: 8 minutes OVEN: 450° MAKES: 16 appetizer servings

4	large pita bread rounds
1	7-ounce container hummus
1	medium tomato, seeded and chopped
½	of a 6-ounce jar marinated artichoke hearts, drained and chopped
½	cup crumbled feta cheese (2 ounces)

½	cup shredded mozzarella cheese (2 ounces)
2	teaspoons olive oil (optional)
1	teaspoon sesame seeds (optional)
8	pitted ripe olives, quartered (optional)
	Fresh oregano leaves (optional)

1 On a large baking sheet place pita rounds. Spread each round with one-fourth of the hummus, leaving a 1-inch border. Sprinkle each with one-fourth of the tomato, artichoke hearts, feta cheese, and mozzarella cheese. If desired, drizzle with olive oil and sprinkle with sesame seeds.

2 Bake in a 450° oven for 8 to 10 minutes or until cheese has melted and edges are light brown. If desired, top with olives and oregano. Cut into quarters.

NUTRITION FACTS PER SERVING: 87 cal., 3 g total fat (1 g sat. fat), 5 mg chol., 184 mg sodium, 12 g carbo., 0 g fiber, 3 g pro. DAILY VALUES: 6% vit. C, 5% calcium, 4% iron

OH, THOSE OLIVES! If your olives come only from a can or speared from the depths of a martini, you're missing a world of good eating. Olives grow on six continents and are cured and dressed in countless ways. Specialty food stores and even some supermarkets now offer them in an exciting variety—fat, slender, round, tapered, black, brown, green, purple, smooth, wrinkled, salt-cured, brine-cured, oil-cured—in bulk and prepackaged. Ask for suggestions and for samples, if possible. It's the best way to choose.

Quick-fix Focaccia Wedges

This 10-minute wonder will have guests clamoring for more. Allow four to five wedges per person if serving dinner shortly after the appetizer course; six to seven if dining later.

PREP: 15 minutes BAKE: 10 minutes OVEN: 450° MAKES: 16 appetizers

3	medium onions, thinly sliced	1	teaspoon dried thyme, crushed
¼	teaspoon coarsely ground black pepper	4	6-inch Italian bread shells (such as Boboli brand)
1	tablespoon olive oil		Red sweet pepper (optional)
¾	cup rinsed and drained canned small white beans		Fresh marjoram (optional)
½	cup dry white wine or reduced-sodium chicken broth		

1 In a large skillet cook and stir onions and black pepper in hot oil over medium-high heat about 7 minutes or until onions turn brown. Remove onions; set aside. Add beans and cook for 1 minute. Add wine and thyme; reduce heat. Simmer, uncovered, for 3 to 4 minutes or until liquid is reduced by half. Mash beans slightly.

2 On a baking sheet place bread shells. Spread each bread shell with bean mixture; top with onions. Bake in a 450° oven for 10 minutes. Cut each round into quarters. If desired, garnish each wedge with sweet pepper and marjoram.

NUTRITION FACTS PER WEDGE: 108 cal., 3 g total fat (0 g sat. fat), 1 mg chol., 211 mg sodium, 16 g carbo., 1 g fiber, 4 g pro. DAILY VALUES: 2% vit. C, 3% calcium, 6% iron

Cheese Triangles

These puffy, crisp appetizers probably got their start as a variation of early Southern cheese straws, which were slim, cylinder-shaped crackers.

PREP: 25 minutes BAKE: 12 minutes OVEN: 400° MAKES: 32 triangles

2 cups all-purpose flour	1 cup finely shredded sharp cheddar cheese (4 ounces)
2 teaspoons baking powder	
³/₄ teaspoon ground red pepper (optional)	³/₄ cup milk
¹/₂ teaspoon salt	1 tablespoon milk
3 tablespoons shortening	

1 Lightly grease baking sheets; set aside. In a large bowl stir together flour, baking powder, red pepper (if using), and salt. Using a pastry blender, cut in shortening until the size of coarse crumbs. Stir in ¹/₂ cup of the cheddar cheese. Add the ³/₄ cup milk, stirring just until dry ingredients are moistened. Form into a ball.

2 On a lightly floured surface, roll dough to a 10-inch square, ¹/₄ inch thick. Brush with the 1 tablespoon milk and sprinkle with the remaining ¹/₂ cup cheddar cheese; press lightly. Cut into sixteen 2¹/₂-inch squares. Cut each square in half diagonally to make 32 triangles.

3 Place triangles on the prepared baking sheets. Bake in a 400° oven for 12 to 15 minutes or until golden brown. Serve warm.

NUTRITION FACTS PER TRIANGLE: 54 cal., 3 g total fat (1 g sat. fat), 4 mg chol., 86 mg sodium, 6 g carbo., 0 g fiber, 2 g pro. DAILY VALUES: 5% calcium, 2% iron

Cheesy Spinach Quesadillas

Oozing with cheese and studded with spinach, dried tomatoes, and nuts, these appetizer wedges are best served hot from the oven.

PREP: 15 minutes BAKE: 6 minutes OVEN: 450° MAKES: 24 appetizers

½	of a 10-ounce package frozen chopped spinach, thawed and well drained
¼	cup purchased basil pesto
2	tablespoons seasoned fine dry bread crumbs
2	teaspoons drained and snipped oil-packed dried tomatoes

1½	cups shredded co-jack cheese or cheddar cheese (6 ounces)
⅓	cup finely chopped toasted pine nuts or pecans
6	8-inch flour tortillas

1 In a small bowl stir together spinach, pesto, bread crumbs, dried tomatoes, 1 cup of the co-jack cheese, and half of the pine nuts.

2 Spread mixture evenly over three of the tortillas. Top each with a remaining tortilla. Place on a very large baking sheet. Sprinkle the remaining ½ cup co-jack cheese and the pine nuts on top of tortillas.

3 Bake in a 450° oven for 6 to 8 minutes or until tortillas are light brown and crisp. Cut each into eight wedges.

NUTRITION FACTS PER APPETIZER: 78 cal., 5 g total fat (2 g sat. fat), 8 mg chol., 109 mg sodium, 5 g carbo., 0 g fiber, 3 g pro. DAILY VALUES: 2% vit. C, 8% calcium, 3% iron

Fruited Cheese Spirals

Finger food gets a fresh new look! Dried fruit lends jewel tones to these clever spirals filled with prosciutto, cream cheese, and the cinnamon-pepper flavor of fresh basil.

PREP: 25 minutes CHILL: 4 to 24 hours MAKES: About 24 slices

½	cup orange juice or apple juice	4	7- to 8-inch flour tortillas
1	cup dried fruit (such as cranberries, snipped tart red cherries, and/or snipped apricots)	4	very thin slices prosciutto or cooked ham
1	8-ounce tub cream cheese		Fresh basil leaves (optional)
½	cup dairy sour cream or plain yogurt		Orange slices (optional)
¼	cup finely snipped fresh basil leaves		

1 In a small saucepan bring orange juice to boiling. Stir in dried fruit; remove from heat. Let stand, covered, about 15 minutes or until fruit is softened. Drain.

2 Meanwhile, in a medium bowl stir together cream cheese, sour cream, and the snipped basil. Spread cream cheese mixture evenly over one side of each tortilla. Sprinkle each with softened fruit. Place some of the prosciutto near an edge of each tortilla. Tightly roll up, beginning with edge closest to meat. Wrap each roll in plastic wrap and chill for 4 to 24 hours.

3 To serve, remove plastic wrap and cut each roll into 1-inch slices. If desired, garnish with basil leaves and orange slices.

NUTRITION FACTS PER SLICE: 115 cal., 6 g total fat (2 g sat. fat), 12 mg chol., 142 mg sodium, 14 g carbo., 0 g fiber, 3 g pro. DAILY VALUES: 4% vit. C, 1% calcium, 2% iron

APPETIZING IDEAS Even for the most casual get-togethers, it's nice to have an assortment of nibbles for your guests to enjoy as a prelude to the main event. But if you're planning a no-fuss evening, just make one simple starter from scratch. Fill in with purchased crudités, bagel chips, tortilla chips with salsa, purchased hummus with warm wedges of pita bread, or marinated olives. Stylish but easy!

Turkey and Vegetable Tortilla Rolls

While the recipe calls for red sweet pepper, try using a variety of colors. A combination of peppers, such as red, yellow, and green, makes these appetizers a visual knockout when sliced and presented cut side up.

COOK: 4 minutes CHILL: up to 12 hours MAKES: 24 to 28 slices

12	medium asparagus spears	1	to 2 teaspoons brown mustard
1	large red sweet pepper	4	7- or 8-inch flour tortillas
1	8-ounce package cream cheese, softened	2	6-ounce packages thinly sliced cooked smoked turkey
2	tablespoons milk		Lettuce leaves
2	teaspoons snipped fresh rosemary or ½ teaspoon dried rosemary, crushed		

1 Snap off and discard woody bases from asparagus. In a large skillet cook asparagus in a small amount of boiling water about 4 minutes or until crisp-tender. Drain thoroughly on paper towels. Cut sweet pepper into strips.

2 In a small mixing bowl beat cream cheese, milk, rosemary, and mustard together with an electric mixer on medium speed until mixture is smooth.

3 To assemble, place one tortilla on a flat surface. Spread one-fourth of the cream cheese mixture on the tortilla. Place one-fourth of the turkey on cream cheese mixture. Arrange three of the asparagus spears and several pepper strips over turkey. Roll up tortilla. Repeat with remaining tortillas and filling ingredients. Wrap each tortilla roll in plastic wrap; chill for up to 12 hours.

4 To serve, remove plastic wrap and cut each tortilla roll into 1-inch slices. Place, cut side up, on a lettuce-lined plate.

NUTRITION FACTS PER SLICE: 86 cal., 6 g total fat (2 g sat. fat), 11 mg chol., 205 mg sodium, 4 g carbo., 0 g fiber, 4 g pro. DAILY VALUES: 17% vit. C, 1% calcium, 3% iron

Nutty Blue Cheese Rolls

These flavorful appetizers get a head start with a refrigerated piecrust.

PREP: 15 minutes BAKE: 15 minutes OVEN: 425° MAKES: 12 appetizers

²/₃ cup finely chopped walnuts	1 tablespoon milk
¹/₃ cup crumbled blue cheese	2 teaspoons grated Parmesan cheese
1 tablespoon finely snipped fresh parsley	Finely snipped fresh parsley
¹/₄ teaspoon ground black pepper	
¹/₂ of a 15-ounce package (1 crust) folded refrigerated unbaked piecrust	

1 For filling, in a small bowl stir together walnuts, blue cheese, the 1 tablespoon parsley, and the pepper. On a lightly floured surface unfold piecrust according to package directions. Spread filling evenly over crust. Cut the pastry circle into 12 wedges. Starting at wide ends, loosely roll up wedges. Place rolls, tip side down, on a greased baking sheet.

2 Brush rolls lightly with milk. Sprinkle with Parmesan cheese and additional parsley. Bake in a 425° oven about 15 minutes or until golden brown. Cool slightly on a wire rack. Serve warm.

NUTRITION FACTS PER APPETIZER: 139 cal., 10 g total fat (1 g sat. fat), 8 mg chol., 130 mg sodium, 9 g carbo., 3 g fiber, 3 g pro. DAILY VALUES: 1% vit. C, 2% calcium, 1% iron

TO MAKE AHEAD: Prepare rolls through step 1. Cover and chill for up to 24 hours. Uncover and continue with step 2.

Italian Pepperoni-Cheese Puffs

Fragrant and airy, these puffs are perfect for appetizers or snacks.

PREP: 30 minutes   BAKE: 15 minutes   OVEN: 450°   MAKES: 48 puffs

1¼ cups water	¾ cup finely shredded pecorino Romano cheese or Parmesan cheese (3 ounces)
⅓ cup shortening	2 tablespoons snipped fresh parsley
1½ cups all-purpose flour	⅛ teaspoon garlic powder
4 eggs	⅛ teaspoon ground black pepper
¾ cup finely chopped pepperoni (3 ounces)	

1 Grease two large baking sheets; set aside. In a large saucepan combine water and shortening. Bring to boiling. Add flour all at once, stirring vigorously. Cook and stir until mixture forms a ball. Remove from heat. Cool for 10 minutes. Add eggs, one at a time, beating well with a wooden spoon after each addition. Stir in pepperoni, pecorino Romano cheese, parsley, garlic powder, and pepper.

2 Drop dough by rounded teaspoons 2 inches apart onto prepared baking sheets. Bake in a 450° oven for 15 to 17 minutes or until golden. Transfer to a wire rack. Serve warm.

NUTRITION FACTS PER PUFF: 48 cal., 3 g total fat (1 g sat. fat), 21 mg chol., 62 mg sodium, 3 g carbo., 0 g fiber, 2 g pro. DAILY VALUES: 1% vit. C, 1% iron

FRESH SNIPPED HERBS In nearly every dish featuring herbs, fresh is best. Here's how to prepare fresh herbs for use in cooking:

Herbs with delicate stems, such as cilantro, parsley, basil, and mint, can simply be snipped—stems and all—in a small bowl with a pair of clean kitchen shears. This is often much faster and neater than chopping the herbs on a cutting board.

Herbs with woodier stems, such as thyme, oregano, and particularly rosemary, should be stripped from their stems before using. Hold the stem in one hand and—starting at the top of the stem—strip off the leaves by running the fingers of your other hand firmly down the stem.

Pecan Potato Balls

Crispy pecan-coated on the outside and bacon-and-jalapeño-studded on the inside, these little bites can be served as an appetizer or a side dish.

PREP: 30 minutes CHILL: 2 to 4 hours COOK: 1½ minutes per batch MAKES: 15 balls

2 cups unseasoned mashed potatoes	½ teaspoon ground cumin
4 slices bacon or turkey bacon, crisp-cooked, drained, and crumbled	⅛ teaspoon ground red pepper
¼ cup butter or margarine, melted and cooled	1 egg, slightly beaten
1 fresh jalapeño pepper, seeded and finely chopped*	1 tablespoon water
1 tablespoon snipped fresh chives	½ cup all-purpose flour
½ teaspoon salt	2 cups finely chopped pecans
	Cooking oil or shortening for deep-fat frying

1 In a medium bowl stir together potatoes, bacon, butter, jalapeño pepper, chives, salt, cumin, and ground red pepper. Cover and chill for 2 to 4 hours.

2 Shape the potato mixture into 1½-inch balls. In a small bowl combine the egg and water. Roll balls in flour, next in egg-water mixture, and finally in pecans.

3 In a heavy saucepan or deep-fat fryer heat 2 inches of cooking oil or melted shortening to 375°. Fry potato balls, a few at a time, for 1½ to 2 minutes or until golden, turning once. Using a slotted spoon, remove potato balls from hot oil. Drain on paper towels. Serve immediately.

*Note: Because chile peppers contain volatile oils that can burn your skin and eyes, avoid direct contact with them as much as possible. When working with chile peppers, wear plastic or rubber gloves. If your bare hands do touch the chile peppers, wash your hands well with soap and water.

NUTRITION FACTS PER POTATO BALL: 225 cal., 19 g total fat (3 g sat. fat), 24 mg chol., 140 mg sodium, 13 g carbo., 1 g fiber, 3 g pro. DAILY VALUES: 11% vit. C, 1% calcium, 5% iron

Mandarin Apricot Chicken Wings

Line the roasting pan with foil for the easiest cleanup possible.

PREP: 15 minutes BAKE: 25 minutes OVEN: 400° MAKES: 24 appetizer servings

2 pounds chicken wing drumettes (about 24)*	2 tablespoons honey
⅔ cup bottled sweet and sour sauce	2 cloves garlic, minced
½ cup snipped dried apricots	¼ teaspoon ground ginger
⅓ cup bottled hoisin sauce	¼ teaspoon five-spice powder
¼ cup soy sauce	1 tablespoon sesame seeds, toasted

1 Arrange drumettes in a single layer in a foil-lined baking pan or roasting pan. Bake drumettes in a 400° oven for 20 minutes.

2 Meanwhile, in a small saucepan stir together the sweet and sour sauce, apricots, hoisin sauce, soy sauce, honey, garlic, ginger, and five-spice powder. Bring to boiling; reduce heat. Simmer, uncovered, for 5 minutes. Remove from heat.

3 Brush about ¼ cup of the sauce mixture over drumettes. Sprinkle with sesame seeds. Bake about 5 minutes more or until drumettes are no longer pink in the center. Serve drumettes with remaining sauce.

*****Note:** If you can't find drumettes, use 12 chicken wings. Cut off and discard wing tips or reserve for making broth. Cut each wing into two sections (drumettes).

NUTRITION FACTS PER SERVING: 86 cal., 5 g total fat (1 g sat. fat), 29 mg chol., 274 mg sodium, 7 g carbo., 0 g fiber, 5 g pro. DAILY VALUES: 4% vit. A, 1% iron

Batter-Dipped Fried Clams

Set a plateful of piping hot fried clams in front of guests and watch them disappear.
Few appetizers can match them for sheer gobble-ability!

PREP: 10 minutes COOK: 1½ minutes per batch MAKES: 8 appetizer servings

½	cup milk	1	egg white
1	egg yolk		Cooking oil for deep-fat frying
1	tablespoon butter, melted and cooled	1	pint shucked clams, rinsed and well drained
¼	teaspoon salt		
½	cup all-purpose flour	1	recipe Tartar Sauce or purchased tartar sauce

1 In a medium bowl combine milk, egg yolk, melted butter, and salt. Sift flour over milk mixture; stir until smooth. In a small mixing bowl beat egg white with an electric mixer on medium to high speed until soft peaks form. Fold egg white into milk mixture.

2 In a deep-fat fryer or saucepan, heat oil to 375°. Poke each clam with a fork; dip into batter. Gently drop clams into hot oil and fry a few at a time about 1½ minutes or until golden brown, turning once. Using a slotted spoon, remove clams from hot oil and drain on paper towels. Keep warm in a 300° oven while frying remaining clams. Serve with Tartar Sauce.

Tartar Sauce: In a small bowl stir together 1 cup mayonnaise, ¼ cup finely chopped sweet pickle relish, 1 tablespoon finely chopped onion, 1 tablespoon snipped fresh parsley, 1 tablespoon diced pimiento, and 1 teaspoon lemon juice.

NUTRITION FACTS PER SERVING: 346 cal., 32 g total fat (6 g sat. fat), 57 mg chol., 336 mg sodium, 11 g carbo., 0 g fiber, 6 g pro. DAILY VALUES: 10% vit. C, 5% calcium, 24% iron

Artichoke-Stuffed New Potatoes

Two popular contemporary appetizers—hot artichoke dip and stuffed potato skins—come together in one great nibble. New potatoes and a sprightly gremolata update this dynamic duo.

PREP: 25 minutes BAKE: 20 minutes OVEN: 450° MAKES: 16 appetizers

16   tiny new potatoes (1½- to 2-inch diameter)

1   tablespoon olive oil

1   14-ounce can artichoke hearts, drained and chopped

½   cup light mayonnaise dressing or salad dressing

¼   cup finely shredded Parmesan cheese
     Dash ground red pepper

1   recipe Gremolata

1 Cut off the top one-third of each potato. Using a melon baller, hollow out the potatoes, leaving ¼-inch shells. Cut a thin slice off the bottom of each potato so it will sit without tipping. (Discard potato trimmings, or cook and use to make potato salad or mashed potatoes.) Lightly brush potatoes all over with oil. Place in a shallow baking pan; set aside.

2 For filling, in a medium bowl combine artichoke hearts, mayonnaise dressing, Parmesan cheese, and ground red pepper. Spoon about 1 tablespoon of the filling into each potato shell.

3 Bake in a 450° oven about 20 minutes or until potatoes are tender and filling is golden brown. Sprinkle Gremolata over potatoes.

Gremolata: In a small bowl stir together ¼ cup snipped fresh parsley, 2 tablespoons finely shredded lemon peel, and 2 cloves minced garlic.

NUTRITION FACTS PER APPETIZER: 70 cal., 4 g total fat (1 g sat. fat), 4 mg chol., 144 mg sodium, 7 g carbo., 1 g fiber, 2 g pro. DAILY VALUES: 2% vit. A, 12% vit. C, 3% calcium, 5% iron

Stuffed Celery Bites

For easiest preparation, spread the cream cheese mixture in the celery first, then slice.

START TO FINISH: 30 minutes MAKES: 8 appetizer servings

Nonstick cooking spray

2 tablespoons pine nuts

1 clove garlic, minced

8 stalks celery

1 8-ounce tub cream cheese with dried tomato or plain cream cheese

¼ cup shredded Italian cheese blend (1 ounce)

2 tablespoons dry-roasted shelled sunflower seeds

Celery leaves (optional)

1 Lightly coat a skillet with nonstick cooking spray. Add pine nuts and garlic. Cook over medium heat for 3 to 5 minutes or until nuts are golden brown, stirring frequently. Set aside.

2 Remove tops and wide base from celery. Using a vegetable peeler, remove two thin strips from the rounded side of the celery, creating a flat surface.

3 In a small bowl stir together the cream cheese and Italian cheese blend. Spread or spoon cheese mixture into celery.

4 Cut each filled stalk of celery into 2-inch pieces. Sprinkle half the pieces with the pine nut mixture and half with the sunflower seeds. If desired, top with celery leaves.

NUTRITION FACTS PER SERVING: 132 cal., 13 g total fat (7 g sat. fat), 31 mg chol., 152 mg sodium, 3 g carbo., 1 g fiber, 4 g pro. DAILY VALUES: 5% vit. C, 6% calcium, 3% iron

TO MAKE AHEAD: Stuff celery up to 4 hours before serving; cover and chill. Just before serving, cut into 2-inch pieces and add nuts and seeds.

Greek Salad Bites

*For ultimate impact, serve these cucumber stacks as
soon as you finish assembling them.*

PREP: 15 minutes CHILL: 2 hours MAKES: 30 appetizers

1	cup crumbled feta cheese (4 ounces)		½	teaspoon cracked black pepper
½	cup dairy sour cream		1½	medium cucumbers
¼	cup snipped fresh parsley		¼	cup finely shredded fresh basil
2	tablespoons oil-packed dried tomatoes, drained and finely chopped		¼	cup chopped pitted kalamata olives
2	cloves garlic, minced			

1 In a small bowl stir together feta cheese, sour cream, parsley, dried tomatoes, garlic, and pepper. Cover and chill for at least 2 hours.

2 Using a sharp knife, trim the ends from cucumbers; discard ends. Bias-slice the cucumbers into ¼-inch slices. Spoon 1½ teaspoons cheese mixture onto each cucumber slice. Arrange cucumber slices on a serving platter.

3 In a small bowl stir together basil and olives. Spoon some of the mixture over each cucumber slice. Serve immediately.

NUTRITION FACTS PER APPETIZER: 22 cal., 2 g total fat (1 g sat. fat), 5 mg chol., 57 mg sodium, 1 g carbo., 0 g fiber, 1 g pro. DAILY VALUES: 2% vit. C, 3% calcium, 1% iron

---

FRESH-HERB INTERCHANGES Fresh herbs turn ordinary dishes into extraordinary ones. Each herb has its own distinct flavor, but you can have one step in for another. Try these substitutions.

SAGE: use savory, marjoram, or rosemary

BASIL: substitute oregano or thyme

THYME: basil, marjoram, oregano, or savory will suffice

MINT: substitute basil, marjoram, or rosemary

ROSEMARY: try thyme, tarragon, or savory

CILANTRO: substitute parsley

Antipasto on a Stick

Salami, vegetables, and cheesy tortellini can be marinated overnight, making this a cinch to fix today for travel tomorrow. Serve slices of crusty bread to catch the drips as you eat your antipasto off skewers (no serving utensils required).

PREP: 25 minutes CHILL: 2 to 24 hours MAKES: 16 appetizer or 8 main-dish servings

8 ounces thinly sliced salami or other desired meat

1/2 of a 9-ounce package refrigerated cheese-filled tortellini, cooked and drained*

1 14-ounce can artichoke hearts, drained and halved

8 large pitted ripe olives

8 pepperoncini salad peppers

8 red or yellow cherry tomatoes

1/2 cup bottled reduced-calorie or fat-free Italian salad dressing

1 large clove garlic, minced

16 thin slices baguette-style French bread

Bottled reduced-calorie or fat-free Italian salad dressing

1 Fold the salami slices in quarters. On 16 short or 8 long wooden skewers, alternately thread salami, tortellini, artichoke halves, olives, pepperoncini, and tomatoes. Place kabobs in a plastic food storage container.

2 In a glass measure or bowl stir together the 1/2 cup salad dressing and garlic; drizzle over kabobs. Cover and chill for 2 to 24 hours.

3 Brush bread slices with additional salad dressing. Broil bread slices on the unheated rack of a broiler pan 4 to 5 inches from the heat about 1 minute or until slices are golden brown. Cool. Serve kabobs with toasted bread.

***Note:** To vary this Italian-style appetizer, substitute 1 cup cubed provolone cheese or mozzarella cheese (4 ounces) for the cheese-filled tortellini.

NUTRITION FACTS PER SERVING: 158 cal., 7 g total fat (2 g sat. fat), 18 mg chol., 729 mg sodium, 17 g carbo., 2 g fiber, 7 g pro. DAILY VALUES: 4% vit. C, 4% calcium, 9% iron

Lemony Herbed Olives

Once the crushed red pepper is stirred in, the mixture of kalamata and green olives goes from mellow to merry. If you like things spicy hot, use the 1 teaspoon crushed red pepper.

PREP: 15 minutes **MARINATE:** 4 to 24 hours **STAND:** 30 minutes **MAKES:** 56 appetizer servings

1 pound pitted kalamata olives and/or green olives (3½ cups)

1 tablespoon olive oil

½ teaspoon finely shredded lemon peel

1 tablespoon lemon juice

2 teaspoons snipped fresh oregano or ½ teaspoon dried oregano, crushed

½ to 1 teaspoon crushed red pepper

Lemon peel curls (optional)

1 In a plastic bag set in a bowl place olives. For marinade, combine olive oil, lemon peel, lemon juice, oregano, and crushed red pepper. Pour over olives; close bag. Marinate in the refrigerator for 4 to 24 hours, turning bag occasionally.

2 To serve, let olives stand at room temperature for 30 minutes. Drain and serve. If desired, garnish olives with curled strips of lemon peel.

NUTRITION FACTS PER SERVING: 21 cal., 2 g total fat (0 g sat. fat), 0 mg chol., 134 mg sodium, 1 g carbo. 1 g fiber, 0 g pro.

Savory Nuts

Combine the flavors and colors of macadamia nuts and walnuts,
and add seasonings for a simple snack.

PREP: 10 minutes BAKE: 12 minutes OVEN: 350° MAKES: 8 (¼ cup) servings

2   cups macadamia nuts and/or walnuts

2   tablespoons white wine Worcestershire
    sauce

1   tablespoon olive oil

2   teaspoons snipped fresh thyme

1   teaspoon snipped fresh rosemary

¼   teaspoon salt

⅛   teaspoon ground red pepper

1 Spread nuts in a 13×9×2-inch baking pan. In a small bowl stir together the Worcestershire sauce, olive oil, thyme, rosemary, salt, and red pepper. Drizzle oil mixture over nuts; toss to coat.

2 Bake in a 350° oven for 12 to 15 minutes or until nuts are toasted, stirring occasionally. Spread on foil; cool. Store in an airtight container.

NUTRITION FACTS PER SERVING: 253 cal., 26 g total fat (4 g sat. fat), 0 mg chol., 100 mg sodium, 5 g carbo., 3 g fiber, 3 g pro. DAILY VALUES: 2% calcium, 5% iron

Chapter Two
Soups&Stews

Mediterranean Minestrone, p. 45

Chicken and Tortellini Stew, p. 69

QUICK & EASY COMFORT COOKING

Country French Beef Stew, p. 64

Black Bean and Sausage Posole, p. 63

Tamale-Topped Lentil Soup, p. 46

Spicy Shrimp and Noodle Soup, p. 55

Potato and Leek Soup, p. 48

▲ Salmon and Potato Chowder, p. 59

▲ Tortilla-Chicken Soup, p. 41

▲ Beef-Vegetable Soup, p. 54

▲ Navy Beans and Pork, p. 61

Tortilla-Chicken Soup

When you put two cuisines together, few are better blends than Tex-Mex, in which Mexican and Southwest flavors meld in spicy friendship. Here's to both sides of the border.
(See photo, page 40.)

START TO FINISH: 45 minutes MAKES: 6 servings

4	skinless, boneless chicken breast halves (about 1 pound total)
2	14-ounce cans reduced-sodium chicken broth
1	14-ounce can beef broth
1	14½-ounce can tomatoes, undrained and cut up
½	cup chopped onion (1 medium)
¼	cup chopped green sweet pepper
1	cup frozen loose-pack whole kernel corn
1	to 2 teaspoons chili powder
½	teaspoon ground cumin
⅛	teaspoon ground black pepper
3	cups tortilla chips, coarsely crushed
1	cup shredded Monterey Jack cheese (4 ounces)
1	avocado, peeled, seeded, and cut into chunks (optional)
	Snipped fresh cilantro (optional)
	Sliced fresh jalapeño peppers (optional)*
	Lime wedges (optional)

1 Cut chicken into bite-size pieces; set aside. In a 4-quart Dutch oven combine chicken broth, beef broth, undrained tomatoes, onion, and sweet pepper. Bring to boiling; add chicken. Return to boiling; reduce heat. Simmer, covered, for 10 minutes.

2 Add corn, chili powder, cumin, and black pepper to chicken mixture in Dutch oven. Return to boiling; reduce heat. Simmer, covered, for 10 minutes more.

3 To serve, place crushed tortilla chips in six soup bowls. Ladle soup over tortilla chips. Sprinkle with Monterey Jack cheese. If desired, top with avocado, cilantro, and jalapeño peppers. If desired, serve with lime wedges.

***Note:** Because chile peppers contain volatile oils that can burn your skin and eyes, avoid direct contact with them as much as possible. When working with chile peppers, wear plastic or rubber gloves. If your bare hands do touch the chile peppers, wash your hands well with soap and water.

NUTRITION FACTS PER SERVING: 259 cal., 10 g total fat (4 g sat. fat), 60 mg chol., 896 mg sodium, 17 g carbo., 2 g fiber, 27 g pro. DAILY VALUES: 23% vit. C, 19% calcium, 8% iron

A to Z Vegetable Soup

Easy to make, this all-in-the-family meal is good for every age—veggie-packed for kids and only 1 gram of saturated fat for health-conscious adults. Little ones just learning their letters will love reciting, then taking a bite out of the alphabet.

START TO FINISH: 35 minutes MAKES: 4 servings

1 tablespoon cooking oil or olive oil

2 cups mixed, cut-up fresh vegetables, such as sliced small zucchini, carrots, celery, and chopped red onions

2 14-ounce cans reduced-sodium chicken broth

2 cloves garlic, minced

1 15-ounce can white kidney (cannellini) beans or Great Northern beans, rinsed and drained

½ cup packaged dried alphabet-shaped pasta or tiny shells

2 tablespoons fresh small oregano leaves

1 ounce Parmesan cheese, thinly sliced (optional)

1 In a large saucepan heat oil over medium-high heat. Add mixed vegetables. Cook, uncovered, about 10 minutes or until vegetables are crisp-tender, stirring occasionally. Remove half the vegetables; set aside.

2 Stir chicken broth and garlic into remaining vegetables in saucepan. Bring to boiling. Stir in drained beans and pasta. Return to boiling; reduce heat. Simmer, covered, about 10 minutes or until pasta is just tender. Stir in fresh oregano leaves.

3 To serve, ladle soup into bowls. Top with reserved vegetables. If desired, sprinkle with Parmesan cheese slices.

NUTRITION FACTS PER SERVING: 188 cal., 4 g total fat (1 g sat. fat), 0 mg chol., 717 mg sodium, 33 g carbo., 6 g fiber, 12 g pro. DAILY VALUES: 79% vit. A, 9% vit. C, 5% calcium, 12% iron

Italian Bean Soup

Blend or puree half of the beans and tomatoes to thicken this home-style soup.

START TO FINISH: 25 minutes MAKES: 8 servings

2	15-ounce cans red kidney beans, rinsed and drained
1	15-ounce can Great Northern beans, rinsed and drained
1	14½-ounce can diced tomatoes with basil, oregano, and garlic, undrained
5	cups water
½	of a 6-ounce can Italian-style tomato paste (⅓ cup)
1	tablespoon instant chicken bouillon granules
1	teaspoon dried basil, crushed
1	teaspoon dried oregano, crushed
½	teaspoon ground white pepper
1	cup packaged dried wide egg noodles
1	tablespoon snipped fresh parsley

1 In a blender container or food processor bowl combine one can of the drained red kidney beans, ²/₃ cup of the drained Great Northern beans, ³/₄ cup of the undrained tomatoes, and 1 cup of the water. Cover and blend or process until nearly smooth. Transfer mixture to a 4-quart Dutch oven.

2 Add the remaining beans, remaining tomatoes, remaining 4 cups water, tomato paste, bouillon granules, basil, oregano, and white pepper to mixture in Dutch oven. Bring to boiling; stir in noodles. Return to boiling; reduce heat. Simmer, covered, for 15 minutes. Stir in parsley. To serve, ladle soup into bowls.

NUTRITION FACTS PER SERVING: 218 cal., 1 g total fat (0 g sat. fat), 7 mg chol., 1,025 mg sodium, 40 g carbo., 11 g fiber, 12 g pro. DAILY VALUES: 18% vit. A, 8% calcium, 17% iron

Root Vegetable Soup

Serve this hearty soup with a country-style bread and a selection of artisan cheeses for a rustic and comforting Sunday supper.

START TO FINISH: 45 minutes   MAKES: 4 to 6 servings

2 14-ounce cans vegetable broth	6 baby carrots, peeled, or 2 small carrots, peeled and cut up
2½ cups water	1 small parsnip, peeled and cut up
2 medium leeks, halved lengthwise and cut into 1- to 2-inch pieces	½ cup dry sherry or vegetable broth
1 medium rutabaga, peeled and cut into 1-inch pieces	1 4-inch sprig fresh rosemary or ½ teaspoon dried rosemary, crushed
1 medium turnip, peeled and cut into 1-inch pieces	

1 In a 4-quart Dutch oven combine vegetable broth, water, leeks, rutabaga, turnip, carrots, parsnip, sherry, and rosemary. Bring to boiling; reduce heat. Simmer, uncovered, for 25 to 30 minutes or until rutabaga and turnip are tender. Remove rosemary sprig, if using. To serve, ladle soup into bowls.

NUTRITION FACTS PER SERVING: 112 cal., 2 g total fat (0 g sat. fat), 0 mg chol., 344 mg sodium, 15 g carbo., 3 g fiber, 2 g pro. DAILY VALUES: 121% vit. A, 29% vit. C, 6% calcium, 6% iron

CLEANING LEEKS The tightly packed leaves of leeks taste delicious but collect soil easily. Properly cleaning them is a must. First remove any wilted outer leaves. Slice the leek lengthwise in half, all the way through the root end. Holding the leek under a faucet with the root end up, rinse the leek under cold running water, lifting and separating the leaves with your fingers to allow the grit to flow down through the top of the leek. Continue rinsing until all grit is removed. Slice off the root end before using.

Mediterranean Minestrone

Arborio rice is an Italian-grown grain that is shorter and plumper than any other short-grain rice. Traditionally used to make creamy risotto, it adds a similar texture to this bean and vegetable soup. (See photo, page 33.)

START TO FINISH: 40 minutes MAKES: 6 servings

1 cup finely chopped celery (2 stalks)	1 15-ounce can Great Northern beans, rinsed and drained
¾ cup finely chopped onion (1 large)	2 cups chopped tomatoes (3 medium)
2 cloves garlic, minced	1½ cups coarsely chopped zucchini (1 medium)
1 tablespoon olive oil	¼ cup snipped fresh thyme
5 cups beef broth	¼ teaspoon cracked black pepper
1 cup water	½ cup crumbled feta cheese (2 ounces)
½ cup uncooked Arborio rice	
6 cups torn fresh spinach	

1 In a 4- to 6-quart Dutch oven cook celery, onion, and garlic in hot oil until tender. Add beef broth, water, and rice. Bring to boiling; reduce heat. Simmer, covered, for 15 minutes.

2 Add the torn spinach, drained beans, tomatoes, zucchini, thyme, and black pepper to rice mixture in Dutch oven. Cook and stir until heated through.

3 To serve, ladle soup into bowls. Sprinkle with feta cheese.

NUTRITION FACTS PER SERVING: 252 cal., 6 g total fat (2 g sat. fat), 8 mg chol., 834 mg sodium, 39 g carbo., 8 g fiber, 13 g pro. DAILY VALUES: 58% vit. C, 15% calcium, 31% iron

THE BEST BROTHS When a recipe calls for chicken, beef, or vegetable broth, use a homemade stock recipe or substitute commercially canned broth. Just remember that the canned varieties usually are saltier than homemade stocks, so hold off on adding extra salt until the end of cooking. Season to taste. Another option is to try a canned reduced-sodium broth. Bouillon cubes and granules diluted according to package directions may be used, but they are also saltier than homemade stocks.

Tamale-Topped Lentil Soup

The cheesy cornmeal topping is a hearty addition to this fiber-rich, meatless lentil-and-vegetable soup. (See photo, page 37.)

PREP: 20 minutes COOK: 35 minutes MAKES: 6 servings

3½	cups water	½	cup chopped green sweet pepper (1 small)
1	cup sliced celery (2 stalks)	1	clove garlic, minced
½	cup chopped onion (1 medium)	¾	teaspoon salt
½	cup dried brown lentils, rinsed and drained	¾	teaspoon chili powder
1	14½-ounce can stewed tomatoes, undrained	¼	teaspoon ground cumin
1	cup sliced carrots (2 medium)	⅛	teaspoon ground black pepper
1	cup frozen loose-pack whole kernel corn	1	recipe Tamale Topper
1	cup frozen loose-pack cut green beans	¼	cup shredded cheddar cheese (1 ounce)
1	cup sliced zucchini and/or yellow summer squash (1 small)		

1 In a 4-quart Dutch oven combine 1½ cups of the water, the celery, onion, and lentils. Bring to boiling; reduce heat. Simmer, covered, about 20 minutes or until lentils are tender; drain.

2 Add the remaining water, the undrained tomatoes, carrots, corn, green beans, zucchini, sweet pepper, garlic, salt, chili powder, cumin, and black pepper to lentil mixture in Dutch oven. Return to boiling; reduce heat.

3 Meanwhile, prepare Tamale Topper. Using a spoon, drop Tamale Topper in six portions onto hot soup. Simmer, covered, about 15 minutes more or until a toothpick inserted in topper comes out clean. (Do not lift cover while cooking.)

4 To serve, ladle soup and a portion of tamale topper into bowls. Sprinkle with cheddar cheese.

Tamale Topper: In a medium saucepan combine ⅔ cup cornmeal and ¼ teaspoon salt. Gradually stir in 1 cup milk. Cook and stir until thickened and bubbly. Gradually stir cornmeal mixture into 1 beaten egg. Stir in ½ cup shredded cheddar cheese (2 ounces).

NUTRITION FACTS PER SERVING: 286 cal., 8 g total fat (4 g sat. fat), 53 mg chol., 666 mg sodium, 43 g carbo., 6 g fiber, 13 g pro. DAILY VALUES: 30% vit. C, 23% calcium, 19% iron

Italian Country Bread Soup

In a few swift strokes, slice off sweet pepper's bothersome stem, seeds, and ribs.
Here's how: Holding the pepper upright on a cutting surface, slice each side with
a sharp knife and presto—four flat pieces of pepper to easily chop.

START TO FINISH: 30 minutes   OVEN: 375° MAKES: 6 servings

8	ounces Italian flatbread (focaccia), cut into ¾-inch cubes (4 cups)	1	tablespoon olive oil
2½	cups chopped zucchini and/or yellow summer squash (2 medium)	2	14-ounce cans chicken broth
¾	cup chopped green sweet pepper (1 medium)	1	14½-ounce can diced tomatoes with basil, oregano, and garlic, undrained
½	cup chopped onion (1 medium)		Finely shredded Parmesan cheese (optional)

1 On an ungreased baking sheet spread bread cubes in a single layer. Bake in a 375° oven for 10 to 15 minutes or until lightly toasted.

2 Meanwhile, in a large saucepan cook zucchini, sweet pepper, and onion in hot oil for 5 minutes. Stir in chicken broth and undrained tomatoes. Bring to boiling; reduce heat. Simmer, uncovered, about 5 minutes or just until vegetables are tender.

3 To serve, ladle soup into bowls. Top with toasted bread cubes and, if desired, Parmesan cheese.

NUTRITION FACTS PER SERVING: 172 cal., 4 g total fat (1 g sat. fat), 9 mg chol., 526 mg sodium, 27 g carbo., 3 g fiber, 8 g pro. DAILY VALUES: 5% vit. A, 45% vit. C, 8% calcium, 6% iron

Potato and Leek Soup

Gourmet cooks love their leeks. Even so, this mellow cousin of onion and garlic is not so fancy if grit lurks in its tightly packed leaves. To clean, see the tip on page 44.
(See photo, page 39.)

PREP: 20 minutes COOK: 25 minutes MAKES: 4 servings

3	cups cubed, peeled russet or Idaho potatoes (1 pound)	2	cups cubed, peeled sweet potatoes
1	14-ounce can chicken broth	¼	teaspoon ground black pepper
1	cup sliced celery (2 stalks)	¼	teaspoon ground nutmeg
⅓	cup thinly sliced leek (1 medium)	1½	cups milk
2	tablespoons butter or margarine	½	teaspoon salt

1 In a medium saucepan combine the russet potatoes and 1 cup of the chicken broth. Bring to boiling; reduce heat. Simmer, covered, about 10 minutes or until potatoes are tender; do not drain. Cool slightly.

2 Transfer potato mixture to a blender container or food processor bowl. Cover and blend or process until smooth; set aside.

3 In a large saucepan cook celery and leek in hot butter for 3 to 4 minutes or until tender. Add sweet potatoes, the remaining chicken broth, pepper, and nutmeg. Bring to boiling; reduce heat. Simmer, covered, for 10 minutes. Stir in pureed potato mixture, milk, and salt. Cook and stir about 5 minutes more or until thickened. Season to taste with salt and pepper. To serve, ladle soup into bowls.

NUTRITION FACTS PER SERVING: 280 cal., 9 g total fat (5 g sat. fat), 30 mg chol., 696 mg sodium, 42 g carbo., 5 g fiber, 9 g pro. DAILY VALUES: 50% vit. C, 16% calcium, 9% iron

PUREED SOUPS Have you ever had a vegetable cream soup that tasted more like butter or cream than vegetables? Most likely, such a soup relied on cream, cornstarch, and/or a mixture of butter and flour to thicken. Such thickening agents work fine in some recipes but can mask the delicate flavors of vegetable-based soups. The thickening agent used for this soup is made by first cooking potatoes in chicken broth, then pureeing or finely mashing the mixture. The resulting puree is all the thickening this soup needs because the starch from the potatoes acts as a thickener. What's more, the puree allows the full flavors of the vegetables to come through. You also can rely on the starch in rice to thicken soups. The next time you make your favorite rice soup, try pureeing some of the cooked rice to act as a thickener.

Springtime Soup

Combine garden-fresh asparagus, snow peas, and spinach for a quick vegetarian treat.
Use a vegetable peeler to remove asparagus scales.

START TO FINISH: 25 minutes MAKES: 8 side-dish or 4 main-dish servings

1 pound asparagus spears	3 cups fresh snow peas, ends and strings removed
½ cup chopped onion (1 medium)	6 cups torn fresh spinach
3 cloves garlic, minced	¼ teaspoon ground black pepper
1 tablespoon olive oil	¼ cup purchased pesto (optional)
1 49½-ounce can chicken broth	¼ cup finely shredded Parmesan cheese
½ cup packaged dried orzo or other tiny pasta	

1 Snap off and discard woody asparagus bases. If desired, scrape off scales. Bias-slice the asparagus into 1-inch pieces; set aside.

2 Meanwhile, in a 4-quart Dutch oven cook the onion and garlic in hot oil until tender. Carefully add chicken broth; bring to boiling. Stir in pasta; reduce heat. Boil gently, uncovered, for 5 minutes. Stir in asparagus and snow peas. Return soup to boiling; cook, uncovered, for 3 minutes more. Stir in spinach and black pepper; cook for 1 minute more.

3 To serve, ladle soup into bowls. If desired, swirl some of the pesto into each bowl of soup. Sprinkle with Parmesan cheese.

NUTRITION FACTS PER SERVING: 133 cal., 4 g total fat (1 g sat. fat), 3 mg chol., 634 mg sodium, 15 g carbo., 3 g fiber, 10 g pro. DAILY VALUES: 31% vit. A, 59% vit. C, 8% calcium, 18% iron

Wild Rice, Barley, and Mushroom Soup

It's hard to resist this enticing soup. The nutty flavor and chewy texture of wild rice and barley are pleasant contrasts to the earthy flavor and soft texture of the mushrooms. Add a splash of Madeira for a sophisticated accent.

START TO FINISH: 25 minutes MAKES: 3 main-dish servings or 6 side-dish servings

1	cup water	3	cups sliced fresh mushrooms
¼	cup quick-cooking barley	1	tablespoon snipped fresh sage or 1 teaspoon dried sage, crushed
1	cup thinly sliced leeks (3)		
½	cup sliced carrot (1 medium)	2½	cups vegetable broth
1	small parsnip, finely chopped	¾	cup cooked wild rice
1	clove garlic, minced	2	tablespoons Madeira wine or dry sherry (optional)
1	tablespoon butter or margarine		

1 In a small saucepan combine water and barley. Bring mixture to boiling; reduce heat. Simmer, covered, for 10 minutes.

2 Meanwhile, in a large saucepan cook leeks, carrot, parsnip, and garlic in hot butter for 5 minutes. Stir in mushrooms and, if using, dried sage. Cook for 5 to 10 minutes more or just until mushrooms are tender. Stir in the vegetable broth, cooked wild rice, cooked barley, and, if desired, Madeira wine. If using, stir in fresh sage. Cook and stir until heated through. Season to taste with salt and pepper. To serve, ladle soup into bowls.

NUTRITION FACTS PER SERVING: 223 cal., 6 g total fat (2 g sat. fat), 10 mg chol., 854 mg sodium, 45 g carbo., 9 g fiber, 7 g pro. DAILY VALUES: 20% vit. C, 5% calcium, 24% iron

SOUP WITH SPIRIT Adding wine to soup often enhances its flavor. Sherry or Madeira blends well with veal or chicken soup. A strongly flavored soup with beef benefits from a tablespoon of dry red table wine. And dry white table wine adds zest to fish soup, crab or lobster bisque, or creamy chowder. Be thrifty with salt in a soup to which wine is added, as the wine intensifies saltiness.

Split Pea and Smoked Turkey Soup

Look for varieties of cooked smoked turkey at your supermarket deli.
Also check out the selection of turkey sausage at the meat counter.

PREP: 20 minutes COOK: 6 hours MAKES: 6 to 8 servings

2 cups dried yellow split peas (1 pound)	1 tablespoon snipped fresh oregano or 1 teaspoon dried oregano, crushed
2 cups chopped cooked smoked turkey or sliced cooked turkey sausage	5 cups chicken broth
1½ cups coarsely shredded carrots	2 cups water
1 cup chopped fresh chives	½ cup snipped dried tomatoes (not oil packed)
1 clove garlic, minced	Fresh chives (optional)
1 tablespoon snipped fresh basil or 1 teaspoon dried basil, crushed	

1 Rinse split peas; drain. In a 3½- or 4-quart crockery cooker combine the split peas, smoked turkey, carrots, chives, garlic, and, if using, dried basil and oregano. Pour chicken broth and water over all.

2 Cover and cook on low-heat setting for 6 to 8 hours or on high-heat setting for 3 to 4 hours. Stir in dried tomatoes; cover and let stand for 10 minutes. If using, stir in fresh basil and oregano.

3 To serve, ladle soup into bowls. If desired, garnish with fresh chives.

NUTRITION FACTS PER SERVING: 204 cal., 2 g total fat (1 g sat. fat), 22 mg chol., 1,313 mg sodium, 26 g carbo., 5 g fiber, 22 g pro. DAILY VALUES: 13% vit. C, 4% calcium, 15% iron

Mixed-Tomato Soup

For the fresh tomatoes in this recipe, use the ripest available. If homegrown or farm-fresh tomatoes are available, they'll make the best soup.

PREP: 45 minutes COOK: 1 hour 5 minutes MAKES: 8 side-dish servings

1	3-ounce package dried tomatoes (not oil packed)	4	cups water
½	cup chopped onion (1 medium)	1	teaspoon salt
¼	teaspoon coarsely ground black pepper	1	cup whipping cream
1	tablespoon olive oil or cooking oil		Olive oil (optional)
8	medium fresh tomatoes, chopped (about 2½ pounds)	8	yellow pear or dried yellow tomato halves (optional)

1 Place the dried tomatoes in a small bowl. Add enough boiling water to cover; let stand for 30 minutes. Drain and rinse. Coarsely chop rehydrated tomatoes.

2 In a Dutch oven cook onion, rehydrated tomatoes, and black pepper in hot oil until onion is tender. Reserve ¾ cup of the chopped fresh tomatoes; set aside. Add remaining fresh tomatoes to onion mixture. Cook, covered, over low heat about 20 minutes or until tomatoes are soft. Add water and salt. Cook, uncovered, over low heat for 40 minutes more, stirring often.

3 Transfer one-fourth of mixture at a time to a blender container or food processor bowl.* Cover and carefully blend or process until smooth. Repeat with remaining soup. Return mixture to Dutch oven. Heat to simmering. Stir in whipping cream. Return just to simmering. Remove from heat.

4 To serve, ladle soup into bowls. Spoon some of the reserved fresh chopped tomatoes into each bowl. If desired, drizzle with some olive oil and top with a yellow teardrop or dried yellow tomato half.

***Note:** When blending or processing heated mixtures, use caution to avoid being splashed by the scalding liquid. Do not fill the blender or food processor bowl completely. Cover the container tightly. Slightly open the center of the lid to vent the hot air. Cover the blender or processor lid with a clean dish towel while operating.

NUTRITION FACTS PER SERVING: 176 cal., 14 g total fat (7 g sat. fat), 41 mg chol., 540 mg sodium, 13 g carbo., 3 g fiber, 3 g pro. DAILY VALUES: 47% vit. C, 4% calcium, 9% iron

TO MAKE AHEAD: Prepare soup as directed up to stirring in the whipping cream. Cool soup. Transfer to an airtight container. Seal, label, and freeze for up to 2 months. To reheat, transfer frozen soup to a saucepan. Cook, covered, over medium heat for 15 to 20 minutes, stirring occasionally. Stir in cream. Cook and stir 5 to 10 minutes more or until heated through. Continue with Step 4.

Chicken 'n' Dumpling Soup

Savor the memory and aroma of your grandmother's cozy kitchen. Recapture the past with a little help from biscuit mix—your secret to keep or reveal.

START TO FINISH: 30 minutes MAKES: 4 servings

12 ounces skinless, boneless chicken breast strips	1 cup purchased julienne or coarsely shredded carrots
Salt and ground black pepper	1 cup water
1 tablespoon olive oil or cooking oil	2/3 cup reduced-fat packaged biscuit mix
2 tablespoons all-purpose flour	1/3 cup yellow cornmeal
1/4 teaspoon dried marjoram, crushed	1/4 cup shredded cheddar cheese (1 ounce)
1 14-ounce can chicken broth	1/2 cup milk
1 medium onion, cut into wedges	
1 cup fresh green beans, trimmed and halved	

1 Season chicken with salt and pepper. In a large saucepan cook and stir chicken in hot oil about 2 minutes or until browned. Sprinkle flour and marjoram over chicken. Stir in chicken broth, onion, green beans, carrots, and the water. Bring to boiling; reduce heat. Simmer, covered, for 5 minutes.

2 In a small bowl stir together biscuit mix, cornmeal, and cheddar cheese. Stir in milk just until mixture is moistened. Using a spoon, drop batter onto hot soup, making eight dumplings. Return to boiling; reduce heat. Simmer, covered, for 10 to 12 minutes until dumplings test done. (Do not lift cover while simmering.) To serve, ladle soup and dumplings into bowls.

NUTRITION FACTS PER SERVING: 338 cal., 10 g total fat (3 g sat. fat), 60 mg chol., 783 mg sodium, 34 g carbo., 3 g fiber, 27 g pro. DAILY VALUES: 12% vit. C, 15% calcium, 14% iron

Beef-Vegetable Soup

This rich and satisfying chili-flavored dish is filled with chunks of beef and a basketful of vegetables. Serve it with slices of crusty bread. (See photo, page 40.)

PREP: 35 minutes COOK: 2½ hours MAKES: 8 servings

3	pounds meaty beef shank crosscuts	2	bay leaves
2	tablespoons cooking oil	1	cup diagonally sliced carrots (2 medium)
6	cups water		
2	cups tomato juice	1	cup sliced celery (2 stalks)
4	teaspoons instant beef bouillon granules	1	cup peeled and cubed potato (1 large)
		1	cup coarsely chopped cabbage
1	tablespoon Worcestershire sauce	⅓	cup coarsely chopped onion (1 small)
1	teaspoon chili powder		

1 In a 4-quart Dutch oven brown beef, half at a time, in hot oil over medium-high heat. Drain off fat. Return all of the meat to Dutch oven.

2 Add the water, tomato juice, beef bouillon granules, Worcestershire sauce, chili powder, and bay leaves to beef in Dutch oven. Bring to boiling; reduce heat. Simmer, covered, for 2 hours. Remove beef crosscuts. Skim fat from broth. When cool enough to handle, remove beef from bones; discard bones. Coarsely chop beef.

3 Stir chopped beef, carrots, celery, potato, cabbage, and onion into broth. Bring to boiling; reduce heat. Simmer, covered, for 30 to 45 minutes or until vegetables and beef are tender. Discard bay leaves. To serve, ladle soup into bowls.

NUTRITION FACTS PER SERVING: 185 cal., 5 g total fat (2 g sat. fat), 55 mg chol., 743 mg sodium, 9 g carbo., 2 g fiber, 26 g pro. DAILY VALUES: 43% vit. A, 31% vit. C, 5% calcium, 21% iron

Spicy Shrimp and Noodle Soup

Here's an easy way to devein shrimp. About two to three sections from the head of the shrimp, insert a toothpick between two shell plates and through meat near the center top. Keeping the meat intact, lift out the vein. (See photo, page 38.)

START TO FINISH: 35 minutes MAKES: 6 servings

1 pound fresh or frozen medium shrimp in shells	1 15-ounce can black beans, rinsed and drained
1 tablespoon lemon juice	1 8¾-ounce can no-salt-added whole kernel corn, drained
¼ teaspoon chili powder	¼ cup snipped fresh cilantro
¼ teaspoon ground cumin	2 tablespoons thinly sliced green onion (1)
⅛ teaspoon ground black pepper	Shredded cheddar cheese (optional)
5 cups water	Fresh cilantro sprigs (optional)
2 3-ounce packages shrimp- or Oriental-flavored ramen noodles	
1 16-ounce jar salsa (about 1¾ cups)	

1 Thaw shrimp, if frozen. Peel and devein shrimp, leaving tails on if desired. In a medium bowl combine lemon juice, chili powder, cumin, and pepper. Add shrimp to lemon juice mixture; toss to coat. Let shrimp stand for 20 minutes at room temperature, stirring occasionally.

2 Meanwhile, in a large saucepan bring the water to boiling. Stir in one of the noodle flavor packets (reserve remaining flavor packet for another use). Break ramen noodles into pieces; add to saucepan. Return to boiling; cook for 1 minute. Add shrimp; cook for 1 to 2 minutes more or until shrimp turn pink. Stir in salsa, drained beans, drained corn, the ¼ cup snipped cilantro, and the green onion. Heat through.

3 To serve, ladle into soup bowls. If desired, sprinkle with cheddar cheese and garnish with cilantro sprigs.

NUTRITION FACTS PER SERVING: 251 cal., 6 g total fat (0 g sat. fat), 92 mg chol., 976 mg sodium, 33 g carbo., 6 g fiber, 20 g pro. DAILY VALUES: 27% vit. C, 9% calcium, 19% iron

Thai-Style Shrimp Soup

To find lemongrass for this simple Asian dish, shop Asian specialty markets or larger supermarkets. The same for coconut milk—but avoid products used to make mixed drinks.

START TO FINISH: 25 minutes   MAKES: 3 to 4 servings

12 ounces fresh or frozen small shrimp	2 tablespoons minced fresh ginger
1 14-ounce can chicken broth	1/4 teaspoon crushed red pepper
1 small zucchini, cut into matchstick-size pieces (about 1 1/2 cups)	1 14-ounce can unsweetened coconut milk
1 green onion, bias-cut into 1 1/4-inch slices	2 tablespoons shredded fresh basil
2 tablespoons minced fresh lemongrass or 1 1/2 teaspoons finely shredded lemon peel	2 tablespoons toasted shaved coconut
	Fresh basil sprigs (optional)

1 Thaw shrimp, if frozen. Peel and devein shrimp; set aside. In a large saucepan bring broth to boiling. Add zucchini, green onion, lemongrass, ginger, and crushed red pepper. Return to boiling; reduce heat. Simmer, uncovered, for 3 minutes, stirring occasionally.

2 Add shrimp to soup mixture in saucepan. Simmer, uncovered, for 1 to 3 minutes or until shrimp turn pink. Add coconut milk. Heat through (do not boil).

3 To serve, ladle soup into bowls. Top with shredded basil, coconut, and, if desired, basil sprigs.

NUTRITION FACTS PER SERVING: 445 cal., 37 g total fat (31 g sat. fat), 115 mg chol., 708 mg sodium, 12 g carbo., 4 g fiber, 21 g pro. DAILY VALUES: 18% vit. C, 8% calcium, 25% iron

STORING AND USING FRESH GINGER Whole ginger stays fresh for two to three weeks in the refrigerator when wrapped loosely in a paper towel and lasts almost indefinitely when frozen. To freeze, place unpeeled ginger in a freezer bag. You can grate or slice the ginger while it's frozen.

Spicy Corn Chowder

Mild corn chowder gets hot with a little salsa.
Extra spicy salsa makes for a fiery evening at the dinner table.

START TO FINISH: 25 minutes MAKES: 4 servings

½ teaspoon ground cumin	½ cup chopped red or green sweet pepper
½ teaspoon chili powder	2 ounces American cheese, cubed
1 cup chicken broth	¾ cup bottled chunky salsa
1½ cups loose-pack frozen whole kernel corn	1 cup half-and-half, light cream, or milk
1 cup frozen loose-pack diced hash brown potatoes	2 tablespoons snipped fresh cilantro and/or snipped fresh chives
½ cup chopped onion (1 medium)	

1 In a large saucepan combine cumin and chili powder. Cook and stir over medium heat until spices are lightly toasted and aromatic. Carefully add chicken broth. Stir in corn, hash brown potatoes, onion, and sweet pepper. Bring to boiling; reduce heat. Simmer, covered, for 5 minutes.

2 Stir American cheese into soup mixture in saucepan. Cook and stir until cheese is melted. Stir in the salsa and half-and-half; heat through.

3 To serve, ladle chowder into soup bowls. Sprinkle with fresh cilantro.

NUTRITION FACTS PER SERVING: 248 cal., 12 g total fat (6 g sat. fat), 30 mg chol., 594 mg sodium, 31 g carbo., 2 g fiber, 9 g pro. DAILY VALUES: 72% vit. C, 14% calcium, 13% iron

Potato-Cauliflower Chowder

Rye bread is a snappy complement to the nutty flavor of Jarlsberg cheese.

START TO FINISH: 30 minutes OVEN: 350° MAKES: 6 servings

1 cup chopped onions (2 medium)	3 cups shredded Jarlsberg cheese (10 ounces)
2 tablespoons butter or margarine	Salt and ground black pepper
4 cups chicken broth	3 slices dark rye bread or pumpernickel bread, halved crosswise (optional)
2 cups diced, peeled Yukon gold potatoes or white potatoes	
2½ cups cauliflower florets	2 tablespoons snipped fresh flat-leaf parsley (optional)
1 cup half-and-half, light cream, or milk	
2 tablespoons all-purpose flour	

1 In a large saucepan or 4-quart Dutch oven cook onions in hot butter until tender. Carefully add chicken broth and potatoes. Bring to boiling; reduce the heat. Simmer, covered, for 6 minutes. Add cauliflower. Return to boiling; reduce heat. Simmer, covered, for 4 to 6 minutes or until vegetables are tender.

2 In a small bowl whisk half-and-half into flour until smooth; add to soup mixture in saucepan. Cook and stir until mixture is thickened and bubbly. Reduce heat to low. Stir in 2½ cups of the Jarlsberg cheese until melted. Do not allow mixture to boil. Season to taste with salt and pepper.

3 Meanwhile, if using bread, trim crusts, if desired. Place the halved bread slices on a baking sheet. Bake in a 350° oven about 3 minutes or until crisp on top. Turn slices over. Sprinkle with the remaining ½ cup Jarlsberg cheese and, if desired, the parsley. Bake about 5 minutes more or until cheese melts.

4 To serve, ladle soup into bowls. Float one cheese-topped bread slice in each bowl.

NUTRITION FACTS PER SERVING: 267 cal., 17 g total fat (12 g sat. fat), 58 mg chol., 533 mg sodium, 14 g carbo., 2 g fiber, 15 g pro. DAILY VALUES: 15% vit. A, 31% vit. C, 39% calcium, 5% iron

Salmon and Potato Chowder

Angling for an innovative way to serve seafood? Forget the fish in the sea, including clams and lobsters, when whipping up chowder. Go for the fresh combination of salmon and potato seasoned with caraway seeds and dillweed. (See photo, page 40.)

START TO FINISH: 35 minutes MAKES: 6 servings

½	cup thinly sliced celery	¼	teaspoon caraway seeds
½	cup chopped onion (1 medium)	¼	teaspoon ground black pepper
1	tablespoon olive oil	⅛	teaspoon salt
4	cups milk	1	large potato, peeled, if desired, and cut into ½-inch cubes (about 1⅓ cups)
1	10-ounce can condensed cream of celery soup	8	ounces fresh or frozen skinless, boneless salmon fillets, cut into ¾-inch cubes
1	tablespoon snipped fresh dill or 1 teaspoon dried dillweed		

1 In a large saucepan cook and stir celery and onion in hot oil over medium-high heat until tender. Carefully stir in milk, condensed soup, dill, caraway seeds, black pepper, and salt. Stir in potato. Bring to boiling; reduce heat. Simmer, covered, for 10 to 15 minutes or until potato is tender.

2 Stir salmon into soup mixture in saucepan. Simmer, uncovered, for 2 to 3 minutes more or until salmon flakes easily with a fork. To serve, ladle chowder into cups or bowls.

NUTRITION FACTS PER SERVING: 215 cal., 9 g total fat (3 g sat. fat), 24 mg chol., 546 mg sodium, 21 g carbo., 1 g fiber, 13 g pro. DAILY VALUES: 12% vit. A, 12% vit. C, 19% calcium, 8% iron

Island-Style Clam Chowder

With clams, onion, celery, tomatoes, and thyme, this dish has its roots in the time-honored Eastern Seaboard tradition. This version features sweet potatoes, chile peppers, and lime juice for Caribbean flair.

START TO FINISH: 35 minutes MAKES: 4 servings

½	pint shucked clams or one 6½-ounce can minced clams	1½	teaspoons snipped fresh thyme or ½ teaspoon dried thyme, crushed
2	cups peeled and cubed sweet potatoes (1 to 2 medium)	1	10-ounce can chopped tomatoes and green chile peppers, undrained
½	cup chopped onion (1 medium)	1	tablespoon lime juice
½	cup chopped celery (1 stalk)	1	tablespoon dark rum (optional)
¼	cup chopped red sweet pepper		
2	cloves garlic, minced		

1 Drain clams, reserving juice. Add enough water to clam juice to make 2½ cups liquid. If using fresh clams, chop clams; set aside.

2 In a large saucepan bring the clam liquid to boiling. Stir in sweet potatoes, onion, celery, sweet pepper, garlic, and, if using, dried thyme. Return to boiling; reduce heat. Cover and simmer about 10 minutes or until sweet potatoes are tender.

3 Mash mixture slightly with a potato masher. Stir in clams, undrained tomatoes, lime juice, and, if using, fresh thyme. If desired, stir in 1 tablespoon dark rum. Return to boiling; reduce heat. Cook for 1 to 2 minutes more. To serve, ladle chowder into bowls.

NUTRITION FACTS PER SERVING: 128 cal., 1 g total fat (0 g sat. fat), 19 mg chol., 337 mg sodium, 22 g carbo., 3 g fiber, 9 g pro. DAILY VALUES: 66% vit. C, 6% calcium, 57% iron

Navy Beans and Pork

Amidst a hearty medley of diced veggies and plump navy beans stand tender barbecued pork spareribs. (See photo, page 40.)

START TO FINISH: 1½ hours OVEN: 350° MAKES: 6 servings

2	pounds meaty pork spareribs or loin-back ribs	½	teaspoon ground black pepper
1	cup chopped onions (2 medium)	1	tablespoon cooking oil
1	cup chopped celery (2 stalks)	2	15-ounce cans navy beans, rinsed and drained
¾	cup chopped carrots	2	14-ounce cans chicken broth
2	teaspoons dried sage, crushed	¼	cup bottled barbecue sauce

1 Trim separable fat from ribs. Cut meat into two-rib portions. In a 4½- to 6-quart Dutch oven cook ribs, onions, celery, carrots, sage, and pepper in hot oil over medium heat for 5 minutes.

2 Add drained navy beans and chicken broth to ribs in Dutch oven. Bring to boiling; reduce heat. Cook, covered, for 20 minutes, stirring often. Remove ribs; cover and reduce heat. Cook for 50 minutes, stirring occasionally.

3 Meanwhile, line a shallow roasting pan with a double thickness of foil. Place ribs, meaty side down, in pan. Brush with half of the barbecue sauce. Bake in a 350° oven for 25 minutes. Turn and brush with remaining sauce. Bake about 25 minutes more or until tender.

4 To serve, place one double-rib piece into each bowl. Slightly mash beans in soup. Ladle soup over ribs.

NUTRITION FACTS PER SERVING: 443 cal., 19 g total fat (7 g sat. fat), 65 mg chol., 1,199 mg sodium, 36 g carbo., 8 g fiber, 31 g pro. DAILY VALUES: 8% vit. C, 12% calcium, 21% iron

SUPER SOUP TOPPERS AND STIR-INS Sometimes a simple ingredient, either stirred in or sprinkled over soup, is all it takes to make a bowl of soup beyond basic. Here are a few ideas to try:

Snipped fresh herbs or purchased or homemade pesto are fragrant and lively when added to creamy soups, such as potato and other vegetable soups or thick stews and chowders.

Crumbled crispy bacon or roasted garlic is just the right addition for hearty concoctions.

Drop some dried tomatoes or a little crumbled Parmigiano-Reggiano cheese into simmering broth-based soups. The hot broth will soften the tomatoes and melt the cheese while bringing out the flavor.

Shrimp Gumbo

Shrimp and sausage team up in this Cajun-style stew.

START TO FINISH: 35 minutes MAKES: 4 servings

1 pound fresh or frozen medium shrimp	1 14½-ounce can tomatoes, undrained and cut up
8 ounces andouille or Cajun sausage, coarsely chopped	1¼ cups water
¾ cup chopped green sweet pepper (1 medium)	½ cup uncooked long grain rice
½ cup chopped onion (1 medium)	3 cloves garlic, minced
	1 teaspoon Cajun seasoning

1 Thaw shrimp, if frozen. Peel and devein shrimp; set aside. In a 4-quart Dutch oven cook sausage, sweet pepper, and onion for 5 to 8 minutes or until vegetables are tender. Stir in undrained tomatoes, water, rice, garlic, and Cajun seasoning. Bring to boiling; reduce heat. Simmer, covered, for 15 to 20 minutes or until rice is tender.

2 Stir shrimp into soup mixture in Dutch oven. Return to boiling; reduce heat. Simmer, covered, for 2 to 3 minutes more or until shrimp are pink. To serve, ladle gumbo into bowls.

NUTRITION FACTS PER SERVING: 424 cal., 20 g total fat (7 g sat. fat), 152 mg chol., 1,164 mg sodium, 30 g carbo., 2 g fiber, 31 g pro. DAILY VALUES: 67% vit. C, 11% calcium, 24% iron

Black Bean and Sausage Posole

*Posole, a traditional dish from Mexico's Pacific Coast region,
gives in-a-hurry cooks cause to celebrate any weeknight. Prepared in 15 minutes,
the soup has a simmering time of 30 minutes. (See photo, page 36.)*

START TO FINISH: 45 minutes MAKES: 6 servings

12	ounces uncooked bulk turkey sausage	1	cup frozen loose-pack diced hash brown potatoes
2	14-ounce cans reduced-sodium chicken broth	½	cup chopped green sweet pepper (1 small)
1	15-ounce can black beans, rinsed and drained	⅓	cup chopped onion (1 small)
1	14½-ounce can golden hominy, rinsed and drained	1	clove garlic, minced
1	14½-ounce can Mexican-style stewed tomatoes, undrained	1	teaspoon dried oregano, crushed
		½	teaspoon chili powder

1 In a large saucepan brown sausage over medium heat. Drain off fat.
Add chicken broth, drained black beans, drained hominy, undrained tomatoes,
hash brown potatoes, sweet pepper, onion, garlic, oregano, and chili powder to
sausage in saucepan. Bring to boiling; reduce heat. Simmer, covered, for
30 minutes. To serve, ladle soup into bowls.

NUTRITION FACTS PER SERVING: 292 cal., 14 g total fat (1 g sat. fat), 45 mg chol., 1,295 mg sodium,
26 g carbo., 4 g fiber, 17 g pro. DAILY VALUES: 30% vit. C, 3% calcium, 15% iron

Country French Beef Stew

There's no glamour in pot roast—it's cheap and reliable, if perhaps a little tough. A Gallic twist, however, lends the recipe cachet, while the stewing technique delivers tender, juicy meat. C'est si bon! (See photo, page 35.)

PREP: 30 minutes COOK: 1 hour 55 minutes MAKES: 6 servings

¼	cup all-purpose flour	1	cup beef broth
½	teaspoon ground black pepper	1	cup chopped tomato
2	pounds boneless beef chuck pot roast, cut into 1-inch pieces	2	teaspoons dried thyme, crushed, or 2 tablespoons snipped fresh thyme
3	tablespoons olive oil	4	medium carrots, cut into ½-inch slices
1	medium onion, cut into thin wedges	2	medium parsnips, cut into ½-inch slices
3	cloves garlic, minced		Snipped fresh parsley (optional)
⅔	cup dry red wine		
1	15-ounce can small white beans, rinsed and drained		

1 In a plastic bag combine flour and pepper. Add beef pieces, a few at a time, shaking to coat. In a 4- to 6-quart Dutch oven brown half of the beef in 1 tablespoon of the oil; remove beef. Add remaining oil, remaining beef, onion, and garlic to Dutch oven. Cook until beef is brown and onion is tender. Drain off fat, if necessary.

2 Add wine to Dutch oven, scraping until the brown bits are dissolved. Return all beef to Dutch oven. Stir in drained beans, beef broth, tomato, and, if using, dried thyme. Bring to boiling; reduce heat. Simmer, covered, for 1½ hours.

3 Add carrots and parsnips to beef mixture in Dutch oven. Return to boiling; reduce heat. Simmer, covered, for 25 to 30 minutes more or until beef and vegetables are tender. Stir in fresh thyme, if using.

4 To serve, ladle stew into bowls. If desired, garnish with parsley.

NUTRITION FACTS PER SERVING: 554 cal., 31 g total fat (10 g sat. fat), 99 mg chol., 295 mg sodium, 29 g carbo., 8 g fiber, 34 g pro. DAILY VALUES: 211% vit. A, 26% vit. C, 8% calcium, 30% iron

STEWING FOR TENDERNESS Stewing is a cooking technique perfectly suited for when you want to make the most of less expensive, tougher cuts of meat such as beef chuck or round. Stewing simply means to cook food in liquid in a covered pot for a long time. You can stew meats either on the range top or in the oven. The long, slow, moist cooking softens the tough fibers of the meat, making it tender, juicy, and delicious. Naturally tender cuts, such as most steaks, however, don't require this sort of cooking. That's why they often are grilled, broiled, or panfried for a short period of time.

Sweet and Sour Stew

Catsup or ketchup? No matter how you spell it, the pronunciation and taste are generally similar. Some aficionados proclaim just a bit more tang to catsup.

PREP: 20 minutes COOK: 1½ hours MAKES: 4 servings

¼ cup all-purpose flour	½ cup catsup
1 teaspoon salt	¼ cup packed brown sugar
Dash ground black pepper	¼ cup vinegar
1½ pounds beef stew meat, cut into 1-inch pieces	1 tablespoon Worcestershire sauce
2 tablespoons cooking oil	1 cup chopped onions (2 medium)
1 cup water	6 medium carrots, cut into ¾-inch pieces

1 In a plastic bag combine flour, salt, and pepper. Add beef pieces, a few at a time, shaking to coat. In a large skillet brown beef, half at a time, in hot oil, adding additional oil, if necessary. Drain off fat. Return all the beef to the skillet.

2 In a medium bowl stir together water, catsup, brown sugar, vinegar, and Worcestershire sauce. Add catsup mixture to beef in skillet; stir in onions. Bring to boiling; reduce heat. Simmer, covered, for 1 hour. Add carrots; simmer, covered, about 30 minutes more or until meat and carrots are tender. To serve, ladle stew into bowls.

NUTRITION FACTS PER SERVING: 479 cal., 17 g total fat (4 g sat. fat), 80 mg chol., 1,122 mg sodium, 42 g carbo., 4 g fiber, 40 g pro. DAILY VALUES: 23% vit. C, 8% calcium, 29% iron

Hearty Beef Stew with Basil

*It's amazing how much time a soup mix can shave off your dinnertime preparation.
Amazing, too, is the fresh flavor a sprinkling of snipped basil brings to a stew.
Convenience and freshness? Talk about the best of both worlds!*

PREP: 20 minutes COOK: 1½ hours MAKES: 6 to 8 servings

1	2-pound boneless beef chuck roast
¼	cup all-purpose flour
½	teaspoon seasoned salt
2	tablespoons butter or margarine
1	pound tiny new potatoes, quartered
2	cups whole fresh mushrooms, halved

1½	cups packaged, peeled baby carrots
1	2.4-ounce envelope (regular-size) tomato-basil soup mix
2	cups water
1	large tomato, chopped
2	tablespoons snipped fresh basil

1 Trim fat from beef. Cut beef into 1½-inch pieces. Place flour and seasoned salt in a plastic bag. Add beef pieces, a few at a time, shaking to coat. In a 4-quart Dutch oven brown beef, half at a time, in hot butter over medium-high heat. Drain off fat. Return all of the beef to Dutch oven.

2 Add potatoes, mushrooms, and carrots to beef in Dutch oven. Sprinkle with soup mix; stir in water. Bring to boiling; reduce heat. Simmer, covered, about 1½ hours or until meat and vegetables are tender. Stir in tomato and basil; heat through. To serve, ladle stew into bowls.

NUTRITION FACTS PER SERVING: 444 cal., 16 g total fat (7 g sat. fat), 120 mg chol., 716 mg sodium, 33 g carbo., 3 g fiber, 40 g pro. DAILY VALUES: 31% vit. C, 3% calcium, 43% iron

TO MAKE AHEAD: Prepare stew, simmering until meat, potatoes, and carrots are tender. Transfer to a bowl. Cool quickly in an ice bath; cover and chill up to 24 hours. To serve, return to Dutch oven and bring to boiling, stirring occasionally. Stir in fresh tomato and basil; heat through.

Beef and Green Chile Stew

Using medium green salsa instead of mild adds an extra kick to this hearty stew.

PREP: 15 minutes COOK: 1¾ hours MAKES: 8 servings

2	pounds beef stew meat		1	teaspoon ground cumin
¼	cup all-purpose flour		3	cups cubed potatoes
¼	cup butter or margarine		1	14½-ounce can hominy, drained
6	cloves garlic, minced		2	4½-ounce cans diced green chile peppers, drained
3	cups beef broth		12	green onions, bias-sliced into 1-inch pieces (1½ cups)
1	12-ounce bottle dark Mexican beer		½	cup snipped fresh cilantro
1	cup bottled mild or medium-hot green salsa			
2	tablespoons snipped fresh oregano or 2 teaspoons dried oregano, crushed			

1 Toss beef cubes with flour. In a 4½-quart Dutch oven brown the beef cubes, half at a time, in hot butter. Using a slotted spoon, remove beef from Dutch oven. Add garlic to drippings; cook for 1 minute. Carefully add beef broth, beer, salsa, oregano, and cumin. Return beef to Dutch oven. Bring to boiling; reduce heat. Simmer, covered, about 1¼ hours or until beef is nearly tender.

2 Add potatoes to beef mixture in Dutch oven. Simmer, covered, about 30 minutes more or until beef and potatoes are tender. Stir in drained hominy, drained chile peppers, green onions, and cilantro; heat through. To serve, ladle stew into bowls.

NUTRITION FACTS PER SERVING: 392 cal., 16 g total fat (6 g sat. fat), 97 mg chol., 720 mg sodium, 28 g carbo., 1 g fiber, 32 g pro. DAILY VALUES: 49% vit. C, 7% calcium, 38% iron

Pork Stew with Hominy

This savory combination could be described as a posole—a thick, hearty Mexican soup traditionally served as a main course at Christmas. Sprinkle shredded radishes over the top for a festive presentation.

START TO FINISH: 25 minutes MAKES: 4 servings

12 ounces boneless pork strips or stir-fry strips	¼ teaspoon ground cumin
¾ cup chopped onion (1 large)	¼ teaspoon crushed red pepper
2 cloves garlic, minced	1 14½-ounce can hominy, drained
1 tablespoon cooking oil	3 tablespoons snipped fresh cilantro
4 cups chicken broth	¼ cup shredded radishes
1 cup thinly sliced carrots (2 medium)	

1 In a large saucepan cook pork, onion, and garlic in hot oil until pork is slightly pink in center. Remove pork mixture from saucepan; set aside.

2 Add chicken broth, carrots, cumin, and red pepper to saucepan. Bring to boiling; reduce heat. Simmer, covered, about 8 minutes or just until carrots are tender. Add drained hominy, cilantro, and pork mixture; cook and stir until heated through.

3 To serve, ladle stew into bowls. Sprinkle with radishes.

NUTRITION FACTS PER SERVING: 290 cal., 12 g total fat (3 g sat. fat), 39 mg chol., 1,056 mg sodium, 26 g carbo., 3 g fiber, 20 g pro. DAILY VALUES: 118% vit. A, 8% vit. C, 4% calcium, 15% iron

FROZEN ASSETS When freezing leftover soups and stews, keep these tips in mind: To freeze leftovers, first cool the hot food by placing it in a bowl set over another bowl filled with ice water. This lets the food cool quickly, which is important. Transfer the food to freezer-safe containers. Use small, shallow containers to allow food to freeze quickly, which slows bacteria growth. Soups and stews expand when they freeze, so leave about ½ inch of space below the rim. Thaw frozen foods in the refrigerator or microwave—never at room temperature. You can also slowly reheat frozen food without thawing by placing it in an appropriate-size saucepan. Cook the food, covered, until it is thawed, stirring occasionally to break it up. Then heat to boiling, stirring frequently. Cornstarch- or flour-thickened soups do not freeze well, as the starch breaks down during freezing, altering the soup's consistency. Cheese soups also do not freeze well.

Chicken and Tortellini Stew

Dress up leftover chicken by stirring it into this easy-to-prepare stew. Chunks of yellow squash and sweet pepper accompany plump tortellini and beet greens. (See photo, page 34.)

START TO FINISH: 35 minutes MAKES: 6 servings

2 cups water	3/4 cup coarsely chopped green sweet pepper (1 medium)
1 14-ounce can reduced-sodium chicken broth	1/2 cup sliced carrot (1 medium)
1 medium yellow summer squash	1 1/2 teaspoons snipped fresh rosemary
6 cups torn beet greens, turnip greens, or spinach	1/2 teaspoon salt-free seasoning blend
1 cup packaged, dried, cheese-filled tortellini pasta	1/4 teaspoon ground black pepper
1 medium onion, cut into thin wedges	2 cups chopped cooked chicken
	1 tablespoon snipped fresh basil

1 In a 4-quart Dutch oven bring water and chicken broth to boiling. Meanwhile, halve summer squash lengthwise and cut into 1/2-inch slices. Add summer squash, greens, pasta, onion, sweet pepper, carrot, rosemary, seasoning blend, and black pepper to broth mixture in Dutch oven. Return to boiling; reduce heat. Simmer, covered, about 15 minutes or until pasta and vegetables are nearly tender.

2 Stir chicken into stew mixture in Dutch oven. Cook, covered, about 5 minutes more or until pasta and vegetables are tender. Stir in fresh basil. To serve, ladle stew into bowls.

NUTRITION FACTS PER SERVING: 234 cal., 6 g total fat (1 g sat. fat), 45 mg chol., 530 mg sodium, 22 g carbo., 3 g fiber, 22 g pro. DAILY VALUES: 55% vit. C, 14% calcium, 13% iron

Easy Oyster Stew

Be sure to rinse the drained oysters to remove any bits of sand or shell. For a richer stew, substitute two additional cups of half-and-half or light cream for the milk.

START TO FINISH: 25 minutes MAKES: 8 servings

⅔ cup sliced leeks (2 medium) (see tip, p. 44)

2 tablespoons butter or margarine

3 tablespoons all-purpose flour

1 teaspoon anchovy paste

2 cups half-and-half or light cream

2 cups milk

3 pints shucked oysters

Several dashes bottled hot pepper sauce (optional)

1 In a 4-quart saucepan or Dutch oven cook leeks in hot butter until tender. Stir in flour and anchovy paste until combined. Add half-and-half and milk. Cook and stir until slightly thickened and bubbly. Cook and stir 1 minute more.

2 Meanwhile, drain oysters, reserving 3 cups liquid. Strain liquid. In a large saucepan combine reserved oyster liquid and oysters. Bring just to simmering over medium heat; reduce heat. Cook, covered, about 1 to 2 minutes or until oysters curl around the edges. Skim surface of cooking liquid. Stir oyster mixture into cream mixture. If desired, add hot pepper sauce. To serve, ladle stew into bowls.

NUTRITION FACTS PER SERVING: 242 cal., 14 g total fat (8 g sat. fat), 105 mg chol., 248 mg sodium, 15 g carbo., 1 g fiber, 14 g pro. DAILY VALUES: 14% vit. C, 17% calcium, 61% iron

HOT FROM THE POT Don't let a cold bowl of chili or soup let you down! Keep soups and stews warm longer by serving them in warmed bowls. Just before ladling, rinse bowls under hot tap water; dry. Or if the vessels are ovenproof, let them sit briefly in the oven at a low temperature.

Turkey and Black Bean Chili

Think you've "bean there, done that" with chili? Try this variation. With black beans instead of red, and turkey instead of beef, it's a whole new stew.

START TO FINISH: 45 minutes MAKES: 6 servings

1	pound turkey breast tenderloins or skinless, boneless chicken breast halves or thighs
2	tablespoons cooking oil
1	cup chopped green sweet pepper (1 large)
1	cup chopped onions (2 medium)
2	cloves garlic, minced
2	28-ounce cans tomatoes, undrained and cut up
2	15-ounce cans black beans or Great Northern beans, rinsed and drained

1	12-ounce can beer
2	tablespoons red wine vinegar
1	tablespoon chili powder
1	teaspoon dried oregano, crushed
1	teaspoon ground cumin
½	teaspoon salt
¼	teaspoon ground black pepper
¼	teaspoon bottled hot pepper sauce
1	bay leaf
1	cup shredded Monterey Jack cheese or cheddar cheese (4 ounces)

1 Cut turkey into bite-size pieces. In a 4-quart Dutch oven heat 1 tablespoon of the oil over medium heat. Cook half of the turkey in hot oil until no longer pink; remove from pan. Repeat with remaining oil and turkey; remove turkey.

2 Add green sweet pepper, onions, and garlic to Dutch oven. Cook about 5 minutes or just until vegetables are tender; stir occasionally. Drain off fat.

3 Return turkey to Dutch oven. Add undrained tomatoes, drained beans, beer, vinegar, chili powder, oregano, cumin, salt, black pepper, hot pepper sauce, and bay leaf. Bring to boiling; reduce heat. Simmer, covered, about 20 minutes or until turkey is tender, stirring occasionally. Discard bay leaf.

4 To serve, ladle chili into bowls. Sprinkle with cheese.

NUTRITION FACTS PER SERVING: 358 cal., 12 g total fat (4 g sat. fat), 63 mg chol., 887 mg sodium, 32 g carbo., 10 g fiber, 34 g pro. DAILY VALUES: 67% vit. C, 26% calcium, 21% iron

full-of-Beans Chili

Not only is there a bounty of chili beans and zesty chipotle pepper in this winter warmer, but refried beans add satisfying body and flavor, making this the quintessential bean-lover's chili.

PREP: 10 minutes COOK: 1½ hours MAKES: 8 to 10 servings

2	pounds ground beef
1	cup chopped onions (2 medium)
2	tablespoons chili powder
2	tablespoons ground cumin
2	cups water
1	16-ounce jar bottled thick and chunky salsa
1	16-ounce can refried beans

1	12-ounce can beer
1	to 2 canned chipotle peppers in adobo sauce, chopped
2	15¾-ounce cans chili beans with chili gravy, undrained
2	tablespoons lime juice
	Dairy sour cream (optional)
	Finely shredded lime peel (optional)

1 In a 4- to 6-quart Dutch oven cook beef and onions until beef is brown and onions are tender, stirring occasionally, leaving some bite-size chunks of beef. Drain off fat. Stir in chili powder and cumin; cook and stir for 3 minutes more.

2 Add the water, salsa, refried beans, beer, and chipotle peppers to beef mixture in Dutch oven. Bring to boiling; reduce heat. Simmer, covered, for 1 hour. Stir in undrained chili beans and lime juice. Cook, covered, for 15 minutes more.

3 To serve, ladle chili into bowls. If desired, garnish with a spoonful of sour cream and sprinkle with finely shredded lime peel.

NUTRITION FACTS PER SERVING: 469 cal., 19 g total fat (6 g sat. fat), 97 mg chol., 1,108 mg sodium, 43 g carbo., 9 g fiber, 34 g pro. DAILY VALUES: 28% vit. A, 66% vit. C, 10% calcium, 52% iron

Chapter Three
Side Dishes

Tomato-Cheese Melts, p. 107

Stuffed Zucchini, p. 108

Corn Cakes with Fresh Corn and Chives, p. 100

Corn Pudding, p. 101

Green Beans in Yellow Pepper Butter, p. 104

Autumn Medley, p. 110

Carrot, Corn, and Bean Salsa, p. 85

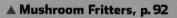

▲ **Mushroom Fritters, p. 92**

▲ **Rice Primavera, p. 81**

▲ **Scalloped New Potatoes, p. 98**

▲ **Caramelized Sweet Potatoes, p. 99**

Rice Primavera

You'll find jasmine rice in larger supermarkets, some Asian and Indian groceries, and health food and gourmet stores. (See photo, page 80.)

START TO FINISH: 45 minutes MAKES: 6 side-dish servings

1⅔ cups water	1 teaspoon finely shredded lemon peel
1 cup jasmine rice	1 tablespoon lemon juice
3 cups assorted fresh vegetables, such as sugar snap peas; asparagus, sliced into 1-inch pieces; red, green, or yellow sweet pepper, cut into 1-inch cubes; and/or cherry tomatoes, quartered	¼ teaspoon coarsely ground black pepper
	1 cup chicken broth
	3 to 4 tablespoons shredded fresh basil or purple basil
	1 tablespoon basil oil or olive oil
¼ cup finely chopped red onion	2 tablespoons pine nuts, toasted
2 teaspoons cornstarch	Purple basil blossoms (optional)

1 In a saucepan bring water to boiling. Stir in rice. Return to boiling; reduce heat. Simmer, covered, 15 minutes or until liquid is absorbed and rice is tender.

2 Meanwhile, in a covered large saucepan cook vegetables (except cherry tomatoes, if using) and red onion in a small amount of boiling lightly salted water for 2 to 3 minutes or until crisp-tender. Drain and keep warm.

3 In a medium saucepan stir together cornstarch, lemon peel, lemon juice, and black pepper. Stir in chicken broth. Cook and stir over medium heat until thickened and bubbly. Cook and stir for 2 minutes more. Remove from heat. Add cooked vegetables and, if using, cherry tomatoes; toss.

4 Add shredded basil and basil oil to rice; toss to combine. Divide rice among six bowls; make an indentation in centers. Fill with vegetable mixture. Sprinkle with pine nuts. If desired, garnish with purple basil blossoms. Serve immediately.

NUTRITION FACTS PER SERVING: 188 cal., 5 g total fat (1 g sat. fat), 0 mg chol., 138 mg sodium, 32 g carbo., 1 g fiber, 6 g pro. DAILY VALUES: 65% vit. C, 2% calcium, 14% iron

---

RAINBOW OF RICES Rice is the most popular grain in the world, and it comes in several forms.

1 Brown rice has only the hull removed. The bran layers left on the grain give it a tan color and a nutty flavor with a slightly chewy texture. **2** White or polished rice is milled to remove both the hull and the bran layers. It is mild, delicately flavored, and comes in several varieties. **3** Precooked (quick-cooking) rice is available in both white and brown varieties and cooks in a few minutes. **4** Parboiled (sometimes called converted) rice is treated by a steam-pressure process before milling to make the white cooked grain extra fluffy. **5** Wild rice is used like rice but isn't rice at all; it's the long, dark brown or black, nutty-flavored seed of a marsh grass.

In addition, there are a host of colored rices. These include Himalayan Red, Chinese Black, Colusari Red, Black Japonica, and Purple Thai, now available for cooks who want to go beyond basic white or brown.

Tossed Crisp Vegetable Salad

The fresher and firmer the vegetables, the better the salad.
Choose any desired vegetable combination.

START TO FINISH: 25 minutes MAKES: 6 side-dish servings

4	thin asparagus spears	1	small celery root
1	small beet	1	small fennel bulb
1	small carrot	¼	to ⅓ cup bottled clear Italian or white
1	small parsnip or parsley root		wine vinaigrette salad dressing

1 Snap off and discard woody bases from asparagus. Wash asparagus and drain. Using a sharp knife, cut spears lengthwise into very thin strips. Wash beet; trim ends. Using a mechanical slicer or sharp peeler, cut thin strips of beet. Rinse under cold water; set aside. Trim carrot, parsnip, celery root, and fennel bulb. Using a mechanical slicer or sharp peeler, cut vegetables into wide, thin strips.

2 In a large salad bowl combine vegetables. Season to taste with salt and freshly ground black pepper. Serve and pass salad dressing.

NUTRITION FACTS PER SERVING: 79 cal., 6 g total fat (1 g sat. fat), 4 mg chol., 159 mg sodium, 6 g carbo., 2 g fiber, 1 g pro. DAILY VALUES: 15% vit. C, 1% calcium, 3% iron

Three-Bread Salad

Try this Italian classic with romaine lettuce and fun toppers such as crumbled bacon or dry-roasted sunflower seeds.

START TO FINISH: 25 minutes MAKES: 6 side-dish servings

1   recipe Dried Yellow Tomato Vinaigrette

6   cups mixed salad greens

2   1-inch-thick slices crusty sourdough bread, cut into irregular pieces

1   8-inch whole wheat pita bread round, cut into 12 wedges

2   slices pumpernickel bread, torn into pieces

1   small sweet onion, very thinly sliced and separated into rings

1   cup yellow and/or red pear-shaped tomatoes or cherry tomatoes

2   ounces shaved dry Monterey Jack cheese or other hard grating cheese

1 Prepare Dried Yellow Tomato Vinaigrette. Transfer to a storage container. Cover and chill.

2 In a large salad bowl combine mixed greens, sourdough pieces, pita wedges, torn pumpernickel, sliced onion, and tomatoes. Stir Dried Yellow Tomato Vinaigrette. Drizzle vinaigrette over salad; toss gently to coat. Sprinkle with cheese.

Dried Yellow Tomato Vinaigrette: In a small bowl place $1/4$ cup snipped dried yellow or red tomatoes (not oil packed). Add 1 cup boiling water; cover and let stand for 10 minutes. Drain tomatoes, reserving $1/2$ cup of the liquid. In a blender container or food processor bowl combine tomatoes and the reserved liquid; $1/4$ cup red wine vinegar; 1 tablespoon Dijon-style mustard; 2 teaspoons snipped fresh thyme or $1/2$ teaspoon dried thyme, crushed; $1/4$ teaspoon salt; and $1/8$ teaspoon coarsely ground black pepper. Cover and blend or process until nearly smooth. Gradually add $1/3$ cup olive oil, processing until combined and slightly thickened.

NUTRITION FACTS PER SERVING: 269 cal., 16 g total fat (4 g sat. fat), 7 mg chol., 599 mg sodium, 24 g carbo., 3 g fiber, 9 g pro. DAILY VALUES: 28% vit. C, 16% calcium, 11% iron

Zesty Fiesta Corn Salad

*Come summertime, serve this sassy salad with grilled chicken or burgers.
In winter, try it with roast turkey or broiled chops.*

PREP: 15 minutes CHILL: 8 hours MAKES: 8 side-dish servings

½	of a 1.25-ounce envelope (about 2 tablespoons) taco seasoning mix	1	15¼-ounce can whole kernel corn, drained
¼	cup water	1½	cups chopped tomatoes
¼	cup cooking oil	½	cup sliced ripe olives
¼	cup vinegar	¼	cup finely chopped green sweet pepper

1 In a large bowl stir together taco seasoning mix and water until well mixed; stir in oil and vinegar. Add corn, tomatoes, olives, and sweet pepper; toss lightly to coat. Cover and chill 8 hours or overnight, stirring mixture occasionally. Serve with a slotted spoon.

NUTRITION FACTS PER SERVING: 132 cal., 9 g total fat (1 g sat. fat), 0 mg chol., 394 mg sodium, 15 g carbo., 2 g fiber, 2 g pro. DAILY VALUES: 26% vit. C, 2% calcium, 6% iron

Carrot, Corn, and Bean Salad

This recipe is a perfect way to use peak-season sweet corn. You also can bring a taste of summer to your wintertime table by making this salad with frozen corn.
(See photo, page 79.)

(See photo, page 79.)

PREP: 20 minutes CHILL: 4 to 24 hours MAKES: 8 side-dish servings

3 cups thinly sliced carrots	¼ cup vinegar
2 cups fresh or frozen whole kernel corn	2 teaspoons snipped fresh thyme or ½ teaspoon dried thyme, crushed
1 15-ounce can kidney beans or black beans, rinsed and drained	1 teaspoon sugar
1 medium green or red sweet pepper, cut into thin strips (1 cup)	¼ teaspoon cracked black pepper
⅓ cup snipped fresh basil or parsley	¼ teaspoon crushed red pepper
¼ cup olive oil or salad oil	

1 In a large saucepan cook carrots and corn in a small amount of boiling salted water for 4 minutes. Drain.

2 In a large bowl combine carrots and corn, drained beans, sweet pepper, and basil. Set aside.

3 For dressing, in a screw-top jar combine oil, vinegar, thyme, sugar, black pepper, and red pepper. Cover and shake to combine. Add dressing to vegetable mixture; toss to coat. Cover and chill for at least 4 hours or up to 24 hours.

NUTRITION FACTS PER SERVING: 165 cal., 7 g total fat (1 g sat. fat), 0 mg chol., 104 mg sodium, 24 g carbo., 6 g fiber, 6 g pro. DAILY VALUES: 33% vit. C, 3% calcium, 7% iron

Pea and Macaroni Salad

It's not necessary to allow the macaroni to cool before mixing with the dressing. Once it's chilled, stir in additional milk to moisten the salad.

PREP: 20 minutes CHILL: 4 to 24 hours MAKES: 12 to 16 side-dish servings

1	cup fresh sugar snap peas	2	cloves garlic, minced
8	ounces packaged dried elbow macaroni	¼	teaspoon salt
1	cup frozen peas, thawed	¼	teaspoon ground black pepper
½	cup mayonnaise or salad dressing	¾	cup thinly sliced celery
½	cup dairy sour cream	2	tablespoons chopped onion
⅓	cup milk		Milk (optional)
¼	cup horseradish mustard		Sugar snap peas (optional)

1 Remove tips and strings from sugar snap peas; diagonally cut sugar snap peas in half. Cook macaroni according to package directions in boiling lightly salted water, adding sugar snap peas and frozen peas during the last 1 minute of cooking. Drain and rinse. Set aside macaroni mixture.

2 In a small bowl stir together mayonnaise, sour cream, milk, mustard, minced garlic, salt, and pepper; set aside.

3 In a large bowl combine cooked macaroni mixture, celery, and onion. Pour mayonnaise mixture over macaroni mixture; stir gently to combine. Cover and chill 4 to 24 hours.

4 Stir mixture before serving. If necessary, add additional milk (1 to 2 tablespoons) to moisten. If desired, top with additional sugar snap peas.

NUTRITION FACTS PER SERVING: 178 cal., 10 g total fat (2 g sat. fat), 7 mg chol., 169 mg sodium, 18 g carbo., 2 g fiber, 4 g pro. DAILY VALUES: 3% vit. A, 11% vit. C, 3% calcium, 5% iron

Barley-Couscous Salad

Quick-cooking barley and couscous trim preparation time. Don't cheat on the chilling time, however. It gives the grains a chance to soak up the lemony dressing.

PREP: 25 minutes CHILL: 2 to 24 hours MAKES: 6 side-dish servings

2	cups chicken broth		¼	cup sliced green onions (2)
½	cup quick-cooking barley*		2	cups shredded fresh spinach
⅔	cup couscous		1	cup cherry tomatoes, quartered
3	tablespoons fresh lemon juice			Lemon wedges (optional)
2	tablespoons olive oil			

1 In a large saucepan bring broth to boiling. Stir in barley; reduce heat. Simmer, covered, for 12 minutes. Stir in couscous; remove from heat. Cover and let stand for 5 minutes.

2 Transfer couscous mixture to a large bowl. Stir in lemon juice and olive oil. Cool completely. Stir in green onions. Cover and chill for 2 to 24 hours.

3 To serve, fluff salad with a fork. Stir in spinach and tomato wedges. If desired, garnish with lemon wedges.

*Note: To heighten barley's nutty flavor, take an extra, easy step—toast it before cooking. In a heavy, dry pan over low heat, cook barley about 10 minutes, stirring often, until golden brown.

NUTRITION FACTS PER SERVING: 183 cal., 6 g total fat (1 g sat. fat), 0 mg chol., 278 mg sodium, 28 g carbo., 4 g fiber, 6 g pro. DAILY VALUES: 15% vit. A, 21% vit. C, 2% calcium, 9% iron

---

HEARTY BARLEY You're missing out if you haven't tried barley. Its toothsome texture and nutty flavor make it a great choice for pilaf, barley "risotto," or for adding to soups and casseroles. Look for barley in these forms:

Pearl barley has the outer hull removed and has been polished or pearled. It is sold in regular or quick-cooking forms.

Scotch or pot barley is less processed than pearl barley. It requires a long soaking period before cooking. Look for it in health food stores.

Barley flakes are similar to rolled oats, but thicker and chewier. Use in homemade granola and in baked goods.

Three-Corner Chicken Salad

Instead of using precooked packaged chicken, you may want to cook boneless chicken breasts by broiling them in the oven for about six minutes on each side. Or cover them with water or chicken stock and simmer on the stove top until cooked through.

START TO FINISH: 25 minutes OVEN: 400° MAKES: 4 side-dish servings

1 10-ounce package refrigerated pizza dough	6 cups torn mixed salad greens
1 9-ounce package frozen cooked chicken strips	1/3 cup bottled salad dressing

1 Grease well the outside sides and bottoms of four 10-ounce custard cups. Invert custard cups on a shallow baking pan; set aside.

2 Unroll refrigerated pizza dough on a cutting board. Shape into a 10-inch square. Cut the square into four triangles. Drape each triangle over a prepared inverted custard cup. Bake in a 400° oven about 15 minutes or until deep golden brown. Remove from cups; cool.

3 Prepare frozen cooked chicken strips according to package directions. To serve, divide the mixed salad greens and the chicken among bread bowls. Drizzle with dressing.

NUTRITION FACTS PER SERVING: 419 cal., 21 g total fat (4 g sat. fat), 43 mg chol., 1,333 mg sodium, 37 g carbo., 2 g fiber, 21 g pro. DAILY VALUES: 16% vit. A, 9% vit. C, 4% calcium, 14% iron

Summer Fruit with Sesame Dressing

A simple three-ingredient dressing livens up a bowl of fresh fruit.
This recipe uses peaches, papaya, strawberries, and raspberries,
but you can create your own fruit combination.

START TO FINISH: 25 minutes MAKES: 6 side-dish servings

2 cups sliced, peeled peaches or sliced nectarines	1 teaspoon honey
1 cup sliced, peeled papaya or mango	½ teaspoon toasted sesame oil
½ cup sliced strawberries	6 cups fresh spinach leaves
½ cup raspberries	2 tablespoons snipped fresh mint
¼ cup rice vinegar	

1 In a large bowl combine the peaches, papaya, strawberries, and raspberries. Set aside.

2 For vinaigrette, in a screw-top jar combine vinegar, honey, and sesame oil. Cover and shake well. Pour vinaigrette over fruit; toss gently to coat.

3 To serve, divide spinach among six salad plates. Top with fresh fruit mixture and sprinkle with fresh mint.

NUTRITION FACTS PER SERVING: 80 cal., 1 g total fat (0 g sat. fat), 0 mg chol., 40 mg sodium, 18 g carbo., 7 g fiber, 2 g pro. DAILY VALUES: 68% vit. C, 4% calcium, 15% iron

Citrus Salad with Glazed Pecans

The hearty flavor of spinach balances the tangy, sweet combination of citrus and maple syrup. Always use fresh spinach—stored in the refrigerator no longer than three days and washed thoroughly.

START TO FINISH: 20 minutes MAKES: 4 side-dish servings

3 tablespoons red wine vinegar	½ of a medium red onion, cut into thin wedges
3 tablespoons olive oil	
3 tablespoons pure maple syrup or maple-flavored syrup	6 ounces fresh baby spinach, washed and stems removed
2 tablespoons Dijon-style mustard	4 blood oranges or oranges, peeled, seeded, and thinly sliced
⅓ cup coarsely chopped pecans	
2 slices bacon, cut up	

1 For dressing, in a screw-top jar combine vinegar, olive oil, 1 tablespoon of the maple syrup, and the Dijon-style mustard. Cover and shake well; set aside.

2 In a medium skillet cook pecans in the remaining 2 tablespoons maple syrup over medium heat for 3 to 4 minutes or until lightly toasted. Spread nuts on foil; cool. Break nuts into clusters.

3 Meanwhile, in a small saucepan cook bacon and red onion wedges until bacon is crisp, stirring occasionally. Remove from heat; drain.

4 To serve, divide spinach and orange slices among four salad plates. Top with bacon-onion mixture and pecans; drizzle with dressing.

NUTRITION FACTS PER SERVING: 254 cal., 19 g total fat (3 g sat. fat), 3 mg chol., 142 mg sodium, 20 g carbo., 6 g fiber, 14 g pro. DAILY VALUES: 64% vit. C, 8% calcium, 19% iron

Italian Salad with Garlic Polenta Croutons

Homemade croutons make any salad more special, and your family and guests don't need to know how easy they are to prepare. Here, a package of refrigerated cooked polenta is quickly cubed and baked into a delicious homey accent for this fresh salad.

START TO FINISH: 25 minutes OVEN: 425° MAKES: 4 side-dish servings

½   of a 16-ounce tube refrigerated cooked polenta or 8 ounces leftover polenta

1   tablespoon olive oil

½   teaspoon garlic-pepper seasoning

6   cups torn romaine or torn mixed greens

½   of a 7-ounce jar roasted red sweet peppers, drained and cut up (½ cup)

½   cup chopped tomato

⅓   cup sliced pitted ripe olives

2   tablespoons grated Parmesan cheese

¼   cup bottled Italian salad dressing

1 Grease a shallow baking pan; set aside. For croutons, cut polenta into ¾-inch cubes. In a small bowl combine cubed polenta, olive oil, and garlic-pepper seasoning; toss to coat. Spread cubes in prepared baking pan. Bake in a 425° oven for 15 to 20 minutes or until golden, turning once halfway through.

2 Meanwhile, in a bowl toss together romaine, roasted sweet peppers, tomato, and olives. Divide salad mixture among four salad plates. Top each salad with warm polenta croutons and sprinkle with Parmesan cheese. Serve with Italian salad dressing.

NUTRITION FACTS PER SERVING: 217 cal., 16 g total fat (2 g sat. fat), 12 mg chol., 724 mg sodium, 16 g carbo., 4 g fiber, 4 g pro. DAILY VALUES: 126% vit. C, 8% calcium, 9% iron

STORING LETTUCE Having plenty of lettuce ready for salad at a moment's notice is convenient. Washing and storing lettuce properly makes a big difference in how long it stays at the peak of freshness.

Remove any brown-edged, bruised, wilted, or old leaves. Wash greens under cold running water, then separate the leaves and rinse them in a colander under cold water. If the leaves are very sandy or gritty, repeat the rinsing step.

Use a salad spinner to dry washed lettuce greens, or shake them dry. Layer the leaves between paper towels and store in a sealable container or plastic bag in the refrigerator. Cleaned lettuce will keep this way for a week.

Mushroom fritters

You can also serve fritters with your favorite bottled ranch salad dressing.
(See photo, page 80.)

PREP: 15 minutes   COOK: 3 to 4 minutes per batch   MAKES: 6 side-dish servings

1 cup all-purpose flour	4½ cups sliced fresh button mushrooms (12 ounces)
2 teaspoons baking powder	Cooking oil for deep-fat frying
½ teaspoon salt	Green onion (optional)
1 egg, beaten	1 recipe Havarti-Pepper Dip
⅔ cup milk	

1 To make fritters, in a medium bowl stir together flour, baking powder, and salt. In a small bowl combine egg and milk. Pour milk mixture all at once into flour mixture; stir just until moistened. Fold in mushrooms.

2 In a large saucepan or deep-fat fryer, heat 3 to 4 inches oil to 365°. Using a tablespoon, carefully drop mushroom mixture into hot oil. Fry a few fritters at a time, for 3 to 4 minutes or until golden, turning once. Using a slotted spoon, remove fritters and drain on paper towels. If desired, garnish with green onion. Serve immediately with Havarti-Pepper Dip.

Havarti-Pepper Dip: In a blender container or food processor bowl combine one 8-ounce carton dairy sour cream, ¾ cup shredded Havarti cheese (3 ounces), 1 to 2 tablespoons cracked black pepper, and ⅛ teaspoon salt. Cover and blend or process until smooth.

NUTRITION FACTS PER SERVING: 362 cal., 27 g total fat (7 g sat. fat), 72 mg chol., 459 mg sodium, 22 g carbo., 2 g fiber, 9 g pro. DAILY VALUES: 6% vit. C, 23% calcium, 16% iron

TO MAKE AHEAD: Make and drain fritters as directed. Wrap fritters and chill for up to 2 days. To reheat, place fritters on a baking sheet. Bake, uncovered, in a 375° oven about 10 minutes or until hot and crisp.

fettuccine with four Cheeses

Three Italian cheeses (Parmigiano-Reggiano, Asiago, and Montasio) and one Spanish cheese (Manchego) provide the flourish to a simple dish of pasta and herbs. Use the cheeses suggested or any combination of hard grating cheeses.

START TO FINISH: 30 minutes MAKES: 4 side-dish servings

5 ounces packaged dried fettuccine	2 tablespoons shaved Asiago cheese
3 cloves garlic, minced	2 tablespoons shaved Montasio cheese
1 tablespoon olive oil	2 tablespoons shaved Manchego cheese
1/8 to 1/4 teaspoon ground white pepper	Snipped fresh oregano (optional)
2 tablespoons shaved Parmigiano-Reggiano cheese	

1 Prepare fettuccine according to package directions, adding minced garlic during last minute of cooking. Drain fettuccine; toss with olive oil and white pepper.

2 Divide fettuccine into four bowls. Sprinkle each serving with 1/2 tablespoon of each of the cheeses. If desired, garnish with snipped oregano.

NUTRITION FACTS PER SERVING: 227 cal., 8 g total fat (3 g sat. fat), 10 mg chol., 176 mg sodium, 29 g carbo., 1 g fiber, 9 g pro. DAILY VALUES: 1% vit. C, 11% calcium, 9% iron

Alfredo-Style Fettuccine: Prepare the dried fettuccine according to package directions. In a large skillet cook the garlic in hot oil for 30 seconds. Add 1/3 cup dry white wine and 1/3 cup chicken broth. Bring to boiling. Cook, uncovered, about 4 minutes or until liquid is reduced by half. Add 2/3 cup whipping cream, 1/8 to 1/4 teaspoon ground white pepper, and 1/8 teaspoon ground mace or nutmeg. Simmer, uncovered, about 6 minutes or until cream thickens. Drain fettuccine. Toss pasta with sauce. Divide into four bowls. Sprinkle each serving with 1/2 tablespoon of each of the cheeses. If desired, garnish with snipped fresh oregano.

Smoky Macaroni and Cheese

Watch those elbows disappear from the table when served in this yummy favorite. This creamy version has half the fat and calories of the typical homemade combo.

PREP: 20 minutes BAKE: 20 minutes STAND: 5 minutes OVEN: 350° MAKES: 8 side-dish servings

8	ounces packaged dried elbow macaroni	1/2	teaspoon dry mustard
3	ounces smoked cheddar cheese or smoked Gouda cheese	1/4	teaspoon ground black pepper
1/2	cup chopped onion (1 medium)	2/3	cup coarsely chopped tart apple (1 medium)
1	cup reduced-sodium chicken broth	1	tablespoon finely shredded Parmesan cheese
3/4	cup fat-free half-and-half		
1	tablespoon all-purpose flour		

1 Cook macaroni according to package directions; drain. If desired, use a vegetable peeler to remove any darker outer layer from smoked cheddar cheese. Shred cheese (you should have about ³/₄ cup); set aside.

2 Meanwhile, for cheese sauce, in a covered small saucepan cook onion in chicken broth over medium-high heat about 5 minutes or until tender. In a screw-top jar combine half-and-half, flour, dry mustard, and pepper; cover and shake. Add to broth in saucepan. Cook and stir over medium heat just until bubbly. Remove from heat; add cheddar cheese, stirring until most of cheese is melted. Pour sauce over macaroni, stirring until combined. Transfer mixture to an ungreased 1¹/₂-quart casserole.

3 Bake, covered, in a 350° oven for 10 minutes. Uncover and bake about 10 minutes more or until bubbly. Let stand for 5 minutes. Sprinkle with chopped apple and Parmesan cheese.

NUTRITION FACTS PER SERVING: 176 cal., 3 g total fat (2 g sat. fat), 9 mg chol., 276 mg sodium, 28 g carbo., 1 g fiber, 7 g pro. DAILY VALUES: 3% vit. C, 10% calcium, 5% iron

Garlic Mashed Potatoes and Parsnips

*The subtly sweet flavor of parsnips makes ordinary
mashed potatoes exceptionally delicious.*

START TO FINISH: 35 minutes OVEN: 350° MAKES: 14 side-dish servings

9	medium baking potatoes, such as russet (3 pounds)	¾	cup milk
1½	pounds parsnips	½	cup butter (no substitutes)
1	head garlic, unpeeled	¾	teaspoon salt
2	teaspoons olive oil	⅛	teaspoon freshly ground black pepper

1 Peel potatoes and parsnips; cut into ½-inch chunks. In a covered Dutch oven or large saucepan cook potatoes and parsnips in boiling salted water about 15 minutes or until tender. Drain.

2 Meanwhile, cut about ½ inch off tip of garlic head and discard. Place garlic in a custard cup. Drizzle with olive oil. Cover with foil and bake in a 350° oven about 20 minutes or until tender when pierced with the tip of a sharp knife. Let cool. Squeeze garlic pulp out of peels and mash with a fork; set aside.

3 Press potatoes and parsnips through a potato ricer or food mill (or mash with a potato masher), and return them to Dutch oven.

4 In a small saucepan heat milk and butter just until boiling. Stir milk mixture into potato mixture. Stir in mashed garlic, salt, and pepper. Heat through. Season to taste with additional salt and pepper. Serve at once.

NUTRITION FACTS PER SERVING: 182 cal., 8 g total fat (5 g sat. fat), 20 mg chol., 252 mg sodium, 26 g carbo., 4 g fiber, 3 g pro. DAILY VALUES: 21% vit. C

Golden Potato Mini Casseroles

*Anyone digging into this luscious combination of Yukon gold potatoes
and cheese will strike it rich, as far as flavor goes.*

PREP: 30 minutes BAKE: 15 minutes OVEN: 350° MAKES: 4 side-dish servings

2 pounds Yukon gold potatoes or other
   yellow-fleshed potatoes,
   peeled and cut up

¼ teaspoon salt

⅛ teaspoon black pepper

Milk (optional)

½ cup whipping cream

⅓ cup shredded American cheese or
   cheddar cheese

1 Grease four 10-ounce casseroles or custard cups or a 1-quart casserole; set aside.
In a covered large saucepan cook potatoes in enough boiling water to cover for
15 to 20 minutes or until tender; drain. Mash with a potato masher or beat with an
electric mixer on low speed. Season with the salt and pepper. If necessary, add a
small amount of milk to make of desired consistency.

2 Spoon potato mixture into prepared casseroles. In a chilled medium mixing
bowl beat whipping cream with chilled beaters of an electric mixer on medium
speed until soft peaks form; fold in cheese. Spoon cheese mixture over potatoes.
Bake in a 350° oven for 15 to 20 minutes or until lightly browned.

NUTRITION FACTS PER SERVING: 366 cal., 15 g total fat (9 g sat. fat), 52 mg chol., 340 mg sodium, 51 g carbo.,
2 g fiber, 8 g pro. DAILY VALUES: 49% vit. C, 12% calcium, 21% iron

Cheese and Garlic Potato Gratin

All-purpose Yukon gold potatoes are a good choice for roasting or using in gratins because they have more moisture than high-starch potatoes and don't fall apart easily.

PREP: 15 minutes BAKE: 1¼ hours OVEN: 350° MAKES: 6 to 8 side-dish servings

1½ **pounds Yukon gold potatoes or other yellow-fleshed potatoes, thinly sliced (about 5 cups)**	2 **teaspoons minced garlic**
⅓ **cup sliced green onions (about 3)**	1 **teaspoon salt**
1½ **cups shredded Swiss cheese (6 ounces)**	¼ **teaspoon black pepper**
	1 **cup whipping cream**

1 Grease a 2-quart square baking dish. Layer half of the sliced potatoes and half of the green onions in prepared dish. Sprinkle with half of the Swiss cheese, garlic, salt, and pepper. Repeat layers. Pour whipping cream over top.

2 Bake, covered, in a 350° oven for 1 hour. Uncover and bake for 15 to 20 minutes more or until potatoes are tender and top is golden brown.

NUTRITION FACTS PER SERVING: 365 cal., 23 g total fat (14 g sat. fat), 80 mg chol., 454 mg sodium, 30 g carbo., 1 g fiber, 12 g pro. DAILY VALUES: 25% vit. A, 31% vit. C, 26% calcium, 10% iron

SELECTING THE BEST POTATO FOR THE JOB Whether you're in the mood for mashed, baked, boiled, or fried potatoes will determine which potato is the best type to use. The starch content of each variety dictates the preparation method that works best for that type of potato.

High-starch potatoes, such as russets—which have a light, mealy texture—are best for baked potatoes, potato pancakes, french fries, and mashed potatoes. The fluffy quality that makes them good for these types of foods makes them a poor choice for salads, however, because they will crumble when boiled.

Medium-starch potatoes, such as yellow Finns and Yukon golds, are all-purpose potatoes. They contain more moisture than high-starch potatoes and don't fall apart as easily. They're a good choice for roasting or making into gratins, such as the recipe above.

Low-starch potatoes, often called waxy potatoes, are dense and hold their shape better than other types, making them the ideal choice for potato salad and roasting. Most round red and round white varieties are low-starch potatoes. All new potatoes are low-starch potatoes.

Scalloped New Potatoes

This side dish might be even better than your grandmother's, with its delicate slices of tiny potatoes and spinach, sweet pepper, and rosemary, which offer heightened interest and color. (See photo, page 80.)

PREP: 25 minutes BAKE: 20 minutes OVEN: 375° MAKES: 10 to 12 side-dish servings

Nonstick cooking spray

2 pounds tiny new potatoes, sliced

3 tablespoons butter or margarine

1 cup chopped onions (2 medium)

3 cloves garlic, minced

3 tablespoons all-purpose flour

1¼ teaspoons dried rosemary, crushed

1 teaspoon dried parsley

½ teaspoon salt

¼ teaspoon ground black pepper

1¾ cups milk

6 cups torn fresh spinach or 4 cups broccoli rabe, cut into 1½-inch pieces

1 small red sweet pepper, cut into thin bite-size strips

¾ cup shredded white cheddar cheese (3 ounces)

¼ cup fine dry bread crumbs

1 Coat a 2-quart oval or rectangular baking dish with cooking spray; set aside. In a covered large saucepan cook potatoes in a moderate amount of boiling salted water about 5 minutes or just until tender. Drain and transfer to an extra-large bowl.

2 For sauce, in same saucepan melt 2 tablespoons of the butter over medium heat. Add onions and garlic and cook about 5 minutes or just until tender. Stir in flour, rosemary, parsley, salt, and black pepper. Stir in milk all at once. Cook and stir over medium heat until thickened and bubbly.

3 Add spinach and sweet pepper to potatoes; toss gently to combine. Pour sauce over potato mixture; stir gently until coated. Spoon potato mixture into prepared baking dish (dish will be very full). Set baking dish on a baking sheet. Sprinkle white cheddar cheese over potato mixture.

4 Melt the remaining 1 tablespoon butter. Add bread crumbs, tossing to coat. Sprinkle over cheese. Bake in a 375° oven about 20 minutes or until edges are bubbly and crumbs are golden brown.

NUTRITION FACTS PER SERVING: 214 cal., 8 g total fat (4 g sat. fat), 13 mg chol., 274 mg sodium, 30 g carbo., 2 g fiber, 8 g pro. DAILY VALUES: 54% vit. C, 14% calcium, 16% iron

Caramelized Sweet Potatoes

Just like other potatoes, sweet potatoes can be baked, mashed, or hashed but are sweetly sublime when sautéed with onions and brown sugar, as in this side dish.
(See photo, page 80.)

START TO FINISH: 30 minutes MAKES: 4 side-dish servings

2 large red or white onions, cut into ¾-inch chunks	2 tablespoons brown sugar
4 teaspoons butter or margarine	¾ teaspoon snipped fresh rosemary or ¼ teaspoon dried rosemary, crushed
2 large sweet potatoes, peeled and sliced ½ inch thick (about 1 pound)	Snipped fresh rosemary (optional)
¼ cup water	

1 In a large skillet cook onions in hot butter over medium-high heat for 3 to 4 minutes or until onions are nearly tender, stirring frequently. Stir in sweet potatoes and water. Cook, covered, over medium heat for 10 to 12 minutes or until sweet potatoes are nearly tender, stirring occasionally.

2 Uncover skillet; add brown sugar and the ¾ teaspoon fresh or ¼ teaspoon dried rosemary. Cook, stirring gently, over medium-low heat for 4 to 5 minutes or until onions and sweet potatoes are glazed. If desired, garnish with additional fresh rosemary.

NUTRITION FACTS PER SERVING: 160 cal., 4 g total fat (3 g sat. fat), 11 mg chol., 56 mg sodium, 29 g carbo., 3 g fiber, 2 g pro. DAILY VALUES: 28% vit. C, 4% calcium, 4% iron

Corn Cakes with Fresh Corn and Chives

*Everything old is new again! That most traditional of American foods,
the corn cake, is updated with fresh corn and just-snipped herbs. (See photo, page 75.)*

START TO FINISH: 30 minutes MAKES: 6 side-dish servings

1	fresh ear of corn or ½ cup frozen whole kernel corn		¼	cup milk
2	tablespoons all-purpose flour		1	egg, slightly beaten
1½	teaspoons baking powder		1	tablespoon snipped fresh chives
1	teaspoon sugar		3	tablespoons cooking oil
½	teaspoon salt		1	teaspoon snipped fresh chives or cilantro (optional)
1	cup boiling water		⅓	cup dairy sour cream
1	cup yellow cornmeal			

1 Cut corn kernels from cob and measure ½ cup; set aside. In a small bowl stir together flour, baking powder, sugar, and salt; set aside.

2 In a medium bowl stir boiling water into cornmeal to make a stiff mush. Stir in milk until smooth. Stir in corn, egg, and the 1 tablespoon chives. Add flour mixture and stir just until combined.

3 In a large skillet heat 2 tablespoons of the oil over medium heat. Drop batter by rounded tablespoons into hot oil. Cook for 3 to 4 minutes or until golden brown, turning once. Transfer to a serving platter; cover and keep warm. Repeat with remaining batter, adding the remaining 1 tablespoon oil.

4 Meanwhile, if desired, stir 1 teaspoon chives into sour cream. Serve with corn cakes.

NUTRITION FACTS PER SERVING: 215 cal., 11 g total fat (3 g sat. fat), 42 mg chol., 295 mg sodium, 25 g carbo., 2 g fiber, 4 g pro. DAILY VALUES: 2% vit. C, 10% calcium, 9% iron

Corn Pudding

Embellish this classic American dish by baking in individual soufflé dishes and adding sliced dried beef and parsley for more color and flavor. (See photo, page 76.)

PREP: 30 minutes BAKE: 30 minutes OVEN: 325° MAKES: 8 side-dish servings

3	egg whites
3	egg yolks
1½	cups water
1	cup yellow cornmeal
1	teaspoon instant beef bouillon granules
½	teaspoon ground cumin
¼	teaspoon salt
1	cup milk
2	teaspoons sugar
1	teaspoon baking powder

1	teaspoon dry mustard
½	of a 2½-ounce jar sliced dried beef, finely chopped (about ⅓ cup)
2	tablespoons butter or margarine, melted
1	tablespoon snipped fresh flat-leaf parsley
	Sliced dried beef
	Snipped fresh parsley (optional)
	Fresh flat-leaf parsley leaves (optional)

1 Let egg whites and yolks stand at room temperature for 30 minutes. Meanwhile, grease eight 1- to 1½-cup soufflé dishes; set aside.

2 In a large mixing bowl beat egg whites with an electric mixer on high speed until stiff peaks form (tips stand straight); set aside. In a medium mixing bowl beat egg yolks with an electric mixer on high speed about 5 minutes or until thick and lemon colored. Set bowl of egg yolks aside.

3 In a medium saucepan combine water, cornmeal, beef bouillon granules, cumin, and salt. Cook and stir over medium-high heat until mixture bubbles around edges. Remove from heat. Stir in milk, sugar, baking powder, and dry mustard. Stir in the chopped dried beef, melted butter, and the 1 tablespoon snipped parsley. Stir in egg yolks. Gradually pour cornmeal-beef mixture over stiffly beaten egg whites, folding to combine. (Batter will be thin with small pockets of egg white showing.)

4 Pour mixture into the prepared soufflé dishes.* Bake in a 325° oven for 25 minutes. Arrange a slice of dried beef on top of each. Bake for 5 to 10 minutes more or until a knife inserted near center comes out clean. If desired, sprinkle with additional snipped fresh parsley and garnish with parsley leaves. Serve immediately.

*Note: Or pour the mixture into a greased 2-quart square baking dish. Bake for 30 minutes. Arrange slices of dried beef on top. Bake for 5 to 10 minutes more. Serve immediately.

NUTRITION FACTS PER SERVING: 204 cal., 8 g total fat (5 g sat. fat), 139 mg chol., 796 mg sodium, 22 g carbo., 1 g fiber, 10 g pro. DAILY VALUES: 2% vit. C, 10% calcium, 14% iron

Coleslaw with Dill and Lime

Green and red cabbage, seasoned with lime juice and fresh dill, make a refreshing version of coleslaw. Serve it with grilled fish or seafood kabobs.

PREP: 20 minutes CHILL: 2 to 24 hours MAKES: 8 to 10 side-dish servings

6	cups finely shredded green cabbage (1¼-pound head)
1	cup finely shredded red cabbage
1	medium carrot, shredded
½	of a small red sweet pepper, cut into thin bite-size strips
⅓	cup light mayonnaise dressing or salad dressing
2	tablespoons lime juice or lemon juice
1	tablespoon snipped fresh dill or 1 teaspoon dried dillweed (optional)
1	teaspoon sugar
¼	teaspoon salt
¼	teaspoon ground black pepper

1 In a large bowl toss together green cabbage, red cabbage, carrot, and sweet pepper; set aside.

2 For dressing, in a small bowl stir together the mayonnaise dressing, lime juice, dill (if desired), sugar, salt, and black pepper.

3 Pour the dressing over cabbage mixture; toss to coat. (Mixture may appear dry at first but will moisten as it chills.) Cover and chill for 2 to 24 hours. Stir before serving.

NUTRITION FACTS PER SERVING: 57 cal., 4 g total fat (1 g sat. fat), 3 mg chol., 146 mg sodium, 7 g carbo., 2 g fiber, 1 g pro. DAILY VALUES: 63% vit. C, 3% calcium, 2% iron

Baby Vegetables with Lemon-Herb Marinade

Be careful not to overcook delicate baby vegetables—they will lose their lovely colors and fresh flavors.

PREP: 20 minutes   CHILL: 2 hours or overnight   MAKES: 8 side-dish servings

2	tablespoons water
1	tablespoon olive oil
½	teaspoon finely shredded lemon peel
2	tablespoons fresh lemon juice
1	teaspoon Dijon-style mustard
2	teaspoons snipped fresh basil or oregano
1	clove garlic, minced

2	pounds tiny, whole vegetables such as carrots, zucchini, and/or pattypan squash
8	ounces sugar snap peas and/or yellow wax beans, trimmed
12	cherry tomatoes
	Fresh oregano (optional)

1 For dressing, in a screw-top jar combine water, olive oil, lemon peel, lemon juice, Dijon-style mustard, basil, and garlic. Cover and shake; set aside.

2 In a covered large saucepan cook carrots, zucchini, and/or pattypan squash in a small amount of water for 3 minutes. Add sugar snap peas; cook for 2 to 3 minutes more or until vegetables are crisp-tender. Drain; rinse vegetables with cold water. Drain again.

3 In a large bowl combine cooked vegetables, tomatoes, and dressing; toss gently to coat. Cover and chill for at least 2 hours or overnight before serving. If desired, garnish with oregano.

NUTRITION FACTS PER SERVING: 59 cal., 2 g total fat (0 g sat. fat), 0 mg chol., 43 mg sodium, 9 g carbo., 3 g fiber, 2 g pro. DAILY VALUES: 36% vit. C

HOW TO KEEP VEGETABLES FRESH Ideally, you would buy your vegetables one day and eat them that night or the next. As a practical matter, however, you'll probably want to store your vegetables for several days. How do you keep vegetables fresh after you buy them? The keys are keeping them chilled (with some exceptions, such as onions, garlic, potatoes, and tomatoes), maintaining an appropriate moisture level (too much and they'll rot, too little and they'll dry out), and limiting oxygen—that is, keeping them wrapped or sealed in plastic bags or other containers. Fresh greens require special handling (see tip, page 91).

Green Beans in Yellow Pepper Butter

When purchasing green beans, look for those without bruises, scars, or rusty brown spots. Bulging, leathery beans are old. Wash fresh beans; then place them in airtight plastic bags for three to four days. (See photo, page 77.)

START TO FINISH: 30 minutes MAKES: 8 side-dish servings

1	tablespoon butter or margarine	¼	teaspoon salt
1	medium yellow sweet pepper, coarsely shredded	⅛	teaspoon ground black pepper
6	tablespoons butter or margarine, softened	1½	pounds green beans, trimmed
¼	cup pine nuts	1	large yellow sweet pepper, cut into thin strips
1	tablespoon lemon juice		

1 In a small saucepan melt the 1 tablespoon butter; add shredded sweet pepper. Cook over medium-high heat for 5 minutes or until crisp-tender; set aside.

2 In a blender container or food processor bowl combine the 6 tablespoons softened butter and the pine nuts. Cover and blend or process until almost smooth. Add cooked sweet pepper, lemon juice, salt, and black pepper. Cover and blend or process until almost smooth; set aside.

3 Meanwhile, in a covered large saucepan cook beans in a small amount of boiling water for 12 minutes. Add the sweet pepper strips for the last 3 minutes of cooking. Drain the beans and sweet pepper strips.

4 To serve, transfer beans and sweet pepper strips to a serving bowl. Add the blended butter mixture; toss to coat.

NUTRITION FACTS PER SERVING: 155 cal., 13 g total fat (7 g sat. fat), 29 mg chol., 186 mg sodium, 9 g carbo., 3 g fiber, 3 g pro. DAILY VALUES: 134% vit. C, 4% calcium, 8% iron

Beans with Hot Ham Dressing

*Use a combination of green and wax beans for extra color.
If wax beans aren't available in your market, use all fresh
green beans and top them with the chunky chickpea mixture.*

START TO FINISH: 15 minutes MAKES: 6 to 8 side-dish servings

1	pound whole green and/or yellow wax beans, ends trimmed	1	cup rinsed and drained cooked or canned chickpeas (garbanzo beans)
½	cup diced cooked smoked ham or Canadian-style bacon	2	tablespoons finely chopped shallot (1 medium)
2	tablespoons olive oil	3	tablespoons red wine vinegar

1 In a covered large saucepan cook green and/or yellow beans in a small amount of boiling salted water about 3 minutes or until crisp-tender. Drain well. Transfer to a serving bowl; keep warm.

2 Meanwhile, in a medium skillet cook ham in 1 tablespoon of the olive oil over medium heat for 3 minutes, stirring occasionally. Add chickpeas and shallot. Cook and stir for 2 to 3 minutes more or until pieces of ham are crisp and golden brown. Reduce heat to medium low; push mixture to one side of skillet.

3 Carefully add vinegar to skillet. Heat just until bubbly, scraping up brown bits in bottom of skillet. Stir in the remaining 1 tablespoon olive oil. Stir together chickpea-ham mixture and the vinegar mixture. Pour over beans; toss gently to coat.

NUTRITION FACTS PER SERVING: 120 cal., 6 g total fat (1 g sat. fat), 7 mg chol., 303 mg sodium, 11 g carbo., 4 g fiber, 7 g pro. DAILY VALUES: 16% vit. C, 4% calcium, 7% iron

Roasted Summer Cherry Tomatoes

Simplicity often is the best strategy in preparing warm-weather veggies. A little olive oil, basil, and garlic complement but never overwhelm garden-ripe tomatoes.

PREP: 20 minutes BAKE: 5 minutes OVEN: 425° MAKES: 4 to 6 side-dish servings

12	ounces cherry and/or other miniature tomatoes (such as grape or pear)
2	tablespoons olive oil or cooking oil
¼	cup snipped fresh basil
1	tablespoon minced garlic
¼	teaspoon salt
⅛	teaspoon ground black pepper
	Snipped fresh basil and/or fresh basil sprigs (optional)

1 Line a 13×9×2-inch baking pan with foil. Wash tomatoes; remove stems. Pat dry with paper towels. Pour olive oil into prepared pan. Roll tomatoes in oil to coat. Sprinkle with the ¼ cup snipped basil, the garlic, salt, and pepper.

2 Bake in a 425° oven about 5 minutes or just until skins begin to split, stirring once. If desired, sprinkle with additional snipped fresh basil and/or garnish with fresh basil sprigs.

NUTRITION FACTS PER SERVING: 87 cal., 7 g total fat (1 g sat. fat), 0 mg chol., 142 mg sodium, 6 g carbo., 1 g fiber, 1 g pro. DAILY VALUES: 29% vit. C, 1% calcium, 3% iron

HOW TO SELECT OLIVE OIL Extra-virgin olive oils are cold-pressed for highest quality and full-bodied flavor, but they aren't always the best choice for cooking. For stir-fries and sautés, use a virgin olive oil or pure olive oil as they're less affected by heat—and more economical. Reserve costly premium olive oils for salad dressings and fresh sauces, where their fruity flavor can shine through.

Tomato-Cheese Melts

Topped with zesty cheese, colorful sweet pepper, and toasted almonds, these tasty tomatoes are so enticing, seconds are hard to refuse. (See photo, page 73.)

PREP: 15 minutes BAKE: 15 minutes OVEN: 350° MAKES: 4 side-dish servings

3 large tomatoes (about 8 ounces each) or assorted small tomatoes (about 1½ pounds total)

1 cup shredded Monterey Jack cheese with jalapeño peppers or Monterey Jack cheese (4 ounces)

½ cup finely chopped green, yellow, purple, or red sweet pepper (1 small)

¼ cup sliced almonds, toasted

1 Line a 15×10×1-inch baking pan with foil; set aside. Cut each large tomato into four slices or halve each small tomato.

2 For each serving, arrange three large tomato slices, overlapping slightly, in the prepared baking pan. (Or if using small tomatoes, arrange in a single layer in the prepared baking pan.) Sprinkle tomatoes with Monterey Jack cheese, sweet pepper, and almonds.

3 Bake in a 350° oven about 15 minutes or until cheese is bubbly. Using a large metal spatula, carefully lift tomatoes to plates, allowing excess juices to drain off.

NUTRITION FACTS PER SERVING: 203 cal., 14 g total fat (6 g sat. fat), 25 mg chol., 172 mg sodium, 13 g carbo., 2 g fiber, 10 g pro. DAILY VALUES: 79% vit. C, 20% calcium, 10% iron

TO GRILL TOMATOES Arrange ingredients as directed in a shallow disposable foil pan. In a grill with a cover arrange medium-hot coals around edge of grill. Test for medium heat above center of grill. Place pan with tomatoes in center of the grill rack. Cover and grill for 12 to 15 minutes or until cheese is bubbly.

Stuffed Zucchini

This variety of squash is almost always available. Choose zucchini that are firm and free of cuts and soft spots. Store them in a plastic bag up to five days, making sure there is no moisture in the bag or on the vegetable. (See photo, page 74.)

PREP: 30 minutes BAKE: 25 minutes OVEN: 350° MAKES: 6 side-dish servings

6	medium zucchini	¼	cup finely chopped onion
1½	cups soft bread crumbs (2 slices)	1	tablespoon snipped fresh parsley
1	egg, slightly beaten	¼	teaspoon salt
½	cup finely shredded cheddar cheese or Parmesan cheese (1 ounce)	⅛	teaspoon ground black pepper

1 Wash zucchini and trim ends; do not peel. In a covered Dutch oven cook whole zucchini in boiling lightly salted water for 5 minutes; drain and cool slightly. Cut a lengthwise slice off top of each zucchini. Remove pulp with a spoon, leaving about a ¼-inch shell.

2 Chop enough of the pulp to measure 2 cups; place chopped pulp in a medium bowl. (Save remaining pulp for another use.) Stir bread crumbs, egg, ¼ cup of the cheese, the onion, parsley, salt, and pepper into chopped pulp until well mixed. Fill zucchini shells with pulp mixture. Place in a shallow baking pan.

3 Bake in a 350° oven for 20 minutes. Sprinkle with the remaining ¼ cup cheese. Bake for 5 to 10 minutes more or until golden brown and heated through.

NUTRITION FACTS PER SERVING: 93 cal., 4 g total fat (2 g sat. fat), 45 mg chol., 229 mg sodium, 8 g carbo., 1 g fiber, 5 g pro. DAILY VALUES: 13% vit. C, 10% calcium, 5% iron

Spiced Vegetable-Stuffed Acorn Squash

Cool weather signals a new crop of produce to enjoy during fall and winter. Spice this bounty of turnips, apple, and acorn squash with a buttery mixture of brown sugar, cinnamon, and nutmeg.

PREP: 20 minutes BAKE: 1 hour 5 minutes OVEN: 350° MAKES: 8 side-dish servings

2 medium acorn squash (about 1 pound each)	1/2 teaspoon ground cinnamon
1 1/2 cups chopped turnips (2 small)	1/4 teaspoon salt
1 cup chopped carrots (2 medium)	1/4 teaspoon ground nutmeg
1 tablespoon butter or margarine	1 cup coarsely shredded peeled apple
1 tablespoon brown sugar	

1 Quarter squash; remove seeds and strings. Place squash, cut sides down, in a 13×9×2-inch baking pan. Cover lightly with foil. Bake in a 350° oven for 30 minutes. Turn cut sides up; bake, covered, for 20 to 30 minutes more or until tender. Carefully scoop pulp out of each squash quarter, keeping shells intact and leaving a 1/4-inch layer of squash in shells. Set shells aside. Place cooked pulp in a large bowl.

2 Meanwhile, in a covered medium saucepan cook turnips and carrots in boiling lightly salted water about 20 minutes or until tender. Drain well. Add turnips and carrots to the squash pulp in bowl. Coarsely mash vegetables with a potato masher.

3 Add butter, brown sugar, cinnamon, salt, and nutmeg to mashed vegetables; stir to combine. Fold in apple. Spoon vegetable-apple mixture evenly into squash shells. Return to baking pan. Bake in the 350° oven for 15 to 20 minutes more or until heated through.

NUTRITION FACTS PER SERVING: 86 cal., 2 g total fat (1 g sat. fat), 4 mg chol., 114 mg sodium, 17 g carbo., 3 g fiber, 2 g pro. DAILY VALUES: 29% vit. C, 5% calcium, 5% iron

Autumn Medley

Fresh pears, dried cranberries, and orange juice have a pleasant fruity flavor that livens this winning combo of parsnips and carrots. (See photo, page 78.)

START TO FINISH: 20 minutes   MAKES: 6 side-dish servings

8   ounces parsnips, peeled and cut into thin bite-size strips (2¼ cups)

8   ounces carrots, peeled and cut into thin bite-size strips (2¼ cups)

¾   cup orange juice

⅓   cup dried cranberries

½   teaspoon ground ginger

2   firm ripe pears, peeled, cored, and cut into ½-inch wedges

⅓   cup pecan halves

3   tablespoons brown sugar

2   tablespoons butter or margarine

1 In a large nonstick skillet combine parsnips, carrots, orange juice, dried cranberries, and ginger. Bring to boiling; reduce heat to medium. Cook, uncovered, for 7 to 8 minutes or until vegetables are crisp-tender and most of the liquid has evaporated, stirring occasionally.

2 Add pears, pecans, brown sugar, and butter to mixture in skillet; stir. Cook, uncovered, for 2 to 3 minutes more or until vegetables are glazed.

NUTRITION FACTS PER SERVING: 230 cal., 8 g total fat (3 g sat. fat), 10 mg chol., 77 mg sodium, 40 g carbo., 7 g fiber, 2 g pro. DAILY VALUES: 43% vit. C, 4% calcium, 7% iron

Butternut Squash Compote

A perfect way to get kids to eat their vegetables—squash candied along with fruit favorites.

PREP: 25 minutes BAKE: 1 hour OVEN: 375° MAKES: 6 side-dish servings

1	2-pound butternut squash, peeled, halved, seeded, and cut into 1½-inch chunks
¼	cup orange juice
¼	teaspoon ground ginger
¼	teaspoon ground nutmeg
1	medium red or green tart apple, cored and cut into 1-inch chunks
1	medium pear, peeled, cored, and cut into 1-inch chunks
⅓	cup golden raisins
2	tablespoons chopped pecans
2	tablespoons butter or margarine, cut up
1	tablespoon light-colored corn syrup
1	tablespoon brown sugar
¼	teaspoon salt

1 In a 2-quart casserole stir together squash, orange juice, ginger, and nutmeg. Bake, covered, in a 375° oven for 40 minutes.

2 Add apple, pear, raisins, pecans, butter, corn syrup, brown sugar, and salt to squash mixture, stirring to coat. Bake, uncovered, for 20 minutes more or until squash is tender, stirring once or twice.

NUTRITION FACTS PER SERVING: 168 cal., 6 g total fat (3 g sat. fat), 10 mg chol., 142 mg sodium, 31 g carbo., 4 g fiber, 2 g pro. DAILY VALUES: 39% vit. C, 4% calcium, 7% iron

Eggplant Casserole

This recipe calls for one pound of traditional pear-shaped eggplant.
If you decide to use round, Japanese, or white eggplant instead, buy slightly
more than a pound so you'll have enough ¹/₂-inch cubes.

PREP: 25 minutes BAKE: 30 minutes OVEN: 375° MAKES: 6 to 8 side-dish servings

1	medium eggplant (1 pound)
3	tablespoons cooking oil
1¹/₂	cups chopped onions (2 large)
2	cups chopped green sweet peppers
1	tablespoon all-purpose flour
¹/₄	teaspoon salt
¹/₄	teaspoon ground black pepper

¹/₂	cup sliced pitted ripe olives
¹/₂	cup shredded sharp American cheese or cheddar cheese (2 ounces)
1	8-ounce can tomato sauce
³/₄	cup soft bread crumbs (1 slice)
1	tablespoon butter or margarine, melted

1 Peel eggplant and cut into ¹/₂-inch cubes. In a large skillet cook eggplant cubes in 2 tablespoons of the oil until tender. Remove from skillet.

2 In the same skillet cook onions and sweet peppers in the remaining 1 tablespoon oil until tender, stirring frequently. Remove from heat. Stir in flour, salt, and black pepper. Add olives.

3 In an ungreased 1¹/₂-quart casserole layer half the eggplant, half the onion mixture, and half the cheese. Repeat layers. Pour tomato sauce over all.

4 In a small bowl stir together bread crumbs and melted butter; sprinkle over tomato sauce. Bake, uncovered, in a 375° oven about 30 minutes or until edges are bubbly.

NUTRITION FACTS PER SERVING: 198 cal., 14 g total fat (4 g sat. fat), 14 mg chol., 606 mg sodium, 17 g carbo., 4 g fiber, 5 g pro. DAILY VALUES: 72% vit. C, 10% calcium, 8% iron

Chapter Four
Entrées

Greek-Style Chicken, p. 138

113

ENTRÉES

Chicken-Artichoke Turnovers, p. 150

114

Pork and Green Chile Bake, p. 136

Italian Beef and Spinach Pie, p. 130

Easy Pot Roast, p. 125

Roast Pork Tangerine, p. 133

Hot Veggie Sandwiches, p. 144

▲ Scallops and Shrimp with Linguine, p. 142

▲ Speedy Stroganoff, p. 121

▲ Molasses-Glazed Pork Tenderloin, p. 134

▲ Creamy Turkey Pie, p. 139

Speedy Stroganoff

Serve with crisp breadsticks, or select seasonal fruit for a refreshing side dish.
(See photo, page 120.)

START TO FINISH: 30 minutes MAKES: 4 servings

3	cups packaged dried wide noodles		1	clove garlic, minced
3	cups broccoli florets		1	tablespoon cooking oil
½	cup light dairy sour cream		4	teaspoons all-purpose flour
1½	teaspoons prepared horseradish		½	teaspoon ground black pepper
½	teaspoon snipped fresh dill		1	14-ounce can beef broth
1	pound beef ribeye steak		3	tablespoons tomato paste
1	small onion, cut into ½-inch slices		1	teaspoon Worcestershire sauce

1 Cook noodles according to package directions, adding broccoli for the last 5 minutes of cooking. Drain and keep warm.

2 Meanwhile, in a small serving bowl stir together sour cream, horseradish, and dill. Cover and chill until serving time.

3 Trim fat from beef. Cut into bite-size strips. In a large skillet cook half of the beef, the onion, and garlic in hot oil until onion is tender and beef has reached desired doneness. Remove from skillet. Add remaining beef and cook and stir until beef has reached desired doneness. Return all beef to skillet. Sprinkle flour and pepper over beef; stir to coat.

4 Stir the beef broth, tomato paste, and Worcestershire sauce into beef mixture in skillet. Cook and stir until thickened and bubbly. Cook and stir for 1 minute more. Remove from heat.

5 To serve, divide noodle-broccoli mixture among four bowls. Spoon beef mixture on top of noodle mixture. Top with a spoonful of horseradish-sour cream mixture.

NUTRITION FACTS PER SERVING: 368 cal., 15 g total fat (5 g sat. fat), 81 mg chol., 454 mg sodium, 32 g carbo., 4 g fiber, 29 g pro. DAILY VALUES: 21% vit. A, 83% vit. C, 9% calcium, 21% iron

TIDBITS OF TOMATO PASTE The bad news: Recipes have a way of calling for a tablespoon or two of tomato paste at a time, leaving cooks with most of a can left over. The good news: Tomato paste can be frozen. Spoon 1-tablespoon portions onto a piece of plastic wrap; freeze until firm. Place in a freezer bag. Seal, label, and freeze until the next time you need a tablespoon or two.

Cobb Salad

This All-American salad won its first fans at the Brown Derby restaurant, the see-and-be-seen destination of Hollywood's golden age. Here's the authentic version except for a convenient secret: Purchased French salad dressing substitutes for the original dressing.

START TO FINISH: 20 minutes MAKES: 4 to 6 servings

6   cups shredded lettuce (½ of a large head)

4   medium skinless, boneless chicken breast halves, cooked, chilled, and cubed, or 3 cups diced cooked chicken

2   medium tomatoes, chopped

3   hard-cooked eggs, chopped

6   slices bacon, crisp-cooked and crumbled

¾   cup crumbled blue cheese (3 ounces)

1   or 2 medium avocados, halved, seeded, peeled, and cut into wedges

1   small Belgian endive

1   tablespoon snipped chives or thinly sliced green onion tops (optional)

½   cup bottled French salad dressing

1 On four salad plates or on a large platter arrange shredded lettuce. On top of the lettuce, arrange a row each of chicken, tomatoes, eggs, bacon, and blue cheese.

2 Just before serving, tuck avocado wedges and endive leaves around the edges of plates or platter. If desired, sprinkle with chives. Serve with dressing.

NUTRITION FACTS PER SERVING: 603 cal., 40 g total fat (12 g sat. fat), 272 mg chol., 1,021 mg sodium, 14 g carbo., 4 g fiber, 47 g pro. DAILY VALUES: 33% vit. C, 17% calcium, 18% iron

FOR A LOWER-FAT VERSION Use a fat-free or reduced-calorie French salad dressing instead of regular salad dressing and omit the bacon and avocado.

Thai-Style Chicken and Nectarine Salad

A peppery-sweet dressing provides the crowning touch to this pasta salad entrée. Warmed crusty French rolls are all you need to complete the meal.

START TO FINISH: 40 minutes   MAKES: 4 servings

¼	cup reduced-sodium chicken broth
3	tablespoons reduced-sodium soy sauce
2	tablespoons bottled hoisin sauce
1	tablespoon sugar
1	tablespoon salad oil or olive oil
2	teaspoons toasted sesame oil
3	cloves garlic, minced
1½	teaspoons grated fresh ginger
1	teaspoon crushed red pepper

⅛	teaspoon ground black pepper
12	ounces skinless, boneless chicken breast halves
4	ounces packaged dried angel hair pasta
3	medium nectarines, plums, or peeled peaches, pitted and sliced
2	cups shredded bok choy
¼	cup thinly sliced green onions (2)

1 For dressing, in a screw-top jar combine chicken broth, soy sauce, hoisin sauce, sugar, salad oil, sesame oil, garlic, ginger, red pepper, and black pepper. Cover and shake well; set aside.

2 In a covered large skillet cook chicken in a small amount of boiling water for 12 to 15 minutes or until tender and no longer pink; drain. Cool slightly; cut into cubes. Cook pasta according to package directions; drain.

3 In a large bowl toss pasta with 3 tablespoons of the dressing. Divide pasta mixture among four plates. Top with the chicken, fruit, bok choy, and green onions. Drizzle with remaining dressing.

NUTRITION FACTS PER SERVING: 359 cal., 9 g total fat (2 g sat. fat), 45 mg chol., 644 mg sodium, 46 g carbo., 2 g fiber, 23 g pro. DAILY VALUES: 29% vit. C, 4% calcium, 15% iron

SESAME OIL—A LITTLE GOES A LONG WAY Toasted sesame oil is a flavoring oil, not a cooking oil. Use it sparingly in recipes because of its strong flavor. A lighter version of the oil has very little sesame flavor. Often toasted sesame oil is drizzled on finished stir-fry dishes for a crowning touch. To prevent the oil from becoming rancid once it's opened, store it in the refrigerator for up to one year.

Creamy Mushroom Pasta

Turn the heat to low before adding the sour cream to the sauce.
Once the sour cream is added, the sauce will curdle if it gets too hot.

START TO FINISH: 25 minutes MAKES: 4 servings

8	ounces packaged dried penne pasta	½	cup dry white wine
3	cups sliced fresh button mushrooms (8 ounces)	1	teaspoon instant chicken bouillon granules
1½	cups sliced fresh shiitake mushrooms (4 ounces)	¼	teaspoon coarsely ground black pepper
4	cloves garlic, minced	½	cup light dairy sour cream
1	tablespoon butter or margarine	¼	cup finely shredded Parmesan cheese

1 Cook pasta according to package directions; drain. Keep warm.

2 In a large skillet cook mushrooms and garlic in hot butter over medium-high heat for 3 minutes, stirring frequently. Stir in white wine, bouillon granules, and pepper. Bring to boiling; reduce heat. Simmer, uncovered, for 5 minutes. Reduce heat to low. Stir in sour cream; add hot cooked pasta. Cook and stir until heated through (do not let boil).

3 To serve, transfer pasta to shallow pasta bowls or plates. Sprinkle with Parmesan cheese.

NUTRITION FACTS PER SERVING: 360 cal., 9 g total fat (5 g sat. fat), 24 mg chol., 408 mg sodium, 51 g carbo., 2 g fiber, 14 g pro. DAILY VALUES: 8% vit. A, 2% vit. C, 14% calcium, 13% iron

Easy Pot Roast

Any noodle will complement this dish, but consider spaetzle—sold packaged in the pasta or baking goods section of supermarkets. (See photo, page 117.)

START TO FINISH: 25 minutes MAKES: 4 servings

1	17-ounce heat-and-serve beef pot roast	2	cups fresh, pitted fruit cut into wedges, such as peaches, green plums, and red plums
2	tablespoons minced shallots (1 medium)		Hot cooked spaetzle (optional)
1	tablespoon butter or margarine	1	teaspoon snipped fresh tarragon
2	tablespoons tarragon vinegar		

1 Remove meat from package, reserving juices. In a large skillet cook shallots in hot butter over medium heat for 1 minute. Add pot roast; reduce heat. Simmer, covered, about 10 minutes or until pot roast is heated through.

2 In a small bowl stir together reserved meat juices and tarragon vinegar. Pour over meat. Sprinkle fruit over top. Cook, covered, for 2 minutes more. If desired, serve with cooked spaetzle. Sprinkle with fresh tarragon.

NUTRITION FACTS PER SERVING: 259 cal., 12 g total fat (6 g sat. fat), 72 mg chol., 459 mg sodium, 19 g carbo., 2 g fiber, 24 g pro. DAILY VALUES: 17% vit. C, 1% calcium, 12% iron

SALAD SERVE-ALONGS Pairing a hearty, steaming bowl of soup or stew with a refreshing, crisp, light salad seems like a match made in heaven. Enhance the meal even more by moving beyond the usual head lettuce, tomato, and shredded carrot combination. Here are just a few ideas: ❶ Toss Bibb lettuce, oranges, avocado, and walnuts with an orange vinaigrette. ❷ Toss strawberries, toasted almonds, spinach, crumbled bacon, and hard-cooked eggs; drizzle with western or French dressing. ❸ Toss romaine lettuce with a fruit-flavored vinaigrette (such as a raspberry); arrange grapefruit sections, red onion slices, and feta cheese over the top.

Beef Tenderloin Steaks with Pepper-Onion Relish

Take an Italian-inspired flight of fancy with this entrée. The aroma and taste of pepper, onion, olive oil, red wine vinegar, garlic, and Parmesan mingle deliciously.

START TO FINISH: 30 minutes MAKES: 6 servings

¼	cup seasoned fine dry bread crumbs		2	tablespoons olive oil or cooking oil
¼	cup grated Parmesan cheese		3	red, green, and/or yellow sweet peppers, cut into bite-size strips
1	tablespoon snipped fresh parsley		2	large onions, thinly sliced and separated into rings (3 cups)
¼	teaspoon salt			
	Dash ground black pepper		1	sprig fresh rosemary or ½ teaspoon dried rosemary, crushed
1	egg, beaten			
1	tablespoon water		3	tablespoons red wine vinegar
3	cloves garlic, minced		1	tablespoon butter or margarine
6	beef tenderloin steaks, cut ½ inch thick (about 3 ounces each)			Snipped fresh rosemary (optional)

1 In a shallow dish stir together bread crumbs, Parmesan cheese, parsley, salt, and black pepper. In another dish stir together the egg and water. Rub about half of the garlic over steaks. Dip steaks in egg mixture; coat with crumb mixture. Set aside.

2 For relish, in a large skillet heat 1 tablespoon of the oil over medium heat. Add the remaining garlic, the sweet peppers, onions, and rosemary sprig or dried rosemary. Cook, covered, for 10 to 15 minutes or until tender, stirring occasionally. If used, remove fresh rosemary. Stir in vinegar. Remove from heat; keep warm.

3 Meanwhile, in a large skillet heat butter and the remaining 1 tablespoon oil over medium-high heat. Add steaks; reduce heat to medium. Cook, uncovered, to desired doneness, turning once. (Allow 6 to 8 minutes for rare and 10 to 12 minutes for medium doneness.) Serve with the relish. If desired, sprinkle with snipped rosemary.

NUTRITION FACTS PER SERVING: 273 cal., 15 g total fat (5 g sat. fat), 91 mg chol., 377 mg sodium, 15 g carbo., 3 g fiber, 21 g pro. DAILY VALUES: 98% vit. C, 10% calcium, 16% iron

Herbed Strip Steak with Balsamic Sauce

Dish up this saucy number to rave reviews. The recipe for success lies in the quick technique of reduction—decreasing by half the volume of drippings, balsamic vinegar, and beef broth by rapid boiling and evaporation.

START TO FINISH: 25 minutes MAKES: 4 servings

1	tablespoon cracked black pepper	1	tablespoon olive oil
1½	teaspoons dried basil, crushed	¼	cup balsamic vinegar
1½	teaspoons dried oregano, crushed	¼	cup beef broth
1	teaspoon garlic powder	1	tablespoon butter or whipping cream
2	boneless beef top loin (strip) steaks, cut ¾ inch thick (about 8 ounces each)	¼	cup snipped fresh parsley

1 For rub, in a small bowl stir together pepper, basil, oregano, and garlic powder. Use your fingers to apply the rub mixture to both sides of steaks.

2 In a heavy large skillet cook steaks in hot oil over medium heat to desired doneness, turning once. (Allow 8 to 11 minutes for medium-rare and 12 to 14 minutes for medium doneness.) Remove steaks from skillet, reserving drippings in the skillet. Keep steaks warm.

3 For sauce, carefully add balsamic vinegar and beef broth to drippings in skillet, scraping up crusty brown bits. Bring to boiling. Boil gently, uncovered, 4 minutes or until sauce is reduced by half. Remove from heat; stir in butter.

4 To serve, slice steaks. Divide sauce among four plates. Top sauce with steak slices and sprinkle with parsley.

NUTRITION FACTS PER SERVING: 346 cal., 26 g total fat (10 g sat. fat), 84 mg chol., 134 mg sodium, 5 g carbo., 0 g fiber, 23 g pro. DAILY VALUES: 6% vit. A, 15% vit. C, 2% calcium, 26% iron

WHAT IS A REDUCTION? Reduction is aptly named. It's a technique that involves decreasing the volume of a liquid by boiling rapidly to cause evaporation. As the liquid evaporates, it thickens and intensifies in flavor. You can make a quick and easy sauce for meats and roasted vegetables by reducing stock or broth, wine, vinegar, or another liquid.

The amount of reduction needed in a recipe usually is specified in one of two ways. A recipe such as the one above may tell you to reduce a liquid by a general amount—one-third or one-half, for example. Or it may say to keep boiling until the liquid has reached a specific volume, such as ½ cup or 3 tablespoons. The size of the pan you use will affect the time it takes to reduce a liquid. A bigger pan has a larger surface area and results in faster evaporation. Be sure to use the pan size recommended in the recipe.

Sausage and Beef Meat Loaf

High-flavor ingredients—such as prepared pasta sauce, sausage, and provolone cheese—provide depth and complexity without requiring extra cooking time.

PREP: 20 minutes BAKE: 55 minutes STAND: 10 minutes OVEN: 350° MAKES: 6 servings

1	egg, beaten	1	pound ground beef
1	cup soft bread crumbs	2	ounces provolone cheese or mozzarella cheese, cubed
½	cup bottled pasta sauce with vegetables and/or herbs	2	tablespoons bottled pasta sauce with vegetables and/or herbs
1	to 2 cloves garlic, minced	2	tablespoons shredded provolone cheese or mozzarella cheese
½	teaspoon dried rosemary, crushed		Fresh rosemary sprigs (optional)
8	ounces Italian sausage or pork sausage links or ground beef		

1 In a large bowl stir together egg, bread crumbs, the ½ cup pasta sauce, garlic, and rosemary. If using, remove casings from sausage. Add sausage and ground beef to egg mixture; mix well. Press two-thirds of the meat mixture evenly in the bottom of an ungreased 8×4×2-inch loaf pan.

2 Make a ½-inch indentation down the center of the meat mixture. Place the cheese cubes in indentation. Pat remaining meat mixture evenly over top.

3 Bake, uncovered, in a 350° oven for 55 to 60 minutes or until no pink remains and a thermometer inserted into the thickest part of the loaf registers 170°. Let stand for 10 minutes before serving.

4 To serve, transfer meat loaf to a platter. Drizzle top with the 2 tablespoons pasta sauce. Sprinkle with the 2 tablespoons shredded cheese. If desired, garnish with fresh rosemary sprigs.

NUTRITION FACTS PER SERVING: 328 cal., 21 g total fat (8 g sat. fat), 113 mg chol., 541 mg sodium, 8 g carbo., 0 g fiber, 25 g pro. DAILY VALUES: 9% vit. C, 10% calcium, 16% iron

TO MAKE AHEAD: Prepare meat loaf as directed, except do not bake. Cover and chill for up to 24 hours. To serve, bake meat loaf, uncovered, about 1 hour or until no pink remains and a thermometer inserted into the thickest part of the meat loaf registers 170°.

Mexican Chef's Salad

The heat is on, thanks to a generous helping of green chile peppers.
Even the faint of heart will dig in. Just keep a pitcher of ice water nearby
to cool and refresh the taste buds.

START TO FINISH: 25 minutes MAKES: 6 servings

6	cups torn mixed greens	3	tablespoons thinly sliced green onions
1	cup shredded carrots (2 medium)	2	cups shredded sharp process American or cheddar cheese (8 ounces)
1	cup chopped celery (2 medium stalks)		
1	cup cooked ham, cut in thin matchsticks	$^2/_3$	cup milk
1	cup cooked chicken, cut in thin matchsticks	1	4$^1/_2$-ounce can diced green chile peppers, drained
2	cups red and/or yellow cherry tomatoes, cut in quarters	3	tablespoons sliced pitted ripe olives
		2	cups corn chips (optional)

1 In a large salad bowl toss together greens, carrots, and celery. Arrange ham, chicken, tomatoes, and green onions on the greens.

2 In a heavy medium saucepan combine cheese and milk. Cook and stir over low heat until cheese is melted and mixture is smooth. Stir in chile peppers and olives.

3 Just before serving, pour cheese mixture over salad. Toss lightly to coat. Serve at once. If desired, serve with corn chips.

NUTRITION FACTS PER SERVING: 282 cal., 17 g total fat (9 g sat. fat), 71 mg chol., 1,028 mg sodium, 11 g carbo., 3 g fiber, 22 g pro. DAILY VALUES: 44% vit. C, 32% calcium, 10% iron

Italian Beef and Spinach Pie

Family members who missed their vegetable quota during the day will make it up by nightfall. This pie is loaded with spinach, sweet pepper, mushrooms, and tomato. (See photo, page 116.)

PREP: 25 minutes BAKE: 47 minutes STAND: 10 minutes OVEN: 450°/350° MAKES: 8 servings

1	10-ounce package frozen chopped spinach, thawed	½	cup tomato paste
1	unbaked 9-inch pastry shell	1½	teaspoons dried Italian seasoning, crushed
½	pound lean ground beef	½	teaspoon salt
¼	pound bulk mild Italian turkey sausage	⅔	cup light ricotta cheese
¾	cup chopped red and/or yellow sweet pepper (1 large)	¾	cup shredded mozzarella cheese (3 ounces)
½	cup sliced fresh mushrooms	1	cup chopped tomato
1	clove garlic, minced		Fresh oregano (optional)
1	cup water		

1 Drain thawed spinach well, pressing out excess liquid; set aside. Line pastry shell with a double thickness of foil. Bake in a 450° oven for 8 minutes. Remove foil. Bake for 4 to 5 minutes more or until set and dry; remove from oven. Reduce oven temperature to 350°.

2 In a large skillet cook the beef, sausage, sweet pepper, mushrooms, and garlic until meat is no longer pink and vegetables are tender. Drain off fat. Stir in the water, tomato paste, Italian seasoning, and salt. Bring to boiling; reduce heat. Simmer, covered, for 10 minutes.

3 Meanwhile, in a medium bowl stir together spinach, ricotta cheese, and ¼ cup of the mozzarella cheese. Spoon the spinach mixture into baked pastry shell. Top with the meat mixture.

4 To prevent overbrowning, cover the edge of pastry with foil. Bake in the 350° oven for 45 minutes. Remove foil. Top pie with tomato and the remaining ½ cup mozzarella cheese. Bake for 2 minutes more or until tomato is heated through and cheese is melted. Let stand for 10 minutes before serving. Cut into wedges to serve. If desired, garnish with fresh oregano.

NUTRITION FACTS PER SERVING: 290 cal., 16 g total fat (5 g sat. fat), 33 mg chol., 417 mg sodium, 22 g carbo., 2 g fiber, 16 g pro. DAILY VALUES: 51% vit. C, 12% calcium, 19% iron

Hot Tamale Pie

Looking for a new idea for Saturday supper? Your search is over. This one-dish favorite serves eight, with plenty to go around even if your children invite a friend or two for a sleepover.

PREP: 25 minutes **BAKE:** 25 minutes **OVEN:** 425° **MAKES:** 8 servings

1½ pounds lean ground beef	½ cup all-purpose flour
1 cup chopped onions (2 medium)	1 teaspoon baking powder
1 10¾-ounce can condensed tomato soup	½ teaspoon baking soda
¾ cup frozen whole kernel corn	½ teaspoon salt
½ cup chopped ripe olives	1 cup buttermilk
3 tablespoons chili powder	1 egg, beaten
½ teaspoon ground black pepper	2 tablespoons cooking oil
¾ cup cornmeal	

1 In a large skillet cook beef and onions until beef is brown and onions are tender. Drain off fat. Stir soup, corn, olives, chili powder, and pepper into beef mixture. Bring to boiling over medium heat. Pour into an ungreased 2-quart square baking dish.

2 In a medium bowl stir together cornmeal, flour, baking powder, baking soda, and salt. In a small bowl stir together buttermilk, egg, and cooking oil. Add buttermilk mixture to flour mixture and stir just until batter is smooth. Pour over hot meat mixture, spreading evenly. Bake in a 425° oven about 25 minutes or until golden brown.

NUTRITION FACTS PER SERVING: 363 cal., 16 g total fat (5 g sat. fat), 98 mg chol., 749 mg sodium, 30 g carbo., 4 g fiber, 27 g pro. DAILY VALUES: 9% vit. C, 10% calcium, 25% iron

Double-Crust Pizza Casserole

Why send out for pizza when your family can share the fun of making its own?
If your kids are too young to pitch in with the crust or filling, put their eager young
fingers to work pressing dough into the baking pan.

PREP: 25 minutes BAKE: 35 minutes STAND: 5 minutes OVEN: 425° MAKES: 12 servings

3	cups all-purpose flour		1	6-ounce can Italian-style tomato paste
3	cups packaged instant mashed potatoes		½	of 1.3- to 1.5-ounce package sloppy joe seasoning mix (about 2 tablespoons)
2	cups milk			
½	cup butter or margarine, melted		1	2¼-ounce can sliced ripe olives, drained (optional)
1	pound lean ground beef			
12	ounces bulk Italian sausage		1	cup shredded mozzarella cheese (4 ounces)
1	cup coarsely chopped onions (2 medium)			
1	8-ounce can tomato sauce		1	tablespoon cornmeal

1 For crust, in a large bowl stir together flour, instant mashed potatoes, milk, and melted butter; set aside. (Mixture stiffens somewhat as it stands.)

2 For filling, in a very large (12-inch) skillet or a 4-quart Dutch oven cook beef, sausage, and onions until meat is no longer pink. Drain off fat. Stir tomato sauce, tomato paste, seasoning mix, and, if desired, olives into beef mixture in skillet.

3 Using floured fingers, press half of the dough into the bottom and about 1½ inches up the sides of an ungreased 13×9×2-inch baking pan or a 3-quart rectangular baking dish. Spread filling over crust; sprinkle with mozzarella cheese.

4 Between two large sheets of waxed paper, roll remaining dough into a 15×11-inch rectangle; remove top sheet and invert over filling. Remove paper. Trim edges as necessary. Turn under edges of top crust and pinch to seal to bottom crust. Sprinkle with cornmeal. Bake in a 425° oven about 35 minutes or until casserole is heated through and crust is golden brown. Let stand for 5 minutes before serving.

NUTRITION FACTS PER SERVING: 428 cal., 20 g total fat (10 g sat. fat), 69 mg chol., 715 mg sodium, 41 g carbo., 2 g fiber, 20 g pro. DAILY VALUES: 27% vit. C, 13% calcium, 16% iron

Roast Pork Tangerine

If you prefer a boneless entrée, buy a 3- to 4-pound boneless pork loin center rib roast.
Cook it until a meat thermometer inserted in the center registers 155°.
(See photo, page 118.)

PREP: 25 minutes ROAST: 2¼ hours STAND: 10 minutes OVEN: 325° MAKES: 10 servings

1	4- to 5-pound pork loin center rib roast, backbone loosened	1	tablespoon brown sugar
			Chicken broth or beef broth
1	teaspoon dry mustard	⅔	cup chicken broth or beef broth
1	teaspoon dried marjoram, crushed	3	tablespoons all-purpose flour
½	teaspoon salt	⅛	teaspoon dry mustard
2	teaspoons finely shredded tangerine peel or orange peel	⅛	teaspoon dried marjoram, crushed
½	cup tangerine juice or orange juice	3	tangerines or 2 oranges, peeled, sectioned, and seeded

1 Place pork, rib side down, in a shallow roasting pan. In a small bowl combine the 1 teaspoon dry mustard, the 1 teaspoon marjoram, and the salt; rub over meat. Insert a meat thermometer in center of meat without touching bone. Roast, uncovered, in a 325° oven for 1¾ hours.

2 In a small bowl stir together peel, juice, and brown sugar; spoon over meat. Roast about 30 minutes more or until thermometer registers 155°, spooning pan juices over meat once or twice. Transfer meat to platter. Let stand, covered, for 10 minutes before slicing. (The meat's temperature will rise 5° during standing time.)

3 Meanwhile, strain pan juices. Skim off fat. Measure juices; add enough broth to juices to equal ¾ cup liquid. Place the liquid in a medium saucepan. In a screw-top jar combine the ⅔ cup broth and the flour; shake well. Add to saucepan along with the ⅛ teaspoon dry mustard and the ⅛ teaspoon marjoram. Cook and stir until thickened and bubbly; cook and stir for 1 minute more. Season to taste with salt and black pepper. Stir in tangerine sections; heat through. Serve with pork.

NUTRITION FACTS PER SERVING: 181 cal., 6 g total fat (2 g sat. fat), 54 mg chol., 219 mg sodium, 7 g carbo., 1 g fiber, 22 g pro. DAILY VALUES: 21% vit. C, 1% calcium, 7% iron

USING A THERMOMETER A thermometer is a grilling essential—using one is the only way to tell whether food is cooked to a safe internal temperature as specified for the doneness given in the recipe. To use a thermometer, insert it into the thickest part of the food, making sure it isn't touching bone, fat, or gristle.
1 A meat thermometer works well for longer-cooking meats, such as a roast or whole poultry. It can be left in the food while it cooks.
2 An instant-read thermometer is used for checking the internal temperature of food at the end of cooking and gives a reading in less than 20 seconds. It must be inserted at least 2 inches into the food.
3 A digital thermometer gives digital readings in 10 seconds. Because the probe is inserted only ½ inch deep, it is perfect for thin foods.

Molasses-Glazed Pork Tenderloin

Old-fashioned corn bread is an appetizing dinner partner for this Southern-inspired dish.
(See photo, page 120.)

START TO FINISH: 30 minutes MAKES: 4 servings

¼ cup finely chopped prosciutto or
2 slices bacon, coarsely chopped

1 16-ounce package frozen lima beans
or two 9-ounce packages frozen
Italian green beans

½ cup chopped onion (1 medium)

¾ cup water

1 tablespoon olive oil

12 ounces pork tenderloin, cut into
½-inch slices

½ cup orange juice

3 tablespoons molasses

1 teaspoon cornstarch

½ teaspoon salt

¼ teaspoon ground black pepper

Steamed spinach or turnip greens
(optional)

2 tablespoons snipped fresh parsley

1 In a large skillet cook prosciutto over medium heat until crisp; drain and set aside. In the same skillet cook beans and onion in the water according to beans' package directions. Drain the beans and onions; set aside.

2 In the same skillet heat oil over medium-high heat. Cook tenderloin in hot oil for 4 to 5 minutes or until just barely pink in center, turning once.

3 Meanwhile, in a small bowl stir together orange juice, molasses, cornstarch, salt, and pepper. Add to meat in skillet. Cook and stir until thickened and bubbly. Cook and stir about 2 minutes more. Stir bean mixture into skillet mixture; heat through.

4 To serve, divide steamed spinach, if desired, among four plates. Spoon meat and bean mixture over steamed spinach, if desired. Top with prosciutto and sprinkle with parsley.

NUTRITION FACTS PER SERVING: 324 cal., 6 g total fat (1 g sat. fat), 52 mg chol., 460 mg sodium, 38 g carbo., 7 g fiber, 29 g pro. DAILY VALUES: 7% vit. A, 44% vit. C, 8% calcium, 2% iron

Raspberry-Pepper-Glazed Ham

Tired of turkey year after year? Holiday entertaining takes on sweet sophistication if you present this ham dressed up with a special raspberry sauce or chutney.

PREP: 20 minutes BAKE: 1¾ hours STAND: 15 minutes OVEN: 325° MAKES: 16 to 20 servings

1	9- to 10-pound cooked bone-in ham (rump half or shank portion)
1	recipe Raspberry Sauce
1	tablespoon pink or black peppercorns, coarsely cracked

Fresh raspberries (optional)

Fresh herb sprigs (optional)

1 If desired, score ham by making diagonal cuts in fat in a diamond pattern. Place ham on a rack in a shallow roasting pan. Insert a meat thermometer into the thickest portion of the meat without touching bone. Bake in a 325° oven until the thermometer registers 130° (allow 1½ to 2¼ hours).

2 Meanwhile, prepare Raspberry Sauce. Brush ham with some of the sauce. Bake ham for 15 to 20 minutes more or until the thermometer registers 135°, brushing once or twice with additional sauce. Remove from oven. Sprinkle with the peppercorns. Cover the ham with foil and let stand for 15 minutes. (The meat's temperature will rise 5° during standing time.)

3 Just before serving, carve ham. Reheat any of the remaining Raspberry Sauce and pass with ham. If desired, garnish with raspberries and herbs.

Raspberry Sauce: In a small saucepan stir together 1½ cups seedless raspberry preserves; 2 tablespoons white vinegar; 2 or 3 canned whole chipotle peppers in adobo sauce, drained and chopped; and 3 cloves garlic, minced. Bring to boiling; reduce heat. Simmer, uncovered, for 5 minutes. Remove from heat.

NUTRITION FACTS PER SERVING: 365 cal., 11 g total fat (4 g sat. fat), 130 mg chol., 107 mg sodium, 21 g carbo., 1 g fiber, 42 g pro. DAILY VALUES: 5% vit. C, 2% calcium, 10% iron

Pork and Green Chile Bake

Diced green chile peppers and a little salsa add spunk to this hearty rice, bean, and pork dish. It will receive a top rating from those who love Mexican food. (See photo, page 115.)

PREP: 25 minutes BAKE: 25 minutes STAND: 3 minutes OVEN: 375° MAKES: 6 servings

1¼	pounds lean boneless pork	1	cup uncooked quick-cooking brown rice
1	tablespoon cooking oil	¼	cup water
1	15-ounce can black beans or pinto beans, rinsed and drained	2	tablespoons bottled salsa
1	14½-ounce can diced tomatoes, undrained	1	teaspoon ground cumin
1	10¾-ounce can condensed cream of chicken soup	½	cup shredded cheddar cheese (2 ounces)
2	4½-ounce cans diced green chile peppers, drained		

1 Cut pork into thin bite-size strips. In a large skillet stir-fry pork, half at a time, in hot oil until no pink remains. Drain off fat. Return all pork to skillet. Stir in drained beans, undrained tomatoes, soup, drained chile peppers, brown rice, water, salsa, and cumin. Heat and stir until bubbly. Pour mixture into an ungreased 2-quart casserole.

2 Bake, uncovered, in a 375° oven for 25 minutes. Remove from oven. Sprinkle with cheese; let stand about 3 minutes to melt cheese.

NUTRITION FACTS PER SERVING: 350 cal., 14 g total fat (5 g sat. fat), 69 mg chol., 1,242 mg sodium, 28 g carbo., 5 g fiber, 30 g pro. DAILY VALUES: 58% vit. C, 15% calcium, 14% iron

Oven-Barbecued Ribs

*Toss out the cutlery and loosen up your fingers so you can eat heartily
of this drippy, succulent fare. Mind your manners: Make sure everybody has
a stack of paper napkins within easy grabbing distance.*

PREP: 15 minutes COOK: 1 hour BAKE: 20 minutes OVEN: 350° MAKES: 4 servings

4	pounds pork loin back ribs or meaty spareribs, cut into serving-size pieces
1	clove garlic, minced
1	tablespoon butter or margarine
½	cup catsup
⅓	cup bottled chili sauce
2	tablespoons brown sugar
2	tablespoons chopped onion
1	tablespoon yellow mustard
1	tablespoon Worcestershire sauce
¾	teaspoon celery seeds
¼	teaspoon salt
	Dash bottled hot pepper sauce

1 In a 6- to 8-quart Dutch oven combine ribs and enough water to cover. Bring to boiling; reduce heat. Simmer, covered, for 1 hour.

2 Meanwhile, for sauce, in a small saucepan cook the garlic in hot butter for 1 minute. Stir in catsup, chili sauce, brown sugar, onion, mustard, Worcestershire sauce, celery seeds, salt, and hot pepper sauce. Bring to boiling, stirring to dissolve sugar. Remove from heat; set aside.

3 Drain ribs. Place ribs, bone side down, in a shallow baking pan. Pour sauce over ribs. Bake, covered, in a 350° oven about 20 minutes or until heated through.

NUTRITION FACTS PER SERVING: 519 cal., 22 g total fat (8 g sat. fat), 132 mg chol., 979 mg sodium, 19 g carbo., 2 g fiber, 59 g pro. DAILY VALUES: 16% vit. C, 5% calcium, 17% iron

Greek-Style Chicken

Accented with olive oil, garlic, tomatoes, and feta cheese, this Mediterranean-style main dish takes only 30 minutes to make. (See photo, page 113.)

START TO FINISH: 30 minutes MAKES: 4 servings

¼	cup toasted wheat germ or fine dry bread crumbs
4	skinless, boneless chicken breast halves (about 1 pound)
2	tablespoons olive oil or cooking oil
1	small zucchini, halved lengthwise and sliced (1 cup)
½	of a medium green sweet pepper, chopped (½ cup)
½	of a medium onion, sliced and separated into rings
2	cloves garlic, minced
⅛	teaspoon salt
	Dash ground black pepper
2	medium tomatoes, cut into wedges
2	tablespoons water
4	teaspoons lime juice or lemon juice
3	cups hot cooked orzo, couscous, or rice
½	cup crumbled feta cheese (2 ounces)

1 Place wheat germ in a shallow bowl; coat chicken with wheat germ. In a large skillet heat 1 tablespoon of the oil over medium heat. Cook chicken in the hot oil for 10 to 12 minutes or until tender and no longer pink, turning once. Remove chicken from skillet; keep warm.

2 In same skillet heat the remaining 1 tablespoon oil. Cook zucchini, sweet pepper, onion, garlic, salt, and black pepper in hot oil for 3 minutes. Add tomato wedges, water, and lime juice. Cook for 1 minute more. Remove from heat.

3 To serve, divide orzo among four plates. Top with vegetable mixture and chicken. Sprinkle with feta cheese.

NUTRITION FACTS PER SERVING: 418 cal., 13 g total fat (4 g sat. fat), 78 mg chol., 299 mg sodium, 38 g carbo., 4 g fiber, 36 g pro. DAILY VALUES: 46% vit. C, 11% calcium, 19% iron

POULTRY: HANDLE WITH CARE When working with raw poultry, keep these food safety tips in mind: Refrigerate chicken in the coldest section, placing it on a tray to catch drips. Thaw frozen, wrapped chicken in the refrigerator—never at room temperature. It's a good idea to designate one cutting board for raw poultry and meats and a separate one for chopping vegetables. Always wash hands, work surfaces, and utensils in hot, soapy water after handling raw poultry to prevent bacteria from spreading to other foods. Never put cooked meat on the same plate that held raw poultry unless the plate has been sanitized.

Creamy Turkey Pie

This turkey-and-mushroom pie sports a tender biscuit crust and a rich cottage cheese topper. If you can't find bulk turkey sausage at your local supermarket, buy uncooked ground turkey and add your own seasonings. (See photo, page 120.)

PREP: 25 minutes BAKE: 30 minutes STAND: 5 minutes OVEN: 350° MAKES: 6 servings

1	pound bulk turkey sausage or uncooked ground turkey*
1/2	cup chopped onion (1 medium)
1	3-ounce package cream cheese, cubed
1	4½-ounce jar sliced mushrooms, drained
1	7½-ounce package refrigerated biscuits (10 biscuits)
1	egg
1	cup cream-style cottage cheese
1	tablespoon all-purpose flour
	Chopped tomato (optional)
	Snipped fresh chives (optional)

1 Lightly grease a 9-inch deep-dish pie plate; set aside. In a large skillet cook turkey sausage and onion over medium-high heat until meat is brown. Drain off fat. Stir in cream cheese until melted. Stir in mushrooms. Cover and keep warm.

2 Meanwhile, for crust, arrange biscuits in prepared pie plate, pressing together onto the bottom and up sides to form an even crust. Spoon turkey mixture into crust, spreading evenly.

3 In a blender container or food processor bowl combine egg, cottage cheese, and flour. Cover and blend or process until smooth. Spread cheese mixture evenly over turkey mixture.

4 Bake, uncovered, in a 350° oven about 30 minutes or until edge is brown and top is set. Let stand for 5 to 10 minutes before serving. Cut into wedges to serve. If desired, garnish with chopped tomato and/or snipped chives.

*Note: If using ground turkey, add 1/4 teaspoon salt; 1/4 teaspoon dried sage, crushed; and 1/4 teaspoon black pepper to meat mixture.

NUTRITION FACTS PER SERVING: 420 cal., 24 g total fat (10 g sat. fat), 85 mg chol., 1,406 mg sodium, 26 g carbo., 2 g fiber, 26 g pro. DAILY VALUES: 1% vit. C, 6% calcium, 17% iron

Maryland Fried Chicken

In this special version of fried chicken, you add milk after partially cooking the chicken so the pieces simmer rather than fry. The results are moist, tender, and scrumptious.
(See photo, front cover.)

PREP: 25 minutes COOK: 55 minutes MAKES: 6 servings

1	egg, beaten	2½	to 3 pounds meaty chicken pieces (breasts, thighs, and drumsticks)
3	tablespoons milk		
1	cup finely crushed saltine crackers (28 crackers)	2	to 3 tablespoons cooking oil
1	teaspoon dried thyme, crushed	1	cup milk
½	teaspoon paprika	1	recipe Cream Gravy
⅛	teaspoon ground black pepper		Fresh thyme sprigs (optional)

1 In a small bowl combine the egg and the 3 tablespoons milk. In a shallow bowl combine the crushed crackers, dried thyme, paprika, and pepper. Set aside.

2 Dip chicken pieces, one at a time, in egg mixture, then roll in cracker mixture.

3 In a large skillet heat oil over medium heat. Add chicken and cook, uncovered, for 10 to 15 minutes, turning occasionally to brown evenly. Drain off the fat.

4 Add the 1 cup milk to skillet. Reduce heat to medium low; cover tightly. Cook for 35 minutes. Uncover; cook for 10 minutes more or until chicken is tender and no longer pink. Transfer chicken to a serving platter; cover and keep warm. Reserve drippings. Prepare Cream Gravy. If desired, garnish with fresh thyme.

Cream Gravy: Skim fat from drippings. Reserve 3 tablespoons of the drippings in skillet. In a screw-top jar combine ³⁄₄ cup milk, 3 tablespoons all-purpose flour, ¹⁄₄ teaspoon salt, and ¹⁄₈ teaspoon pepper; cover and shake until well mixed. Add to skillet. Stir in additional ³⁄₄ cup milk. Cook over medium heat, stirring constantly, until thickened and bubbly. Cook and stir 1 minute more. (If desired, thin with additional milk.) Makes about 1¹⁄₂ cups.

NUTRITION FACTS PER SERVING: 409 cal., 23 g total fat (5 g sat. fat), 118 mg chol., 398 mg sodium, 17 g carbo., 1 g fiber, 30 g pro. DAILY VALUES: 9% vit. A, 1% vit. C, 13% calcium, 13% iron

Upside-Down Pizza Pie

Put some pizzazz into this main dish. To make the lattice crust, start at the center of the baking dish moving outward, cutting or piecing pastry strips to fit.

PREP: 20 minutes BAKE: 25 minutes OVEN: 350° STAND: 5 minutes MAKES: 4 servings

1	14½-ounce can diced tomatoes with basil, garlic, and oregano; undrained
2	cups cubed cooked chicken
1½	cups quartered fresh mushrooms, such as brown, white, or button
1	8-ounce can pizza sauce
1	cup shredded pizza cheese (4 ounces)
¼	cup grated Parmesan cheese (1 ounce)

1 11-ounce package refrigerated breadsticks (12)

Milk

1 tablespoon grated Parmesan cheese

Desired toppings, such as sliced green onions, snipped fresh chives, sliced pitted black or green olives, chopped green or yellow sweet pepper, and/or shredded pizza cheese

1 Grease four 12- to 16-ounce baking dishes. In a medium bowl stir together undrained tomatoes, chicken, mushrooms, and pizza sauce. Spoon mixture into the prepared baking dishes. Sprinkle pizza cheese evenly over tomato mixture. Sprinkle with the ¼ cup Parmesan cheese.

2 Unroll breadstick dough. Separate along perforations to form 12 strips. Weave strips over filling to form a lattice crust on each baking dish. Depending on the width of your dishes, you may need to cut strips to length or piece strips together. Brush dough with a little milk. Sprinkle with the remaining 1 tablespoon Parmesan cheese.

3 Bake in a 350° oven about 25 minutes or until breadsticks are golden brown and filling is bubbly. Let stand for 5 minutes before serving. Serve in dishes or loosen edges and invert onto plates; remove dishes. Sprinkle with desired toppings.

NUTRITION FACTS PER SERVING: 562 cal., 20 g total fat (8 g sat. fat), 88 mg chol., 1,865 mg sodium, 52 g carbo., 3 g fiber, 40 g pro. DAILY VALUES: 21% vit. A, 33% vit. C, 40% calcium, 29% iron

Scallops and Shrimp with Linguine

Elegant, yet simple to make, this deftly seasoned dish combines seafood with vegetables and pasta. (See photo, page 120.)

START TO FINISH: 35 minutes MAKES: 6 servings

1 pound fresh or frozen sea scallops	3 cloves garlic, minced
½ pound fresh or frozen medium shrimp in shells	2 tablespoons snipped fresh parsley or 2 teaspoons dried parsley
¼ teaspoon crushed red pepper	1 tablespoon snipped fresh basil or 1 teaspoon dried basil, crushed
2 cups fresh snow peas or one 6-ounce package frozen snow peas	¼ cup oil-packed dried tomatoes, drained and chopped, or 1 small tomato, seeded and chopped
10 ounces packaged dried linguine	
2 tablespoons olive oil or cooking oil	3 tablespoons shaved Parmesan cheese or Romano cheese (optional)
2 tablespoons butter or margarine	
½ cup sliced green onions (4)	Fresh basil (optional)

1 Thaw scallops and shrimp, if frozen. Cut scallops in half. Peel and devein shrimp. In a medium bowl combine scallops, shrimp, and red pepper; set aside.

2 Thaw snow peas, if frozen. Cut snow peas in half; set aside. Cook pasta according to package directions. Drain and return hot pasta to saucepan.

3 Meanwhile, in a large skillet heat oil and butter over medium-high heat. Add green onions and garlic and cook for 30 seconds. Add half of the seafood mixture. If using, stir in dried parsley and dried basil. Cook and stir for 3 to 4 minutes or until scallops and shrimp turn opaque. Using a slotted spoon, remove seafood mixture; set aside. Repeat with remaining seafood mixture.

4 Return all of the seafood mixture to skillet. Add snow peas and tomatoes. Cook and stir for 2 minutes more. Add seafood mixture, and, if using, fresh parsley and snipped fresh basil to pasta. Toss to combine. If desired, sprinkle with Parmesan cheese and garnish with additional fresh basil.

NUTRITION FACTS PER SERVING: 366 cal., 12 g total fat (3 g sat. fat), 84 mg chol., 367 mg sodium, 41 g carbo., 3 g fiber, 22 g pro. DAILY VALUES: 41% vit. C, 6% calcium, 17% iron

Lamb Chops and Lima Beans

*This recipe also works well with medallions of turkey tenderloin or pork
instead of the lamb chops.*

START TO FINISH: 25 minutes MAKES: 4 servings

⅓ cup fine dry bread crumbs	⅓ cup finely chopped red sweet pepper
4 teaspoons mustard seeds, crushed	1 tablespoon butter or margarine
¼ teaspoon salt	1 tablespoon snipped fresh thyme
¼ teaspoon ground ground black pepper	Several dashes bottled green hot pepper sauce
8 lamb chops, cut ½ inch thick (2 to 3 ounces each)	1 tablespoon cooking oil
¼ cup chicken broth	Fresh thyme sprigs (optional)
12 ounces shelled fresh or frozen baby lima beans (2¼ cups)	

1 In a small bowl combine bread crumbs, mustard seeds, salt, and black
pepper. Trim and discard fat from chops. Coat chops with bread crumb mixture,
pressing firmly to coat evenly. Cover and set aside.

2 In a medium saucepan bring chicken broth to boiling; reduce heat. Add
lima beans and sweet pepper. Cook, covered, over medium-low heat for
8 to 10 minutes or just until tender for fresh lima beans, or according to
package directions for frozen lima beans. Remove from heat; drain. Stir butter,
snipped thyme, and hot pepper sauce into lima bean mixture. Set aside and
keep warm.

3 Meanwhile, in a large skillet heat oil over medium-high heat. Cook chops in
hot oil for 6 to 9 minutes, turning once. Reduce heat to prevent overbrowning,
if needed. (An instant-read thermometer inserted into the thickest portion of
the chop should register 145° for medium-rare or 155° for medium doneness).
Drain on paper towels.

4 To serve, spoon cooked beans onto plates. Serve two chops on each plate
alongside beans. If desired, garnish with thyme sprigs.

NUTRITION FACTS PER SERVING: 452 cal., 30 g total fat (12 g sat. fat), 70 mg chol., 448 mg sodium, 24 g carbo.,
5 g fiber, 22 g pro. DAILY VALUES: 57% vit. C, 8% calcium, 24% iron

Hot Veggie Sandwiches

Sometimes veggies satisfy more than a meat or chicken dish. Using cumin-flavored mayonnaise renders a stylishly simple sandwich. (See photo, page 119.)

PREP: 20 minutes GRILL: 17 minutes MAKES: 4 servings

1	small onion, cut into ½-inch slices
1	small eggplant, cut lengthwise into ½-inch slices
1	medium zucchini, cut lengthwise into ¼-inch slices
1	medium yellow summer squash, cut lengthwise into ¼-inch slices
1	medium red sweet pepper, seeded and cut into ½-inch strips
⅓	cup olive oil
4	kaiser rolls, split
¼	cup Cumin Mayo

1 Brush onion, eggplant, zucchini, yellow squash, and sweet pepper with some of the olive oil. Place onion slices on a long metal skewer. Grill onions on the rack of an uncovered grill directly over medium coals for 5 minutes.* Arrange remaining vegetables on the grill rack. Grill for 12 to 15 minutes more or until vegetables are tender, turning once. (If some vegetables cook more quickly than others, remove and keep warm.)

2 Meanwhile, brush the split sides of the rolls with remaining olive oil. Grill rolls, split sides down, about 1 minute or until toasted.

3 To assemble, layer grilled vegetables on the bottom halves of the rolls. Spread top layer of each roll with 1 tablespoon of the Cumin Mayo. Cover sandwiches with tops of rolls.

Cumin Mayo: In a small bowl stir together 1 cup light mayonnaise dressing; 2 tablespoons lime juice; 1 clove garlic, minced; and 1 teaspoon cumin seeds, crushed. Makes about 1 cup.

***Note:** To use the broiler instead of the grill, brush vegetables with some of the oil. Place half of the vegetables on the unheated rack of a broiler pan. Broil 3 to 4 inches from the heat for 12 to 15 minutes or until vegetables are tender, turning once. Remove and cover broiled vegetables to keep warm. Repeat with remaining vegetables. Toast rolls under broiler about 1 minute.

NUTRITION FACTS PER SERVING: 420 cal., 26 g total fat (4 g sat. fat), 5 mg chol., 405 mg sodium, 42 g carbo., 5 g fiber, 8 g pro. DAILY VALUES: 96% vit. C, 8% calcium, 15% iron

Artichoke and Basil Hero

Basil, spinach, tomato, and artichoke hearts combine with cheese for a hearty sandwich. The caper vinaigrette takes it out of the realm of the ordinary.

START TO FINISH: 30 minutes MAKES: 6 servings

1	cup fresh basil (leaves only)
¼	cup olive oil or salad oil
2	tablespoons grated Parmesan cheese
1	tablespoon capers, drained
1	tablespoon white wine vinegar
2	teaspoons Dijon-style mustard
1	clove garlic, quartered

1	16-ounce loaf unsliced French bread
1	14-ounce can artichoke hearts, drained and sliced
4	ounces sliced provolone cheese
1	medium tomato, thinly sliced
2	cups torn fresh spinach

1 In a blender container or food processor bowl combine the basil, oil, Parmesan cheese, drained capers, vinegar, mustard, and garlic. Cover and blend or process until nearly smooth. Set aside.

2 To assemble, using a long serrated knife, cut bread in half lengthwise. Hollow out each half, leaving a $1/2$- to 1-inch shell. (Save bread crumbs for another use.) Spread the basil mixture over cut side of each bread half. On the bottom half, layer artichoke hearts, provolone cheese, tomato, and spinach. Cover with bread top. Cut sandwich crosswise into six pieces.

NUTRITION FACTS PER SERVING: 396 cal., 17 g total fat (5 g sat. fat), 14 mg chol., 887 mg sodium, 46 g carbo., 4 g fiber, 15 g pro. DAILY VALUES: 18% vit. C, 24% calcium, 23% iron

Smoked Turkey Dagwood with Chile Mayonnaise

To seed an avocado, cut it lengthwise through the flesh down to the seed. Separate the halves by placing one hand on each side and twisting in opposite directions. Tap the seed with the knife blade and lift out. Use a knife to remove the skin.

START TO FINISH: 25 minutes MAKES: 4 servings

½ cup mayonnaise or salad dressing	8 ½-inch slices sourdough bread, toasted
2 tablespoons snipped fresh cilantro	16 thin slices smoked turkey (about 8 ounces)
1 fresh jalapeño pepper, seeded and finely chopped*	8 slices tomato
½ teaspoon ground cumin	8 slices bacon, crisp-cooked and drained
1 avocado, seeded, peeled, and thinly sliced	
1 tablespoon lime juice	

1 For chile mayonnaise, in a small bowl stir together mayonnaise, cilantro, jalapeño pepper, and cumin. Cover and chill for up to 2 days.

2 In a small bowl toss avocado slices with lime juice; set aside.

3 To assemble, spread chile mayonnaise evenly over toasted bread slices. On four of the bread slices layer turkey, tomato, avocado, and bacon. Top with remaining bread slices. Serve immediately.

***Note:** Because chile peppers contain volatile oils that can burn your skin and eyes, avoid direct contact with them as much as possible. When working with chile peppers, wear plastic or rubber gloves. If your bare hands do touch the chile peppers, wash your hands well with soap and water.

NUTRITION FACTS PER SERVING: 560 cal., 40 g total fat (8 g sat. fat), 56 mg chol., 1,245 mg sodium, 33 g carbo., 2 g fiber, 21 g pro. DAILY VALUES: 7% vit. A, 34% vit. C, 4% calcium, 20% iron

THE RIGHT AVOCADO If you're after neat little cubes or slices of avocado, choose firm fruits—not rock-hard ones—that give a little under gentle pressure. If you plan to mash the avocado to make guacamole, choose fruits that feel soft to your fingers. If you want to shop ahead, buy very firm avocados. Stored at room temperature, they'll ripen in three to four days. Speed ripening by placing avocados in a brown paper bag or in a fruit ripening bowl. When they're ripe, put them in the refrigerator and use within a few days.

Beef and Sweet Onion Sandwiches

Seek the just-right onion and the first bite will reward. From April through August, use Vidalia, Walla Walla, Maui, Texas Spring Sweet, Imperial Sweet, or Carzalia Sweet varieties. In winter, shop for South American imports, such as Oso Sweet and Rio Sweet.

START TO FINISH: 20 minutes MAKES: 4 servings

12	ounces boneless beef sirloin or top round steak, cut 1 inch thick
½	teaspoon coarsely ground black pepper
2	teaspoons cooking oil
1	medium sweet onion (such as Vidalia or Walla Walla), sliced
2	tablespoons Dijon-style mustard

½	of a 7-ounce jar roasted red sweet peppers, drained
8	1-inch slices sourdough bread or marbled rye bread
1½	cups torn packaged prewashed spinach or other salad greens

1 Trim fat from steak. Sprinkle both sides of steak with black pepper; press in lightly. In a large skillet cook steak in hot oil over medium-high heat about 8 minutes or until slightly pink in center, turning once. Remove from skillet; keep warm. Add onion to drippings in skillet. (Add more oil, if necessary.) Cook and stir about 5 minutes or until onion is crisp-tender. Stir in mustard; remove from heat.

2 Meanwhile, cut drained roasted sweet peppers into ½-inch strips. Toast bread, if desired, and shred spinach.

3 Just before serving, cut steak into bite-size strips. To assemble, top four of the bread slices with spinach, steak strips, roasted pepper strips, and onion mixture. Top with remaining bread slices.

NUTRITION FACTS PER SERVING: 335 cal., 12 g total fat (4 g sat. fat), 57 mg chol., 553 mg sodium, 30 g carbo., 1 g fiber, 25 g pro. DAILY VALUES: 96% vit. C, 5% calcium, 28% iron

Feta-Stuffed Pita Burgers

Take the ho-hum out of hamburgers with a Lebanese touch: lamb-beef patties seasoned with red pepper, cumin, and oregano plus a bit of feta in the center.

PREP: 15 minutes GRILL: 15 minutes MAKES: 4 servings

2 tablespoons cornmeal	1/8 teaspoon lemon-pepper seasoning
2 tablespoons milk	8 ounces lean ground lamb
1 tablespoon finely chopped onion	8 ounces lean ground beef
1 clove garlic, minced	1/4 cup finely crumbled feta cheese (1 ounce)
1/4 teaspoon salt	2 large pita bread rounds, split
1/4 teaspoon dried oregano, crushed	1 1/2 cups shredded fresh spinach
1/4 teaspoon ground cumin	
1/8 teaspoon ground red pepper	

1 In a medium bowl stir together cornmeal, milk, onion, garlic, salt, oregano, cumin, red pepper, and lemon-pepper seasoning. Add ground lamb and ground beef; mix well. Shape meat mixture into eight oval patties, each about 1/4 inch thick. Place 1 tablespoon feta in center of each of four of the ovals. Top with remaining ovals; press edges to seal. Reshape patties as necessary.

2 Grill patties on the rack of an uncovered grill directly over medium-hot coals for 7 minutes. Turn and grill for 8 to 10 minutes more or until no pink remains. Serve burgers in pitas with shredded spinach.

NUTRITION FACTS PER SERVING: 345 cal., 17 g total fat (7 g sat. fat), 80 mg chol., 493 mg sodium, 22 g carbo., 1 g fiber, 25 g pro. DAILY VALUES: 6% vit. C, 10% calcium, 17% iron

CRUSHING DRIED HERBS You'll get more flavor out of dried herbs if you crush them before adding them in recipes.

For the correct amount of herb, first measure it in a measuring spoon, then empty the spoon into your hand. Crush the herb with the fingers of your other hand to release the herb's flavor, and add it to the specified ingredients.

Some dried herbs, such as rosemary and thyme, are more easily crushed with a mortar and pestle—but if you don't have one, try crushing them with a wooden spoon against the inside of a bowl. This is not an ideal substitute for a mortar and pestle but should do in a pinch.

Grilled Beef Tacos

Try the real flavors of Mexico with these soft tacos filled with grilled sirloin, peppers, and onion. True caballeros enjoy their tacos and burritos made with carne asada (grilled meat) and a little picante sauce.

PREP: 20 minutes GRILL: 10 minutes MAKES: 4 servings

2 tablespoons lemon juice	1 tablespoon olive oil
1 avocado, seeded, peeled, and cut into ½-inch cubes	½ cup bottled picante sauce
1 pound boneless beef sirloin or eye of round steak, cut 1 inch thick	2 cups shredded lettuce
	4 7- to 8-inch flour tortillas
1 medium onion, cut into wedges	Bottled picante sauce (optional)
2 fresh cubanelle, anaheim, or poblano peppers, cut into 1-inch squares*	

1 Drizzle lemon juice over avocado; toss gently to coat. Set aside.

2 Trim fat from steak. Cut steak into thin 2-inch strips. On four 12-inch skewers thread steak, accordion-style. On four 12-inch skewers alternately thread onion and peppers. Brush vegetables with olive oil.

3 Grill the kabobs on the rack of an uncovered grill directly over medium coals for 10 to 12 minutes or until steak is cooked to desired doneness, turning kabobs once and brushing occasionally with the ½ cup picante sauce.

4 To serve, divide the steak, onion, peppers, avocado, and lettuce among the tortillas. Fold tortillas over filling. If desired, serve with additional picante sauce.

***Note:** Because chile peppers contain volatile oils that can burn your skin and eyes, avoid direct contact with them as much as possible. When working with chile peppers, wear plastic or rubber gloves. If your bare hands do touch the chile peppers, wash your hands well with soap and water.

NUTRITION FACTS PER SERVING: 425 cal., 24 g total fat (6 g sat. fat), 76 mg chol., 403 mg sodium, 24 g carbo., 3 g fiber, 30 g pro. DAILY VALUES: 105% vit. C, 5% calcium, 32% iron

Chicken-Artichoke Turnovers

Next time you grill or broil chicken, make extra so you'll have enough left over for these plump poultry turnovers filled with cheese, artichokes, and green chile peppers. Frozen patty shells make them easy to prepare. (See photo, page 114.)

PREP: 30 minutes BAKE: 25 minutes OVEN: 400° MAKES: 6 turnovers

1	10-ounce package frozen patty shells (6)	¾	cup coarsely chopped, drained artichoke hearts (half of a 14-ounce can)
¼	cup light dairy sour cream		
1	to 1½ teaspoons chili powder	1	4½-ounce can diced green chile peppers, drained
2	cloves garlic, minced		
1	teaspoon lemon juice	¼	cup thinly sliced green onions (2)
1½	cups chopped cooked chicken	1	tablespoon snipped fresh parsley
¾	cup shredded Monterey Jack cheese (3 ounces)		Milk

1 Thaw patty shells; set aside. For filling, in a medium bowl stir together sour cream, chili powder, garlic, and lemon juice. Stir in chicken, Monterey Jack cheese, artichoke hearts, drained chile peppers, green onions, and parsley.

2 On a lightly floured surface, roll each patty shell to a 7-inch circle. Place about ½ cup filling on half of each circle. For each turnover, moisten edge of circle with water; fold other half of circle over filling. Press with tines of a fork to seal.

3 Line a baking sheet with foil; place turnovers on baking sheet. Cut slits in the top of each turnover for steam to escape. Brush tops with milk. Bake in a 400° oven for 25 to 30 minutes or until golden brown.

NUTRITION FACTS PER TURNOVER: 367 cal., 23 g total fat (4 g sat. fat), 48 mg chol., 378 mg sodium, 22 g carbo., 1 g fiber, 18 g pro. DAILY VALUES: 17% vit. C, 13% calcium, 7% iron

COOKED CHICKEN CHOICES, YOUR WAY When a recipe calls for cooked chicken, use a package of frozen chopped cooked chicken or purchase a deli-roasted chicken. A cooked whole chicken yields 1½ to 2 cups boneless chopped meat. If you have more time, you can poach chicken breasts. For 2 cups cubed cooked chicken, in a large skillet place 12 ounces skinless, boneless chicken breasts and simmer for 12 to 14 minutes or until chicken is tender and no longer pink. Drain chicken well and cut up.

Potato Crust Vegetable Pizza

*Gourmet pizza—with a crust made of shredded potatoes and heaped with zucchini,
summer squash, sweet pepper, and goat cheese—tops take-out any night.*

PREP: 20 minutes BAKE: 32 minutes OVEN: 500° MAKES: 6 to 8 servings

3	medium baking potatoes, peeled (1 pound)
1	small onion
1	egg yolk, beaten
2	teaspoons all-purpose flour
	Dash salt
6	teaspoons olive oil
1	cup thinly sliced zucchini (1 small)
1	cup thinly sliced yellow summer squash (1 small)
½	cup chopped yellow sweet pepper (1 small)
1	small red onion, halved and thinly sliced
1	clove garlic, minced
½	of a 5.3-ounce package soft goat cheese (chèvre)
8	cherry tomatoes, quartered
¾	cup shredded mozzarella cheese (3 ounces)
1	tablespoon shredded fresh basil
	Fresh basil sprigs (optional)

1 Into a bowl of cold water, shred potatoes and onion. Drain potato mixture well, squeezing out excess moisture. In a medium bowl combine potato mixture, egg yolk, flour, and salt; mix well.

2 In an 11×7×1½-inch baking pan heat 2 teaspoons of the olive oil in a 500° oven for 1 to 2 minutes. Remove from oven. Carefully press potato mixture into bottom and up sides of pan. Brush top of potato mixture with 2 teaspoons of the olive oil. Bake in the 500° oven about 30 minutes or until golden brown and crisp.

3 Meanwhile, in a medium bowl toss together zucchini, summer squash, sweet pepper, red onion, and garlic. In a large skillet heat the remaining 2 teaspoons olive oil. Cook zucchini mixture in hot oil until vegetables are crisp-tender, stirring often.

4 Carefully spread goat cheese over potato crust. Top cheese with the hot zucchini mixture and cherry tomatoes. Sprinkle with mozzarella cheese. Bake for 1 minute more to melt cheese. Sprinkle with shredded basil. If desired, garnish with fresh basil sprigs.

NUTRITION FACTS PER SERVING: 216 cal., 11 g total fat (4 g sat. fat), 55 mg chol., 169 mg sodium, 21 g carbo., 2 g fiber, 8 g pro. DAILY VALUES: 91% vit. C, 10% calcium, 4% iron

Tostada Pizza

*Being penny-wise does not mean cheating your family out of a good meal.
The proof is in this Mexican-style pizza, concocted with biscuit-mix crust, seasoned
ground meat, and American cheese.*

PREP: 25 minutes BAKE: 21 minutes OVEN: 450° MAKES: 6 servings

2	tablespoons cornmeal	½	cup cold water
1	pound lean ground beef	1	15-ounce can refried beans
¾	cup water	1	cup shredded sharp American cheese or cheddar cheese (4 ounces)
1	4½-ounce can diced green chile peppers, drained	1	cup shredded lettuce
½	of a 1.5-ounce envelope taco seasoning mix (about 2 tablespoons)	1	medium tomato, chopped
1	teaspoon chili powder	½	cup thinly sliced green onions (4)
2	cups packaged biscuit mix		Bottled taco sauce (optional)

1 Generously grease a 12- to 14-inch pizza pan. Sprinkle pan with cornmeal; set aside. In a large skillet cook ground beef until brown. Drain well. Stir the ¾ cup water, the chile peppers, taco seasoning mix, and chili powder into beef in skillet. Simmer, uncovered, about 15 minutes or until thick.

2 Meanwhile, in a medium bowl stir together the biscuit mix and the ½ cup cold water with a fork until dough follows fork around the bowl. With floured fingers, pat dough into bottom and up edge of prepared pan. Spread refried beans over dough. Spoon meat mixture over refried beans.

3 Bake, uncovered, in a 450° oven for 18 to 20 minutes or until crust is golden brown. Sprinkle with the cheese. Bake for 3 to 5 minutes more or until cheese is melted. Top with lettuce, tomato, and green onions. Cut into wedges to serve. If desired, serve with taco sauce.

NUTRITION FACTS PER SERVING: 500 cal., 21 g total fat (9 g sat. fat), 87 mg chol., 1,473 mg sodium, 45 g carbo., 6 g fiber, 32 g pro. DAILY VALUES: 30% vit. C, 23% calcium, 28% iron

Chapter Five

Easy Breads

Super-Big Cinnamon-Pecan Ring, p. 178

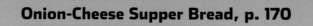

Onion-Cheese Supper Bread, p. 170

Cinnamon Fantans, p. 179

Dried Cherry-Orange Scones, p. 189

Peppery Cheese Bread, p. 169

Crispy Corn Bread with Dried Tomatoes, p. 175

Mostly Mushrooms Popovers, p. 165

▲ Banana-Apple Butter Bread, p. 192

▲ Cucumber Buns, p. 161

▲ Berry Breakfast Rolls, p. 182

▲ Double-Chocolate Scones, p. 188

Cucumber Buns

Cucumber, dill, and chives provide these fluffy yeast rolls garden-fresh flavor.
(See photo, page 160.)

PREP: 25 minutes RISE: 1¼ hours BAKE: 20 minutes OVEN: 350° MAKES: 12 buns

3¼ to 3¾ cups all-purpose flour	1 medium cucumber, peeled and cut up (1½ to 2 cups)
1 package active dry yeast	
2 tablespoons snipped fresh chives or 1 tablespoon dried chives	½ cup dairy sour cream
	¼ cup water
1 teaspoon snipped fresh dill or ¼ teaspoon dried dillweed	1 tablespoon sugar
	1¼ teaspoons salt

1 In a large mixing bowl stir together 1¼ cups of the flour, the yeast, chives, and dill; set aside. In a food processor bowl or blender container place cucumber. Cover and process or blend until smooth (you should have ³⁄₄ cup).

2 In a small saucepan heat and stir the cucumber puree, sour cream, water, sugar, and salt until warm (120° to 130°). (Mixture may look curdled.) Add cucumber mixture to the flour mixture. Beat with an electric mixer on low to medium speed for 30 seconds, scraping the sides of the bowl constantly. Beat on high speed for 3 minutes. Using a wooden spoon, stir in as much of the remaining flour as you can.

3 Turn out onto a lightly floured surface. Knead in enough of the remaining flour to make a moderately stiff dough that is smooth and elastic (knead for 6 to 8 minutes total). Shape dough into a ball. Place in a lightly greased bowl; turn once to grease surface. Cover and let rise in a warm place until double (about 45 minutes).

4 Grease a 13×9×2-inch baking pan; set aside. Punch dough down. Turn out onto a lightly floured surface. Cover and let rest for 10 minutes. Divide dough into 12 pieces. Shape each piece into a ball; arrange in prepared pan, allowing space between balls. Cover and let rise in a warm place until nearly double (about 30 minutes).

5 Bake in a 350° oven for 20 to 25 minutes or until golden. Remove rolls from baking pan and cool on a wire rack. Serve warm or cool.

NUTRITION FACTS PER BUN: 140 cal., 2 g total fat (1 g sat. fat), 4 mg chol., 248 mg sodium, 26 g carbo., 1 g fiber, 4 g pro. DAILY VALUES: 3% vit. C, 2% calcium, 9% iron

Quick Whole Wheat Hot Cross Buns

Greasing the baking pan on the bottom and only ¹/₂ inch up the sides will prevent rims from forming around the edges of quick-bread loaves.

PREP: 15 minutes BAKE: 25 minutes COOL: 20 minutes OVEN: 400° MAKES: 16 buns

1 cup whole wheat flour	¹/₄ cup dried blueberries or snipped dried tart cherries
1 cup all-purpose flour	
2 tablespoons toasted wheat germ	1 egg, beaten
2¹/₂ teaspoons baking powder	1 cup milk
¹/₄ teaspoon ground cinnamon	¹/₂ cup sugar
³/₄ teaspoon salt	¹/₃ cup cooking oil
¹/₂ cup raisins	¹/₃ cup purchased white frosting
¹/₃ cup chopped almonds	

1 Grease the bottom and ¹/₂ inch up the sides of a 9×9×2-inch baking pan; set aside. In a large bowl stir together whole wheat flour, all-purpose flour, wheat germ, baking powder, cinnamon, and salt. Stir in raisins, almonds, and dried fruit until coated with flour. Make a well in the center of flour mixture; set aside.

2 In a medium bowl stir together the egg, milk, sugar, and oil. Add egg mixture all at once to flour mixture. Stir just until moistened (batter should be lumpy). Spoon batter into the prepared pan, spreading evenly.

3 Bake in a 400° oven about 25 minutes or until golden brown. Cool in pan on a wire rack for 20 minutes. Cut into sixteen squares. Pipe a frosting X on top of each square. Serve warm.

NUTRITION FACTS PER BUN: 195 cal., 8 g total fat (1 g sat. fat), 14 mg chol., 192 mg sodium, 29 g carbo., 2 g fiber, 4 g pro. DAILY VALUES: 1% vit. A, 1% vit. C, 7% calcium, 5% iron

Italian Muffins

Button mushrooms, mild in flavor, work in this recipe. For a richer, earthier taste, experiment with morels, shiitakes, or portobellos.

PREP: 20 minutes BAKE: 20 minutes COOL: 5 minutes OVEN: 400° MAKES: 12 muffins

¼	cup oil-packed dried tomatoes	½	teaspoon garlic salt
	Olive oil	¼	teaspoon baking soda
1	cup fresh mushrooms, coarsely chopped	⅛	teaspoon ground black pepper
1¾	cups all-purpose flour	1	egg, beaten
½	cup finely shredded Asiago cheese or Romano cheese (2 ounces)	¾	cup milk
2	tablespoons sugar	2	to 3 tablespoons finely shredded Asiago or Romano cheese (optional)
2	teaspoons baking powder		

1 Grease twelve 2½-inch muffin cups or coat with nonstick cooking spray; set aside. Drain tomatoes, reserving oil. Chop tomatoes; set aside. Add enough additional olive oil to reserved oil to equal ⅓ cup.

2 In a medium skillet cook mushrooms in 1 tablespoon of the oil until mushrooms are tender and most of the liquid has evaporated. Remove from heat; cool slightly.

3 In a medium bowl stir together flour, the ½ cup Asiago cheese, the sugar, baking powder, garlic salt, baking soda, and pepper. Make a well in the center of flour mixture; set aside.

4 In a small bowl stir together egg, milk, and remaining oil. Stir in mushrooms and chopped tomatoes. Add egg mixture all at once to flour mixture. Stir just until moistened (batter should be lumpy). Spoon batter into prepared muffin cups, filling each two-thirds full. If desired, sprinkle with additional Asiago cheese.

5 Bake in a 400° oven about 20 minutes or until golden. Cool in muffin cups on a wire rack for 5 minutes. Remove from muffin cups and cool slightly on a wire rack; serve warm.

NUTRITION FACTS PER MUFFIN: 165 cal., 9 g total fat (2 g sat. fat), 24 mg chol., 244 mg sodium, 17 g carbo., 1 g fiber, 4 g pro. DAILY VALUES: 4% vit. C, 9% calcium, 7% iron

SIZING UP MUFFINS Muffin cups come in all shapes and sizes—from bite-size minis and standard 2½-inch cups to Texas-size mega-muffins. You'll need to adjust the baking time according to the pan you choose. Minimuffins will bake about 8 minutes less than standard-size muffins. For jumbo muffins, lower the oven temperature to 350° and bake for about 30 minutes.

Some muffin-lovers like their muffins to be all tops—and there's a special pan for that too. Muffin-top or muffin-crown pans make flat muffin rounds. Look for these pans in specialty cookware stores or department stores. Bake muffin tops about 10 minutes less than regular-size muffins.

Cream Cheese Savory Muffins

To avoid tough, chewy muffins, do not overstir the batter. To test for doneness, check after the minimum baking time by inserting a wooden toothpick near the centers. If it comes out clean, they're ready.

PREP: 15 minutes BAKE: 20 minutes OVEN: 400° MAKES: 12 muffins

2	cups all-purpose flour		¼	cup finely chopped onion
1	tablespoon sugar		¼	cup snipped fresh parsley
2½	teaspoons baking powder		1	egg, beaten
¼	teaspoon salt		¾	cup milk
1	3-ounce package cream cheese		¼	cup butter or margarine, melted

1 Grease twelve 2½-inch muffin cups or line with paper bake cups; set aside. In a large bowl stir together flour, sugar, baking powder, and salt. Using a pastry blender, cut in cream cheese until mixture resembles coarse crumbs. Stir in onion and parsley.

2 In a small bowl stir together egg, milk, and melted butter. Add egg mixture all at once to flour mixture. Stir just until moistened (batter should be lumpy). Spoon batter into prepared muffin cups, filling each two-thirds full.

3 Bake in a 400° oven for 20 to 25 minutes or until golden. Remove from muffin cups and cool slightly on a wire rack. Serve warm.

NUTRITION FACTS PER MUFFIN: 150 cal., 7 g total fat (4 g sat. fat), 38 mg chol., 208 mg sodium, 17 g carbo., 1 g fiber, 4 g pro. DAILY VALUES: 3% vit. C, 8% calcium, 6% iron

Mostly Mushrooms Popovers

For crisp popovers that keep their shape, put the batter-filled pan in a preheated oven. Once the popovers are baked and firm, remove them from the oven and gently prick each with a fork. (See photo, page 159.)

PREP: 15 minutes BAKE: 35 minutes OVEN: 400° MAKES: 6 popovers

	Nonstick cooking spray	1/8	teaspoon ground black pepper
1/3	cup dried mushrooms, such as shiitake or porcini	1	cup milk
		2	eggs, beaten
1/2	teaspoon salt	1	tablespoon cooking oil
1/4	teaspoon dried thyme leaves, crushed	1	cup all-purpose flour

1 Coat the cups of a popover pan or six 6-ounce custard cups with nonstick cooking spray. Place the custard cups on a 15×10×1-inch baking pan; set aside. In a small bowl pour boiling water over the dried mushrooms to cover; let stand for 5 minutes. Drain, pressing out the liquid. Finely chop mushrooms.

2 In a medium mixing bowl stir together mushrooms, salt, thyme, and pepper. Add milk, eggs, and oil. Using a rotary beater, beat until mixed. Add flour and beat just until mixture is smooth. Spoon batter into prepared cups, filling each half full.

3 Bake in a 400° oven about 35 to 40 minutes or until very firm. Remove from oven. Immediately prick each popover with a fork to let steam escape. Loosen edges. Remove popovers from cups. Serve immediately.

NUTRITION FACTS PER POPOVER: 150 cal., 5 g total fat (1 g sat. fat), 74 mg chol., 219 mg sodium, 20 g carbo., 1 g fiber, 6 g pro. DAILY VALUES: 5% calcium, 8% iron

RISING TO THE OCCASION Just what is the "pop" in popovers? It's not magic, though it may appear to be. Muffin cups a scant half-full of batter that contains no leavening suddenly explode into airy, cloudy puffs that are crisp on the outside and delectably soft on the inside. Why? The answer is simple: The heat is on. Popovers pop because of the steam that forms inside them as they bake. In the mid-19th century, popovers were one of the few breads cooks could make quickly. They became known as popovers because the batter "popped over" the edge of the pan.

Cheesy Whole Wheat Fingers

Capture the chewy, nutty goodness of home-baked bread in these cheese-topped breadsticks made with frozen whole wheat bread dough. If you prefer, white bread dough works just as well.

PREP: 15 minutes RISE: 1½ hours BAKE: 18 minutes OVEN: 375° MAKES: 30 breadsticks

1   16-ounce loaf frozen whole wheat bread dough, thawed

1   teaspoon dried oregano, crushed

½   teaspoon garlic salt

½   teaspoon paprika

¼   teaspoon celery seeds

¼   teaspoon onion powder

1½   cups shredded cheddar cheese (6 ounces)

1 Grease a 15×10×1-inch baking pan; set aside. On a lightly floured surface roll thawed bread dough to a 15×10×1-inch rectangle. (For easier rolling, partially roll out dough. Cover dough and let rest for 10 minutes. Finish rolling.) Place dough in prepared pan. Cover and let rise in a warm place until nearly double (about 1½ hours).

2 In a medium bowl stir together oregano, garlic salt, paprika, celery seeds, and onion powder. Add cheddar cheese; toss to mix. Sprinkle cheese mixture evenly over dough.

3 Bake in a 375° oven for 18 to 20 minutes or until golden brown. Cool slightly in pan on a wire rack. Cut into 3×1½-inch pieces. Serve warm.

NUTRITION FACTS PER BREADSTICK: 62 cal., 2 g total fat (1 g sat. fat), 6 mg chol., 144 mg sodium, 7 g carbo., 1 g fiber, 3 g pro. DAILY VALUES: 4% calcium, 1% iron

Quick Focaccia Breadsticks

Refrigerated pizza dough takes the time and labor out of making homemade breadsticks. Easy to prepare, these soft and tender delicacies are loaded with traditional focaccia flavors of tomatoes, rosemary, and cheese.

PREP: 15 minutes BAKE: 12 minutes OVEN: 350° MAKES: 10 breadsticks

¼	cup oil-packed dried tomatoes	⅛	teaspoon cracked black pepper
¼	cup grated Romano cheese	2	teaspoons water
1½	teaspoons snipped fresh rosemary or ½ teaspoon dried rosemary, crushed	1	10-ounce package refrigerated pizza dough

1 Lightly grease a baking sheet; set aside. Drain tomatoes, reserving 2 teaspoons of the oil. Finely snip tomatoes. In a small bowl stir together tomatoes, Romano cheese, rosemary, pepper, water, and the reserved oil. Set aside.

2 Unroll pizza dough. On a lightly floured surface roll dough into a 10×8-inch rectangle. Spread tomato mixture crosswise over half of the dough.

3 Fold plain half of dough over filling; press lightly to seal edges. Cut folded dough lengthwise into ten ½-inch strips. Fold each strip in half and twist two or three times. Place 1 inch apart on prepared baking sheet.

4 Bake in a 350° oven for 12 to 15 minutes or until golden brown. Remove from baking sheet and cool on a wire rack.

NUTRITION FACTS PER BREADSTICK: 113 cal., 3 g total fat (1 g sat. fat), 3 mg chol., 263 mg sodium, 18 g carbo., 1 g fiber, 5 g pro. DAILY VALUES: 5% vit. C, 3% calcium, 5% iron

Buttermilk Biscuit Sticks

Hints of lemon and tarragon come through in every bite of these flaky, savory sticks. For lunch on the porch, serve them alongside a fresh green salad and a glass of iced lemonade.

PREP: 20 minutes BAKE: 10 minutes OVEN: 425° MAKES: 24 biscuit sticks

2	cups all-purpose flour	¼	cup butter
2	tablespoons sugar	1	egg, beaten
2	teaspoons baking powder	½	cup buttermilk
2	teaspoons finely shredded lemon peel		Buttermilk
2	teaspoons snipped fresh tarragon or ½ teaspoon dried tarragon, crushed		Poppy seeds (optional)
¼	teaspoon baking soda		

1 Lightly grease a baking sheet; set aside. In a medium bowl stir together flour, sugar, baking powder, lemon peel, tarragon, and baking soda. Using a pastry blender, cut in butter until mixture resembles coarse crumbs. Make a well in center of flour mixture. Add egg and the ½ cup buttermilk all at once. Using a fork, stir until moistened.

2 Turn dough out onto a lightly floured surface. Quickly knead dough by gently folding and pressing for 10 to 12 strokes or until dough is nearly smooth. Lightly roll dough into a 12×6-inch rectangle. Cut into twenty-four 6-inch strips.

3 Place strips ½ inch apart on prepared baking sheet. Brush with additional buttermilk. If desired, sprinkle sticks with poppy seeds.

4 Bake in a 425° oven about 10 minutes or until golden. Remove from baking sheet and cool slightly on a wire rack. Serve warm.

NUTRITION FACTS PER BISCUIT STICK: 61 cal., 2 g total fat (1 g sat. fat), 14 mg chol., 71 mg sodium, 9 g carbo., 0 g fiber, 1 g pro. DAILY VALUES: 3% calcium, 3% iron

Peppery Cheese Bread

Spicy brown mustard, plenty of pepper, cheddar cheese, and yogurt provide luscious contrasts in this loaf. (See photo, page 157.)

PREP: 15 minutes BAKE: 45 minutes COOL: 1 hour 10 minutes OVEN: 350° MAKES: 1 loaf (16 servings)

2½	cups all-purpose flour	1	8-ounce carton plain low-fat yogurt
1	tablespoon sugar	½	cup cooking oil
1½	to 2 teaspoons cracked black pepper	¼	cup milk
1	teaspoon baking powder	1	tablespoon spicy brown mustard
¾	teaspoon salt	1	cup shredded cheddar cheese (4 ounces)
½	teaspoon baking soda	¼	cup thinly sliced green onions (2)
2	eggs, beaten		

1 Grease bottom and ½ inch up sides of an 8×4×2-inch loaf pan; set aside. In a large bowl stir together flour, sugar, pepper, baking powder, salt, and baking soda. Make a well in center of flour mixture; set aside.

2 In a medium bowl stir together eggs, yogurt, oil, milk, and mustard. Add egg mixture all at once to flour mixture. Add cheddar cheese and green onions. Stir just until moistened (batter should be lumpy). Spoon batter into prepared pan, spreading evenly.

3 Bake in a 350° oven for 45 to 50 minutes or until a wooden toothpick inserted near center comes out clean. Cool in pan on a wire rack for 10 minutes. Remove bread from pan. Cool for 1 hour on a wire rack. Serve warm. Wrap any leftovers and store in refrigerator for up to 3 days.

NUTRITION FACTS PER SERVING: 179 cal., 10 g total fat (3 g sat. fat), 35 mg chol., 239 mg sodium, 16 g carbo., 1 g fiber, 5 g pro. DAILY VALUES: 1% vit. C, 9% calcium, 7% iron

Onion-Cheese Supper Bread

Biscuit mix minimizes preparation time for this hearty bread. Pair with chili or homemade vegetable soup and a mixed green salad. (See photo, page 154.)

PREP: 15 minutes BAKE: 20 minutes OVEN: 400° MAKES: 8 servings

½   cup chopped onion (1 medium)

2   tablespoons butter or margarine

1½   cups packaged biscuit mix

1   egg, slightly beaten

½   cup milk

1   cup shredded sharp American cheese or cheddar cheese (4 ounces)

1   tablespoon poppy seeds

Cooked, thinly sliced onion (optional)

1 Grease an 8×1½-inch round baking pan; set aside. In a small skillet cook onion in 1 tablespoon of the butter until onion is tender. Set aside.

2 In a medium bowl place biscuit mix. In a small bowl stir together egg and milk. Add egg mixture all at once to biscuit mix. Stir just until moistened. Stir onion mixture, half of the cheese, and half of the poppy seeds into biscuit mix mixture. Spoon batter into prepared pan, spreading evenly. Sprinkle with the remaining cheese and the remaining poppy seeds. If desired, arrange cooked, thinly sliced onion on top. Melt remaining butter; drizzle over batter in pan.

3 Bake in a 400° oven about 20 minutes or until a wooden toothpick inserted near center comes out clean. Cool slightly in pan on a wire rack. Cut into wedges to serve. Serve warm.

NUTRITION FACTS PER SERVING: 204 cal., 12 g total fat (6 g sat. fat), 50 mg chol., 540 mg sodium, 17 g carbo., 1 g fiber, 7 g pro. DAILY VALUES: 1% vit. C, 17% calcium, 5% iron

Dill and Cheese Beer Bread

*You don't have to be an experienced bread baker to make this savory loaf.
It's as easy as stirring and baking.*

PREP: 15 minutes BAKE: 45 minutes COOL: 10 minutes OVEN: 350° MAKES: 1 loaf (16 servings)

3 cups self-rising flour*	2 tablespoons sugar
½ cup shredded cheddar cheese (2 ounces)	1 tablespoon dillseed
½ cup shredded Monterey Jack cheese with jalapeño peppers (2 ounces)	1 teaspoon dried dillweed
	1 12-ounce can beer

1 Grease bottom and ½ inch up sides of a 9×5×3-inch loaf pan; set aside. In a large bowl stir together flour, cheddar cheese, Monterey Jack cheese, sugar, dillseed, and dillweed. Add beer and stir until combined. Spoon batter into prepared pan, spreading evenly.

2 Bake in a 350° oven about 45 minutes or until bread sounds hollow when lightly tapped. Cool in pan on a wire rack for 10 minutes. Remove bread from pan. Cool completely on a wire rack. Serve or wrap and store in the refrigerator for up to 3 days.

***Note:** Substitute 3 cups all-purpose flour plus 1 tablespoon baking powder, 1 teaspoon salt, and ¾ teaspoon baking soda.

NUTRITION FACTS PER SERVING: 128 cal., 2 g total fat (1 g sat. fat), 7 mg chol., 373 mg sodium, 21 g carbo., 1 g fiber, 4 g pro. DAILY VALUES: 11% calcium, 8% iron

Rye Skillet Bread with Toasted Caraway

You may not use rye flour frequently, so store it carefully. The flour will keep in an airtight container in a cool, dry place up to one month or in a refrigerator or freezer up to three months.

PREP: 20 minutes COOK: 20 minutes MAKES: 8 servings

1	teaspoon caraway seeds	¼	teaspoon baking soda
1⅓	cups all-purpose flour	2	tablespoons cold butter
⅔	cup rye flour	1	cup buttermilk
1½	teaspoon baking powder		Nonstick cooking spray
½	teaspoon salt		

1 In a heavy large skillet heat caraway seeds over medium-low heat for 3 to 5 minutes or until toasted, shaking skillet occasionally to prevent seeds from burning. Remove seeds from skillet; set skillet aside to cool.

2 In a large bowl stir together toasted seeds, all-purpose flour, rye flour, baking powder, salt, and baking soda. Using a pastry blender, cut butter into flour mixture until mixture resembles coarse crumbs. Make a well in center of flour mixture. Using a fork, stir in buttermilk just until moistened.

3 Turn dough out onto a well-floured surface. Quickly knead by gently folding and pressing for 10 to 12 strokes until dough is nearly smooth. Roll or pat dough into a circle about 7 inches in diameter and ¾ inch thick. Cut into eight wedges.

4 Coat the cool skillet with nonstick cooking spray. Heat skillet over medium-low heat for 1 to 3 minutes or until a drop of water sizzles. Carefully place dough wedges in skillet. Cook, covered, about 20 minutes or until golden brown and a wooden toothpick inserted into the side of a wedge comes out clean, turning wedges several times to brown both sides. Sides may still look moist. Check bottoms occasionally and decrease heat, if necessary, to prevent overbrowning. Remove from skillet and cool on a wire rack. Serve warm or at room temperature.

NUTRITION FACTS PER SERVING: 140 cal., 4 g total fat (2 g sat. fat), 9 mg chol., 323 mg sodium, 23 g carbo., 2 g fiber, 4 g pro. DAILY VALUES: 1% vit. C, 9% calcium, 6% iron

Simple Focaccia

Make easy work of this flat Italian yeast bread by using a package of hot-roll mix; flavor with desired toppings, such as onions, herbs, olives, dried tomatoes, nuts, or cheese.

PREP: per package directions RISE: 30 minutes BAKE: 15 minutes OVEN: 375° MAKES: 12 servings

1	16-ounce package hot-roll mix	3	tablespoons olive oil
1	egg		Coarse salt

1 Lightly grease a 15×10×1-inch baking pan, a 12- to 14-inch pizza pan, or two 9×1½-inch round baking pans; set aside. Prepare hot-roll mix according to package directions for basic dough, using the 1 egg and substituting 2 tablespoons of the olive oil for the margarine. Knead dough; allow to rest as directed. If using large baking pan, roll dough into a 15×10-inch rectangle. If using a pizza pan, roll dough into a 12-inch round. If using round baking pans, divide dough in half; roll into two 9-inch rounds. Place dough in prepared pan(s).

2 With fingertips, press indentations randomly in dough. Brush dough with the remaining 1 tablespoon olive oil; sprinkle lightly with coarse salt. Cover and let rise in a warm place until nearly double (about 30 minutes).

3 Bake in a 375° oven for 15 to 20 minutes or until golden. Cool 10 minutes on wire rack(s). Remove from pan(s) and cool completely on wire rack(s). Cut into wedges to serve.

NUTRITION FACTS PER SERVING: 176 cal., 4 g total fat (1 g sat. fat), 18 mg chol., 306 mg sodium, 29 g carbo., 0 g fiber, 6 g pro. DAILY VALUES: 6% iron

Parmesan and Pine Nut Focaccia: Prepare as directed, except omit topping with 1 tablespoon of the olive oil and the coarse salt. After making indentations, brush the dough with mixture of 1 egg white and 1 tablespoon water. Sprinkle with ¼ cup pine nuts, pressing lightly into dough. Sprinkle with 2 tablespoons freshly grated Parmesan cheese. Bake as directed.

Lemon and Savory Focaccia: Prepare as directed, except omit the topping of coarse salt. Add ¼ cup coarsely chopped pitted ripe olives, 3 tablespoons snipped fresh savory, and 1 teaspoon finely shredded lemon peel to the dough along with the 2 tablespoons olive oil. Continue as directed.

FOCACCIA MADE EASY Focaccia (foh-KAH-chee-uh) is a flat Italian yeast bread that often is baked with a variety of toppers, such as onions, herbs, olives, dried tomatoes, nuts, or cheese. Simple Focaccia (above) eliminates a lot of the work of making focaccia because it starts with a hot-roll mix.

Serve focaccia as you would garlic bread. It's a great accompaniment to pasta dishes and soups. Cut in thin wedges, it also makes a tasty appetizer or snack.

When it comes to making sandwiches, focaccia is terrific too. To cut focaccia for sandwiches, slice the rounds in half horizontally, then stack the two halves and cut them into wedges.

Country Skillet Corn Bread

Northerners and Southerners still debate the merits of their corn bread.
This version—without sugar and baked in a skillet—is thoroughly Southern.
Baking corn bread in a cast-iron skillet renders a crisp crust.

PREP: 10 minutes BAKE: 15 minutes COOL: 5 minutes OVEN: 450° MAKES: 8 servings

2	tablespoons cooking oil	¼	teaspoon baking soda
3	eggs	½	teaspoon salt
1	cup buttermilk	1½	cups yellow cornmeal
1½	teaspoons baking powder		

1 Pour the cooking oil into a 9-inch cast-iron skillet or a 9×1½-inch round baking pan. Place pan in oven while preheating oven to 450°.

2 Meanwhile, in a large mixing bowl combine eggs and buttermilk with a wire whisk. Add baking powder, baking soda, and salt; stir to combine. Pour hot oil from pan into egg mixture and mix well. Stir in the 1½ cups cornmeal. Carefully pour batter into hot skillet, spreading evenly.

3 Bake in the 450° oven for 15 to 20 minutes or until a wooden toothpick inserted near the center comes out clean. Cool in skillet for 5 minutes. Loosen edges. Carefully invert to remove from skillet. Turn bread browned side up and cool slightly on a wire rack. Cut into wedges to serve. Serve warm.

NUTRITION FACTS PER SERVING: 165 cal., 6 g total fat (1 g sat. fat), 81 mg chol., 316 mg sodium, 22 g carbo., 2 g fiber, 6 g pro. DAILY VALUES: 1% vit. C, 9% calcium, 8% iron

Crispy Corn Bread with Dried Tomatoes

For a full-flavored, crunchy corn bread, buy stone-ground cornmeal, which is available at your grocery store or a health food store. (See photo, page 158.)

PREP: 15 minutes BAKE: 18 minutes COOL: 10 minutes OVEN: 425° MAKES: 8 servings

1	tablespoon shortening	½	teaspoon baking soda
1¼	cups stone-ground or regular yellow cornmeal	2	eggs, beaten
¾	cup all-purpose flour	1	cup buttermilk
2	tablespoons sugar	¼	cup cooking oil
2	teaspoons baking powder	2	tablespoons finely snipped dried tomatoes (not oil packed)
½	teaspoon salt		

1 Place shortening in a 9-inch cast-iron skillet. Place skillet in oven while preheating to 425°.

2 Meanwhile, in a large bowl stir together cornmeal, flour, sugar, baking powder, salt, and baking soda. Make a well in the center of cornmeal mixture; set aside. In a small bowl stir together eggs, buttermilk, oil, and dried tomatoes. Add egg mixture all at once to cornmeal mixture. Stir just until moistened. Remove skillet from oven. Carefully pour batter into hot skillet, spreading evenly. Return skillet to oven.

3 Bake in the 425° oven for 18 to 20 minutes or until a wooden toothpick inserted near center comes out clean. Cool in skillet on a wire rack for 10 minutes. (For a crispier bottom crust, immediately loosen edges and use a wide metal spatula to slide corn bread onto a wire rack.) Cut into wedges to serve. Serve warm.

NUTRITION FACTS PER SERVING: 171 cal., 10 g total fat (2 g sat. fat), 54 mg chol., 390 mg sodium, 16 g carbo., 1 g fiber, 4 g pro. DAILY VALUES: 1% vit. C, 10% calcium, 5% iron

CRISPY CORN BREAD Everyone has an opinion about what makes good corn bread, but a penchant for a crisp crust is almost universal. The secret to crispiness in corn bread lies in how you bake it.

For a crisp-crusted corn bread, bake it in an oven-going skillet, such as the cast-iron skillet called for in the recipe above. Place the fat—butter, shortening, olive oil, or bacon drippings—in the pan. Place the pan in the oven while it preheats. Test the pan to see if it's ready by dropping a tiny amount of batter into it. If it sizzles, it's ready. Pour the batter into the skillet and bake.

Serve corn bread warm with butter or honey. If you like, use corn bread to make stuffing for poultry or to serve with beef or pork roasts.

Peanut Butter Coffee Cake

If you crave treats made of peanut butter and chocolate, this recipe is irresistible—and far superior to candy out of a vending machine.

PREP: 30 minutes BAKE: 25 minutes COOL: 15 minutes OVEN: 375° MAKES: 9 servings

¼	cup all-purpose flour	1	cup all-purpose flour
¼	cup packed brown sugar	½	cup packed brown sugar
2	tablespoons peanut butter	½	cup milk
1	tablespoon butter	1	egg
½	cup miniature semisweet chocolate pieces	1	teaspoon baking powder
¼	cup peanut butter	¼	teaspoon baking soda
2	tablespoons butter	¼	teaspoon salt

1 Grease an 8×8×2-inch baking pan; set aside. For streusel topping, in a small bowl stir together the ¼ cup flour, the ¼ cup brown sugar, the 2 tablespoons peanut butter, and the 1 tablespoon butter. Stir together until crumbly. Stir in ¼ cup of the miniature chocolate pieces; set aside.

2 In a large mixing bowl beat the ¼ cup peanut butter and the 2 tablespoons butter with an electric mixer on medium to high speed for 30 seconds or until combined. Add about half of the 1 cup flour, the ½ cup brown sugar, half of the milk, the egg, baking powder, baking soda, and salt. Beat with an electric mixer on low speed until combined, scraping sides of bowl constantly. Add the remaining flour and remaining milk. Beat on low to medium speed just until combined. Stir in the remaining ¼ cup miniature chocolate pieces. Spread batter evenly into prepared pan. Sprinkle with streusel topping.

3 Bake in a 375° oven for 25 to 30 minutes or until a wooden toothpick inserted near center comes out clean. Cool in pan on a wire rack for 15 minutes. Cut into squares to serve. Serve warm. Cover leftovers and store at room temperature or in the refrigerator for up to 3 days.

NUTRITION FACTS PER SERVING: 269 cal., 13 g total fat (4 g sat. fat), 35 mg chol., 243 mg sodium, 36 g carbo., 1 g fiber, 6 g pro. DAILY VALUES: 5% vit. A, 6% calcium, 10% iron

Crumb-Topped Dried Cherry Coffee Cake

A subtle hint of cardamom flavors the tender, fruit-studded cake that hides beneath a layer of crumb topping.

PREP: 30 minutes BAKE: 40 minutes COOL: 30 minutes OVEN: 350° MAKES: 9 servings

1/3 cup butter, softened	1/4 teaspoon baking soda
1/3 cup granulated sugar	1/4 teaspoon salt
1/3 cup packed brown sugar	3/4 cup buttermilk
2 eggs	1 cup dried tart red cherries
2 cups all-purpose flour	1 recipe Crumb Topping
1 1/2 teaspoons baking powder	
1/2 teaspoon ground cardamom	

1 Grease an 8×8×2-inch baking pan; set aside. In a large mixing bowl beat butter with an electric mixer on medium speed for 30 seconds. Add granulated sugar and brown sugar; beat until light and fluffy. Add eggs, one at a time, beating well after each.

2 In a medium bowl stir together flour, baking powder, cardamom, baking soda, and salt. Add flour mixture alternately with buttermilk to sugar mixture. Beat on low speed after each addition just until combined. Fold in dried cherries. Spread batter evenly into prepared pan. Sprinkle with Crumb Topping.

3 Bake in a 350° oven about 40 minutes or until a wooden toothpick inserted near center comes out clean. Cool in pan on a wire rack at least 30 minutes. Cut into squares to serve. Serve warm or at room temperature.

Crumb Topping: In a bowl combine 1/2 cup all-purpose flour, 1/2 cup packed brown sugar, and 1/4 cup softened butter. Stir with a fork until mixture is crumbly.

NUTRITION FACTS PER SERVING: 402 cal., 14 g total fat (8 g sat. fat), 82 mg chol., 339 mg sodium, 63 g carbo., 2 g fiber, 6 g pro. DAILY VALUES: 10% calcium, 11% iron

COFFEE CAKE 101 How to get even the sleepiest heads up and at 'em: Pop a coffee cake into the oven. There's nothing quite like a piece of warm, fresh-baked coffee cake to go with your morning coffee or tea, as anyone who awakens to the wonderful, homey aroma will heartily agree. Here's how to make a coffee cake just right every time:

1 If you're baking in a metal pan, be sure it's a shiny one. Shiny pans reflect heat, which produces a golden, delicate, and tender crust.

2 Most coffee cakes are at their best served warm. Let your coffee cake cool for 20 to 30 minutes before cutting and serving—it will be at its just-right-for-eating stage.

3 Save leftover coffee cake for an afternoon snack or tomorrow's breakfast in a tightly covered container stored at room temperature. If the coffee cake contains cream cheese, store it in the refrigerator.

4 To reheat coffee cake, wrap it in heavy foil and heat in a 350° oven for about 15 minutes.

Super-Big Cinnamon-Pecan Ring

*Coffee tastes all the more fresh and fragrant when paired
with this beauty of a breakfast bread. (See photo, page 153.)*

PREP: 30 minutes **RISE:** 30 minutes **BAKE:** 25 minutes **COOL:** 15 minutes **OVEN:** 350° **MAKES:** 12 servings

2	16-ounce loaves frozen white bread dough, thawed
1/3	cup butter or margarine, melted
1/3	cup granulated sugar
1/3	cup packed brown sugar
2	teaspoons ground cinnamon
1/2	cup chopped pecans
2/3	cup sifted powdered sugar
1/4	teaspoon vanilla
	Milk

1 Grease a 14-inch pizza pan; set aside. On a lightly floured surface flatten thawed dough slightly. Cut each loaf of dough into four pieces (eight pieces total). Form each piece into a rope about 18 inches long. Brush entire surface of each rope with melted butter.

2 Stir together granulated sugar, brown sugar, and cinnamon. Place mixture in shallow pan or on large sheet of foil. Roll one rope in sugar mixture to coat evenly. Shape rope into coil in center of prepared pan. Roll another rope in sugar mixture. Attach securely to end of first rope and coil around first coil. Continue coating remaining ropes with sugar mixture and attaching them to form a 10- to 11-inch circle. Sprinkle any remaining sugar mixture over ring. Sprinkle chopped pecans on top.

3 Cover and let rise in a warm place until nearly double (30 to 40 minutes). (Or cover with plastic wrap and let rise overnight in the refrigerator. Before baking, remove from the refrigerator and let stand at room temperature for 15 to 20 minutes.)

4 Bake in a 350° oven for 25 to 30 minutes or until bread sounds hollow when lightly tapped. If necessary, cover with foil the last 10 minutes of baking to prevent overbrowning. Remove from pizza pan and cool on a wire rack for 15 minutes.

5 Meanwhile, in a small bowl stir together powdered sugar, vanilla, and enough milk (about 2 teaspoons) to make a thick glaze. Spoon glaze over ring. Cut into wedges to serve. Serve warm.

NUTRITION FACTS PER SERVING: 317 cal., 8 g total fat (3 g sat. fat), 13 mg chol., 62 mg sodium, 49 g carbo., 0 g fiber, 6 g pro. DAILY VALUES: 8% calcium, 3% iron

Cinnamon Fantans

The unique shaping of these cinnamon rolls makes them company-special. Serve them with your favorite flavored coffee or tea. (See photo, page 155.)

PREP: 30 minutes RISE: 2 hours BAKE: 12 minutes OVEN: 350° MAKES: 8 fantans

2½	to 3 cups all-purpose flour	1	egg
1	package active dry yeast	2	tablespoons butter or margarine, melted
¾	cup milk		
¼	cup sugar	½	cup sugar
¼	cup butter or margarine	⅓	cup chopped walnuts
1	teaspoon salt	1½	teaspoons ground cinnamon

1 In a large mixing bowl stir together 1¼ cups of the flour and the yeast; set aside. In a small saucepan heat and stir milk, the ¼ cup sugar, the ¼ cup butter, and the salt just until warm (120° to 130°) and butter almost melts. Add milk mixture to flour mixture; add egg. Beat with an electric mixer on low to medium speed for 30 seconds, scraping sides of bowl constantly. Beat on high speed for 3 minutes. Using a wooden spoon, stir in as much of the remaining flour as you can.

2 Turn dough onto a floured surface. Knead in enough of the remaining flour to make a moderately soft dough that is smooth and elastic (2 to 3 minutes total). Shape dough into a ball. Place dough in a lightly greased bowl; turn once to grease surface. Cover and let rise in a warm place until double (about 1½ hours).

3 Grease a baking sheet; set aside. Punch dough down. Turn out onto a lightly floured surface. Cover and let rest for 10 minutes. Roll out to a 20×10-inch rectangle. Brush with the melted butter.

4 In a small bowl stir together the ½ cup sugar, the walnuts, and cinnamon. Sprinkle sugar mixture evenly over dough. Starting from a long side, roll up dough. Cut into eight 2½-inch slices. With slices sitting on edge, snip or cut each slice in thirds without cutting all the way through. Place 3 inches apart on prepared baking sheet, seam sides down; spread each slightly to form a fan. Cover and let rise until almost double (30 to 45 minutes).

5 Bake in a 350° oven for 12 to 15 minutes or until golden brown. Remove from baking sheet and cool slightly on a wire rack. Serve warm.

NUTRITION FACTS PER SERVING: 338 cal., 14 g total fat (6 g sat. fat), 53 mg chol., 405 mg sodium, 48 g carbo., 2 g fiber, 6 g pro. DAILY VALUES: 1% vit. C, 5% calcium, 12% iron

Baked Doughnut Twists

Packaged biscuit mix makes these cinnamon- and coffee-flavored twists simple to stir together.

PREP: 25 minutes BAKE: 10 minutes OVEN: 400° MAKES: 8 to 10 doughnuts

2 cups packaged biscuit mix	2 tablespoons butter or margarine, melted
2 tablespoons sugar	1/3 cup sugar
2 teaspoons instant coffee crystals	1/2 teaspoon ground cinnamon
1/4 cup milk	1/8 teaspoon ground nutmeg
1 egg, beaten	
1 teaspoon finely shredded orange peel	

1 In a medium bowl stir together biscuit mix and the 2 tablespoons sugar; set aside. In a small bowl dissolve coffee crystals in milk; stir in egg and orange peel. Add coffee mixture all at once to biscuit mixture. Stir just until moistened.

2 Turn dough out onto a well-floured surface. Quickly knead by gently folding and pressing for 10 to 20 strokes or until nearly smooth. Pat or lightly roll dough to 1/2-inch thickness. Cut dough with a floured 2 1/2-inch doughnut cutter, dipping the cutter into flour between cuts. Holding opposite sides of the doughnut, twist once, forming a figure 8. Place on an ungreased baking sheet.

3 Bake in a 400° oven for 10 to 12 minutes or until golden brown. Brush each twist with melted butter. In a shallow dish stir together the 1/3 cup sugar, the cinnamon, and nutmeg. Dip each twist into sugar mixture. Serve warm.

NUTRITION FACTS PER TWIST: 213 cal., 8 g total fat (3 g sat. fat), 35 mg chol., 407 mg sodium, 31 g carbo., 0 g fiber, 3 g pro. DAILY VALUES: 1% vit. C, 5% calcium, 6% iron

Pumpkin-Pecan Muffins

Follow ingredient measurements carefully to ensure the success of muffins. Too much liquid can cause the bread to sink in the middle, and too much fat can result in a coarse texture.

PREP: 20 minutes BAKE: 20 minutes COOL: 5 minutes OVEN: 375° MAKES: 12 to 14 muffins

1/3	cup packed brown sugar		1/4	teaspoon ground nutmeg
2	tablespoons dairy sour cream		1/8	teaspoon ground cloves
2/3	cup chopped pecans		1	beaten egg
2	cups all-purpose flour		3/4	cup buttermilk
2	teaspoons baking powder		3/4	cup canned pumpkin
1	teaspoon ground cinnamon		2/3	cup packed brown sugar
1/2	teaspoon baking soda		1/3	cup butter, melted
1/4	teaspoon salt			

1 Grease twelve to fourteen 2½-inch muffin cups or line with paper bake cups; set aside. In a small bowl stir together the ⅓ cup brown sugar and sour cream. Stir in pecans; set aside.

2 In medium bowl stir together flour, baking powder, cinnamon, baking soda, salt, nutmeg, and cloves. Make a well in center of flour mixture.

3 In another medium bowl stir together egg, buttermilk, pumpkin, the ⅔ cup brown sugar, and melted butter. Add pumpkin mixture all at once to the flour mixture. Stir until moistened (batter should be lumpy). Spoon batter into prepared muffin cups, filling each almost full. Spoon about 2 teaspoons of the pecan mixture on top of each muffin.

4 Bake in a 375° oven for 20 to 25 minutes or until lightly browned. Cool in muffin cups on a wire rack for 5 minutes. Remove from muffin cups and cool slightly on a wire rack. Serve warm.

NUTRITION FACTS PER MUFFIN: 234 cal., 10 g total fat (4 g sat. fat), 33 mg chol., 237 mg sodium, 33 g carbo., 1 g fiber, 4 g pro. DAILY VALUES: 40% vit. A, 1% vit. C, 8% calcium, 12% iron

MIXING MUFFIN AND QUICK BREAD BATTER The trick to making tender and finely crumbed muffins and quick breads is all in the measuring and mixing.

Measuring ingredients accurately is vital for quick breads because if the ingredient proportions aren't correct, the breads will fail. If there's too much liquid, quick breads can sink in the middle. Or too much fat can make them coarsely textured.

Proper mixing also is important for quick breads. If the batter is overmixed, quick breads will have peaked tops and tunnels inside. To avoid these problems, combine the dry ingredients in a bowl and make a well in the center. The well creates a large surface area for the dry ingredients so they can be moistened with a minimum of stirring. Use a rubber spatula because its wide blade will make you less prone to overmix. To ensure that your quick breads turn out beautifully, stop mixing the batter while is still has lumps.

Berry Breakfast Rolls

This recipe uses an all-time-great quick-fix strategy—dressing up a convenience item, such as a package of refrigerated rolls, with a few easy-to-add ingredients. In a flash, off-the-shelf foods can taste bakery fresh! (See photo, page 160.)

PREP: 15 minutes BAKE: 12 minutes COOL: 10 minutes OVEN: 375° MAKES: 16 rolls

1 11½-ounce package refrigerated cinnamon rolls with icing (8)	⅓ cup blueberry preserves
1 cup fresh blueberries	1 teaspoon finely shredded lemon peel
	¼ cup chopped pecans

1 Lightly grease sixteen 2½-inch muffin cups. Cut each cinnamon roll in half horizontally. Press each roll in bottom and halfway up sides of a muffin cup.

2 For filling, in a small bowl stir together blueberries, preserves, and lemon peel. Spoon filling into muffin cups. Sprinkle with pecans.

3 Bake in a 375° oven about 12 minutes or until golden. Cool in cups on a wire rack for 10 minutes. Remove from cups and place on a wire rack.

4 For icing, in a small bowl stir a little milk into packaged icing to make of drizzling consistency. Drizzle over rolls. Serve warm.

NUTRITION FACTS PER ROLL: 110 cal., 4 g total fat (1 g sat. fat), 0 mg chol., 173 mg sodium, 18 g carbo., 0 g fiber, 1 g pro. DAILY VALUES: 3% vit. C, 3% iron

Quaker Bonnet Biscuits

These hat-shaped biscuits will remind you of tender yeast rolls. Don't worry that the tops of these biscuits are slightly off-center. It adds to their old-fashioned charm.

PREP: 20 minutes RISE: 1½ hours BAKE: 13 minutes OVEN: 400° MAKES: 24 biscuits

1⅓	cups warm milk (105° to 115°)		2	eggs, beaten
1	package active dry yeast		1	tablespoon butter, melted
4	cups all-purpose flour		1	egg yolk
1	teaspoon salt		1	teaspoon milk
⅓	cup butter, shortening, or lard			

1 In a bowl combine warm milk and yeast; let stand about 5 minutes for yeast to soften.

2 In a large bowl stir together flour and salt. Using a pastry blender, cut in the ⅓ cup butter until pieces are the size of small peas. Make a well in center of flour mixture; add yeast mixture and eggs all at once. Stir until all dough is moistened. Transfer the dough to a lightly greased bowl. Cover and let rise in a warm place until double in size (1 to 1¼ hours).

3 Lightly grease baking sheets; set aside. Turn dough out onto a well-floured surface. Knead dough 10 to 12 times. Roll dough to ¼-inch thickness. Cut dough with floured round cutters, making twenty-four 2¼-inch rounds and twenty-four 2-inch rounds. Arrange larger rounds about 2 inches apart on prepared baking sheets. Brush tops with melted butter. Top each with a smaller round, stacking slightly off-center. Cover and let rise in a warm place for 30 minutes.

4 In a small bowl stir together egg yolk and milk. Brush tops of biscuits with egg-milk mixture.

5 Bake in a 400° oven for 13 to 15 minutes or until tops are golden. Remove from baking sheet and cool slightly on a wire rack. Serve warm.

NUTRITION FACTS PER BISCUIT: 115 cal., 4 g total fat (2 g sat. fat), 36 mg chol., 142 mg sodium, 16 g carbo., 1 g fiber, 3 g pro. DAILY VALUES: 2% calcium, 6% iron

South-of-the-Border Cornmeal Biscuits

Store cornmeal in an airtight container in a cool, dry place for up to six months, or in the freezer for up to one year.

PREP: 20 minutes BAKE: 12 minutes OVEN: 450° MAKES: 10 to 12 biscuits

1½	cups all-purpose flour	½	cup shredded cheddar cheese (2 ounces)
½	cup yellow cornmeal		
2	teaspoons baking powder	½	cup buttermilk or sour milk
¼	teaspoon baking soda	1	4½-ounce can diced green chile peppers, undrained
¼	teaspoon salt		
½	cup butter or margarine		

1 In a medium bowl stir together flour, cornmeal, baking powder, baking soda, and salt. Using a pastry blender, cut in butter until mixture resembles coarse crumbs. Stir in cheddar cheese. Make a well in the center of flour mixture; set aside.

2 In a small bowl stir together buttermilk and undrained chile peppers. Add buttermilk mixture all at once to flour mixture. Using a fork, stir just until moistened.

3 Turn dough out onto a lightly floured surface. Quickly knead dough by gently folding and pressing dough for 10 to 12 strokes or until dough is nearly smooth. Pat or lightly roll dough to ½-inch thickness. Cut the dough with a floured 2½-inch biscuit cutter, dipping the cutter into flour between cuts. Arrange biscuits 1 inch apart on an ungreased baking sheet.

4 Bake in a 450° oven for 12 to 15 minutes or until golden. Remove biscuits from baking sheet. Serve hot.

NUTRITION FACTS PER BISCUIT: 204 cal., 12 g total fat (7 g sat. fat), 33 mg chol., 359 mg sodium, 20 g carbo., 1 g fiber, 4 g pro. DAILY VALUES: 4% vit. C, 12% calcium, 6% iron

Flaky Biscuits

*Self-rising flour is the key to these Sunday-best biscuits.
The flour has salt and some leavening already added.*

PREP: 15 minutes BAKE: 10 minutes OVEN: 425° MAKES: 10 to 12 biscuits

2	cups self-rising flour*	¼	cup butter or margarine
¼	teaspoon baking soda	¾	cup buttermilk

1 Lightly grease a baking sheet; set aside. In a medium bowl stir together flour and baking soda. Using a pastry blender, cut in butter until mixture resembles coarse crumbs. Make a well in center of flour mixture. Add buttermilk all at once. Stir until moistened.

2 Turn dough out onto a lightly floured surface. Quickly knead dough by gently folding and pressing for 10 to 12 strokes or until nearly smooth. Pat or lightly roll dough to ½-inch thickness. Cut dough into circles with a floured 2½-inch biscuit cutter, dipping the cutter into flour between cuts. Arrange biscuits 1 inch apart on prepared baking sheet.

3 Bake in a 425° oven for 10 to 15 minutes or until golden. Remove biscuits from baking sheet and serve hot.

***Note:** Substitute 2 cups all-purpose flour plus 2 teaspoons baking powder, 1 teaspoon salt, and ½ teaspoon baking soda.

NUTRITION FACTS PER BISCUIT: 136 cal., 5 g total fat (3 g sat. fat), 13 mg chol., 415 mg sodium, 19 g carbo., 3 g fiber, 3 g pro. DAILY VALUES: 8% calcium, 6% iron

Pepper Cheese Biscuits: Prepare as directed, except stir ¾ cup shredded Monterey Jack cheese with jalapeño peppers (3 ounces), 2 tablespoons snipped fresh chives, and ⅛ teaspoon ground red pepper into flour and butter mixture.

Up-and-Down Biscuits

A bit of sweet—sugar and cinnamon—and a lot of love go a long way in the golden-brown goodness of these biscuits.

PREP: 25 minutes BAKE: 10 minutes OVEN: 450° MAKES: 12 biscuits

2	cups all-purpose flour	1/2	cup shortening
3	tablespoons sugar	2/3	cup milk
4	teaspoons baking powder	1/4	cup butter or margarine, melted
1/2	teaspoon cream of tartar	1/4	cup sugar
1/2	teaspoon salt	2	to 3 teaspoons ground cinnamon

1 Grease twelve 2$\frac{1}{2}$-inch muffin cups; set aside. In a medium bowl stir together flour, the 3 tablespoons sugar, baking powder, cream of tartar, and salt. Using a pastry blender, cut in shortening until mixture resembles coarse crumbs. Make a well in center of flour mixture. Add milk all at once. Stir just until moistened.

2 Turn dough out onto a lightly floured surface. Quickly knead dough by gently folding and pressing for 10 to 12 strokes or until nearly smooth. Divide dough in half. Roll half of dough to a 12×10-inch rectangle. Brush dough with half of the melted butter. In a small bowl stir together the 1/4 cup sugar and the cinnamon; sprinkle half over dough.

3 Cut rectangle into five 12×2-inch strips. Stack the strips on top of each other. Cut stack into six 2×2-inch squares. Place squares, cut sides down, in prepared muffin cups. Repeat with remaining dough, remaining butter, and remaining cinnamon mixture.

4 Bake in a 450° oven for 10 to 12 minutes or until golden brown. Remove from muffin cups and cool slightly on a wire rack. Serve warm.

NUTRITION FACTS PER BISCUIT: 220 cal., 13 g total fat (5 g sat. fat), 12 mg chol., 279 mg sodium, 24 g carbo., 1 g fiber, 3 g pro. DAILY VALUES: 1% vit. C, 11% calcium, 7% iron

Maple Sugar Biscuits

Imagine the sweetness of sugar infused with the flavor of natural maple syrup. Maple sugar is worth the effort to track down in specialty food stores or by mail order.

PREP: 15 minutes BAKE: 12 minutes OVEN: 375° MAKES: 14 biscuits

2¼   cups all-purpose flour

¾   teaspoon baking soda

⅛   teaspoon salt

1   8-ounce carton dairy sour cream

1   egg, beaten

1   cup granulated maple sugar or ¾ cup granulated sugar and ¼ teaspoon maple flavoring

½   teaspoon ground allspice

1 Grease a very large baking sheet; set aside. In a large bowl stir together flour, baking soda, and salt. Make a well in center of flour mixture. In a medium bowl stir together sour cream, egg, maple sugar, and allspice. Add sour cream mixture all at once to flour mixture. Stir just until combined.

2 Turn dough out onto a well-floured surface. Quickly knead dough by gently folding and pressing for 10 to 12 strokes or until nearly smooth. Pat or lightly roll dough to a ½-inch thickness. Cut dough with a floured 2½-inch round cutter, dipping cutter into flour between cuts. Arrange biscuits 1 inch apart on prepared baking sheet.

3 Bake in a 375° oven for 12 to 15 minutes or until bottoms are brown. Remove from baking sheet and cool slightly on a wire rack. Serve warm.

NUTRITION FACTS PER BISCUIT: 148 cal., 4 g total fat (2 g sat. fat), 22 mg chol., 102 mg sodium, 25 g carbo., 1 g fiber, 3 g pro. DAILY VALUES: 2% calcium, 5% iron

Double-Chocolate Scones

Chocoholics take notice—these scones contain both cocoa powder and semisweet chocolate pieces for extra chocolate flavor. (See photo, page 160.)

PREP: 20 minutes BAKE: 18 minutes OVEN: 375° MAKES: 10 scones

2 cups all-purpose flour	1 egg yolk, beaten
1/3 cup unsweetened cocoa powder	1 8-ounce carton plain yogurt
1/3 cup packed brown sugar	1/2 cup miniature semisweet chocolate pieces
2 teaspoons baking powder	1 recipe Powdered Sugar Glaze
3/4 teaspoon baking soda	Powdered sugar (optional)
1/8 teaspoon salt	
1/2 cup butter	

1 In a large bowl stir together flour, cocoa powder, brown sugar, baking powder, baking soda, and salt. Using a pastry blender, cut in butter until mixture resembles coarse crumbs. Make a well in center of flour mixture; set aside.

2 In a small bowl stir together egg yolk and yogurt. Add egg yolk mixture all at once to flour mixture. Add chocolate pieces. Stir just until moistened.

3 Turn dough out onto a lightly floured surface. Quickly knead dough by gently folding and pressing for 10 to 12 strokes or until nearly smooth. Roll or pat dough into a 9-inch circle. Cut into 10 wedges. Arrange wedges 1 inch apart on an ungreased baking sheet.

4 Bake in a 375° oven about 18 minutes or until bottoms are lightly browned. Remove from baking sheet and cool slightly on a wire rack. Drizzle with Powdered Sugar Glaze. If desired, sprinkle tops of glazed scones with powdered sugar. Serve warm.

Powdered Sugar Glaze: In a small bowl stir together 1/2 cup sifted powdered sugar, 1 tablespoon melted butter or margarine, 1 teaspoon milk, and 1 teaspoon vanilla. Stir in enough additional milk, 1/4 teaspoon at a time, to make a glaze of drizzling consistency.

NUTRITION FACTS PER SCONE: 289 cal., 14 g total fat (7 g sat. fat), 50 mg chol., 317 mg sodium, 37 g carbo., 1 g fiber, 5 g pro. DAILY VALUES: 13% calcium, 13% iron

Dried Cherry-Orange Scones

These biscuitlike quick breads originated in Scotland. Often made with eggs, butter, and cream or sour cream, they're richer than ordinary biscuits. (See photo, page 156.)

PREP: 30 minutes BAKE: 10 minutes COOL: 10 minutes OVEN: 400° MAKES: 12 scones

1/2	cup snipped dried sweet cherries or raisins	1/2	teaspoon baking soda
2	cups all-purpose flour	1/4	cup butter
3	tablespoons brown sugar	1	teaspoon finely shredded orange peel
2	teaspoons baking powder	1	egg yolk, beaten
1/2	teaspoon salt	1	8-ounce carton dairy sour cream
		1	recipe Orange Glaze

1 In a small bowl pour enough boiling water over dried cherries to cover. Let stand for 5 minutes; drain well. In a large bowl stir together flour, brown sugar, baking powder, salt, and baking soda. Using a pastry blender, cut in butter until mixture resembles coarse crumbs. Add drained cherries and orange peel; toss lightly to coat. Make a well in center of flour mixture; set aside.

2 In a small bowl stir together egg yolk and sour cream. Add yolk mixture all at once to flour mixture. Using a fork, stir until combined (mixture may seem dry).

3 Turn dough out onto a lightly floured surface. Quickly knead dough by gently folding and pressing for 10 to 12 strokes or until nearly smooth. Pat or lightly roll dough into a 7-inch circle. Cut into 12 wedges. Arrange wedges 1 inch apart on an ungreased baking sheet.

4 Bake in a 400° oven for 10 to 12 minutes or until light brown. Remove from baking sheet and cool on a wire rack for 10 minutes. Drizzle warm scones with Orange Glaze. Serve warm.

Orange Glaze: In small mixing bowl stir together 1 cup sifted powdered sugar, 1 tablespoon orange juice, and 1/4 teaspoon vanilla. Stir in enough additional orange juice, 1 teaspoon at a time, to make a glaze of drizzling consistency.

NUTRITION FACTS PER SCONE: 214 cal., 9 g total fat (4 g sat. fat), 31 mg chol., 249 mg sodium, 32 g carbo., 1 g fiber, 3 g pro. DAILY VALUES: 13% vit. A, 2% vit. C, 7% calcium, 7% iron

GREAT SCONES To ensure light, tender, flaky scones, it's important the butter be in small pieces and be cold when it's added to the flour mixture. A pastry blender is handy for cutting in the butter, but if you don't have one, freeze the butter and cut it using a coarse shredder. Here's how: Remove the paper from a half stick of frozen butter. Using the paper to hold the end of the stick, shred the butter using a shredder with large openings. Immediately stir the shredded butter into the flour.

You also can use two knives, cutting with a crossing motion, to cut the butter into the flour.

Oatmeal Carrot Bread

For an on-the-run breakfast or for a simple snack, spread some softened cream cheese between two thin slices of this wholesome bread.

PREP: 20 minutes BAKE: 55 minutes COOL: 10 minutes OVEN: 350° MAKES: 1 loaf (16 servings)

1½	cups all-purpose flour	2	eggs, beaten
⅔	cup packed brown sugar	1	cup finely shredded carrots
½	cup quick-cooking oats	¾	cup milk
2	teaspoons baking powder	⅓	cup cooking oil
1	teaspoon ground cinnamon	½	cup raisins
¼	teaspoon baking soda	½	cup chopped walnuts
¼	teaspoon salt		

1 Grease bottom and ½ inch up sides of an 8×4×2-inch loaf pan; set aside. In a large bowl stir together flour, sugar, oats, baking powder, cinnamon, baking soda, and salt. Make a well in center of flour mixture; set aside.

2 In a medium bowl stir together eggs, carrots, milk, and oil. Add carrot mixture to flour mixture, stirring just until moistened. Stir in raisins and walnuts. Spoon batter into the prepared pan, spreading evenly.

3 Bake in a 350° oven for 55 to 60 minutes or until a wooden toothpick inserted near center comes out clean. Cool in pan on a wire rack for 10 minutes. Remove bread from pan. Cool completely on a wire rack. Wrap and store overnight for easier slicing.

NUTRITION FACTS PER SERVING: 180 cal., 8 g total fat (1 g sat. fat), 27 mg chol., 126 mg sodium, 24 g carbo., 1 g fiber, 3 g pro. DAILY VALUES: 1% vit. C, 7% calcium, 6% iron

STORING QUICK BREADS Do quick breads keep well? Absolutely. To store quick breads for the short term, let the loaves cool completely on a wire rack after baking. Wrap them in foil or plastic wrap, or place them in plastic bags. Store them in the refrigerator for up to one week. Or place completely cooled loaves in freezer containers or bags and freeze for up to three months. Thaw the wrapped loaves overnight in the refrigerator.

QUICK & EASY COMFORT COOKING

Rhubarb Bread

Harvest a crop of tender new rhubarb and stir it into this coffee cakelike bread.

PREP: 20 minutes BAKE: 50 minutes COOL: 10 minutes OVEN: 350° MAKES: 2 loaves (32 servings)

2¾	cups all-purpose flour	½	cup bran cereal flakes
1	teaspoon baking soda	⅓	cup applesauce
1	teaspoon salt	¼	cup cooking oil
1	teaspoon ground cinnamon	2	cups finely chopped fresh rhubarb
1	egg, slightly beaten	1	recipe Streusel Topping
1⅓	cups packed brown sugar		
1	8-ounce carton plain low-fat yogurt		

1 Grease bottom and ½ inch up sides of two 8×4×2-inch loaf pans; set aside. In a large bowl stir together flour, baking soda, salt, and cinnamon. Make a well in center of flour mixture; set aside.

2 In a medium bowl stir together egg, brown sugar, yogurt, bran cereal flakes, applesauce, and oil. Add egg mixture all at once to flour mixture. Stir just until moistened. Gently stir in rhubarb. Spoon batter into prepared pans, spreading evenly. Sprinkle with Streusel Topping.

3 Bake in a 350° oven about 50 minutes or until a wooden toothpick inserted near center comes out clean. Cool in pans on a wire rack for 10 minutes. Remove bread from pans. Cool completely on a wire rack. Wrap and store overnight for easier slicing.

Streusel Topping: In a small bowl stir together ¼ cup packed brown sugar, ¼ cup rolled oats, 1 tablespoon all-purpose flour, ¼ teaspoon ground cinnamon, and 2 tablespoons melted butter or margarine.

NUTRITION FACTS PER SERVING: 115 cal., 3 g total fat (1 g sat. fat), 8 mg chol., 130 mg sodium, 21 g carbo., 1 g fiber, 2 g pro. DAILY VALUES: 1% vit. C, 2% calcium, 8% iron

Banana-Apple Butter Bread

Bake a loaf or two to slice and tuck into your children's lunches or as a homemade gift for your neighbors. (See photo, page 160.)

PREP: 25 minutes BAKE: 45 minutes COOL: 10 minutes OVEN: 350° MAKES: 1 loaf (16 servings)

1½	cups all-purpose flour	2	eggs, slightly beaten
1½	teaspoons baking powder	¾	cup sugar
½	teaspoon ground cinnamon	½	cup mashed ripe banana
¼	teaspoon baking soda	½	cup apple butter
¼	teaspoon salt	¼	cup cooking oil
⅛	teaspoon ground nutmeg		

1 Grease and flour bottom and ½ inch up sides of a 9×5×3-inch loaf pan; set aside. In a large bowl stir together flour, baking powder, cinnamon, baking soda, salt, and nutmeg. Make a well in center of flour mixture; set aside.

2 In a medium bowl stir together eggs, sugar, banana, apple butter, and oil. Add egg mixture all at once to flour mixture. Stir just until moistened. Spoon batter into prepared pan, spreading evenly.

3 Bake in a 350° oven about 45 minutes or until a wooden toothpick inserted near center comes out clean. Cool in pan on a wire rack for 10 minutes. Remove bread from pan. Cool completely on a wire rack. Wrap and store overnight for easier slicing.

NUTRITION FACTS PER SERVING: 168 cal., 4 g total fat (1 g sat. fat), 27 mg chol., 103 mg sodium, 31 g carbo., 1 g fiber, 2 g pro. DAILY VALUES: 2% vit. A, 1% vit. C, 3% calcium, 5% iron

PREPARING PANS To get quick breads and muffins out of their pans easily, prepare the pans before you pour in the batter. Grease the pans lightly but carefully, greasing the corners too. For nicely rounded tops rather than ledges around the edges of your loaves or muffins, grease only the bottoms of the pans and ½ inch up the sides. The batter will then cling to the sides of the pans instead of sliding down during baking.

 Cool breads or muffins in the pans after they're baked so the steam that accumulates as the breads cool will help release the breads from the pans. Cool muffins 5 minutes and quick bread loaves 10 minutes before removing them.

Chapter Six

Brunches

Eggs Sonoma, p. 205

Brunch Turnovers, p. 224

Hash Brown Omelet, p. 203

Stuffed French Toast, p. 225

Basil-Tomato Tart, p. 223

197

Turkey-Asparagus Brunch Bake, p. 207

Egg and Black Bean Breakfast Burritos, p. 204

▲ Mexican-Style Egg Skillet, p. 217

▲ Windowpane Eggs, p. 201

▲ Herbed Ham and Vegetable Quiche, p. 221

▲ Brunch Scrambled Eggs, p. 215

Windowpane Eggs

When grape or cherry tomatoes are not available, substitute a chopped roma or beefsteak tomato. (See photo, page 200.)

START TO FINISH: 20 minutes MAKES: 2 servings

½ cup fresh sugar snap peas, strings and tips removed

½ cup grape tomatoes and/or yellow cherry tomatoes, halved

1 teaspoon cooking oil

2 teaspoons snipped fresh dill or ½ teaspoon dried dillweed

Salt and ground black pepper

2 tablespoons butter or margarine

2 ½-inch slices sourdough bread, approximately 5×4-inch rectangles

2 eggs

1 In a very large (12-inch) skillet cook and stir sugar snap peas and tomatoes in hot oil until the peas are crisp-tender and heated through. Stir in dill. Season with salt and black pepper. Remove from skillet; cover and keep warm.

2 In same skillet melt butter over medium heat. Cut or tear a hole in each slice of bread, leaving about ½ inch of bread around perimeter. Place bread slices in hot skillet. Crack an egg into center of each bread slice. Sprinkle with salt and black pepper. Cook, covered, for 3 minutes. Using a pancake turner, turn bread and egg over. Cook about 1 minute more or until reaches desired doneness.

3 To serve, place egg and bread on plates. Serve with pea-tomato mixture.

NUTRITION FACTS PER SERVING: 282 cal., 20 g total fat (6 g sat. fat), 228 mg chol., 499 mg sodium, 17 g carbo., 2 g fiber, 9 g pro. DAILY VALUES: 30% vit. C, 6% calcium, 11% iron

Zucchini Frittata

Go cosmopolitan at the breakfast table. With zucchini, leek, and Camembert, this Italian omelet offers a distinctly European flavor.

START TO FINISH: 15 minutes OVEN: 400° MAKES: 4 to 6 servings

1 cup thinly sliced zucchini (1 small)	½ teaspoon snipped fresh rosemary or ⅛ teaspoon dried rosemary, crushed
½ cup thinly sliced leek (1 medium)	½ teaspoon salt
1 tablespoon butter or margarine	⅛ teaspoon ground black pepper
6 eggs	½ of a 4½-ounce package Camembert cheese or 2 tablespoons freshly shredded Parmesan cheese
2 tablespoons snipped fresh parsley	
2 tablespoons water	

1 In an omelet pan or 10-inch ovenproof skillet cook zucchini and leek in hot butter just until tender.

2 Meanwhile, in a medium mixing bowl beat together eggs, parsley, water, rosemary, salt, and pepper with a wire whisk or rotary beater. Pour egg mixture over vegetables. Cook over medium-low heat. As mixture sets, run a spatula around edge of skillet, lifting egg mixture to allow uncooked portion to flow underneath. Continue cooking and lifting until egg mixture is almost set (surface will be moist).

3 Bake, uncovered, in a 400° oven about 4 minutes or until top is set. If using, cut the half circle of Camembert horizontally; cut each half into two or three wedges and place Camembert wedges on frittata. Or sprinkle with Parmesan cheese. Let cheese melt slightly before serving. Cut into wedges to serve.

NUTRITION FACTS PER SERVING: 198 cal., 13 g total fat (7 g sat. fat), 338 mg chol., 555 mg sodium, 4 g carbo., 1 g fiber, 13 g pro. DAILY VALUES: 19% vit. A, 10% vit. C, 11% calcium, 9% iron

---

MAKING A GREAT FRITTATA The wonderful thing about frittatas is you can tailor them to please many tastes. Here are some of the options you can select: cooked meat, poultry, seafood, cheeses, fresh and dried herbs, olives, garlic, and vegetables. Grate, shred, chop, or slice all ingredients into bite-size pieces; drain well any ingredients that come in a juice or brine, such as olives. If you're using vegetables, you may want to precook items such as zucchini, carrots, potatoes, broccoli, or mushrooms. To add even more flavor, substitute chicken, beef, or vegetable broth for the milk normally used to make a frittata. Add a topper, such as a spoonful of sour cream, salsa, or heated spaghetti sauce.

Hash Brown Omelet

Four traditional breakfast favorites—bacon, hash browns, eggs, and cheese—come together in this hearty breakfast skillet. (See photo, page 195.)

START TO FINISH: 15 minutes MAKES: 4 servings

4 slices bacon	¼ cup milk
2 cups refrigerated shredded hash brown potatoes (about half of a 20-ounce package)	½ teaspoon salt
	Dash ground black pepper
¼ cup chopped onion	1 cup shredded cheddar cheese (4 ounces)
¼ cup chopped green sweet pepper	Bias-sliced green onions (optional)
4 eggs	

1 In a large skillet cook bacon until crisp. Drain bacon on paper towels, reserving 2 tablespoons drippings in skillet. Crumble bacon; set aside.

2 In a large bowl stir together potatoes, chopped onion, and sweet pepper. Pat potato mixture into the skillet. Cook, uncovered, over low heat about 7 minutes or until crisp and brown, turning once.

3 Meanwhile, in a small mixing bowl beat together eggs, milk, salt, and black pepper with a wire whisk or rotary beater. Pour egg mixture over potato mixture. Sprinkle with cheddar cheese and bacon. Cook, covered, over low heat for 5 to 7 minutes or until egg mixture is set. Loosen omelet; fold in half. Turn out of skillet onto plate. Cut into wedges to serve. If desired, garnish with green onions.

NUTRITION FACTS PER SERVING: 325 cal., 18 g total fat (9 g sat. fat), 249 mg chol., 661 mg sodium, 22 g carbo., 2 g fiber, 18 g pro. DAILY VALUES: 19% vit. A, 27% vit. C, 26% calcium, 12% iron

Egg and Black Bean Breakfast Burritos

Savor the luxury of sleeping in late, followed by a grand breakfast: a burrito, cooked chorizo patties, and grapefruit and orange sections. Then ease into a comfy chair and read the paper—comics first. (See photo, page 199.)

START TO FINISH: 25 minutes MAKES: 4 servings

1 cup rinsed and drained canned black beans	1 medium tomato, thinly sliced
1/3 cup bottled chunky salsa	1/2 cup crumbled queso fresco or shredded Monterey Jack cheese (2 ounces)
4 eggs, slightly beaten	1/4 cup dairy sour cream
2 tablespoons milk	4 teaspoons snipped fresh mint
1/4 teaspoon ground black pepper	Bottled chunky salsa (optional)
1/8 teaspoon salt	
Nonstick cooking spray or cooking oil	

1 In a small saucepan slightly mash black beans. Stir in the 1/3 cup salsa; heat through over low heat. Cover and keep warm.

2 In a medium bowl stir together eggs, milk, pepper, and salt. Coat a 10-inch nonstick omelet pan (or skillet with flared sides) with nonstick cooking spray, or brush lightly with a little cooking oil. Preheat pan over medium heat until a drop of water sizzles.

3 For each of the egg tortillas pour about 1/4 cup of the egg mixture into pan. Lift and tilt pan to spread egg mixture over bottom. Return to heat. Cook for 1 1/2 to 2 minutes or until lightly browned on bottom (do not turn).

4 To serve, loosen edges of egg tortilla with spatula. Carefully slide it onto a plate, brown side down. On half of the tortilla, spread one-fourth of the bean-salsa mixture. Top with tomato and 1 tablespoon of the cheese. Fold in half and then into quarters to form burrito. Keep warm while preparing remaining tortillas and burritos. Top each with a spoonful of sour cream; sprinkle with some of the remaining 1/4 cup cheese and the mint. If desired, serve with additional salsa.

NUTRITION FACTS PER SERVING: 179 cal., 9 g total fat (4 g sat. fat), 223 mg chol., 389 mg sodium, 14 g carbo., 4 g fiber, 14 g pro. DAILY VALUES: 14% vit. C, 12% calcium, 12% iron

Eggs Sonoma

Even the bleary-eyed will rise and shine to the enticing aromas of this Mexican-inspired breakfast. Serve with fresh fruit and strong coffee. (See photo, page 193.)

START TO FINISH: 25 minutes MAKES: 4 servings

1/3 cup seeded, chopped tomato	1/8 teaspoon dried rosemary, crushed
1 4 1/2-ounce can chopped green chile peppers, drained	6 eggs
2 tablespoons finely chopped celery	1/4 teaspoon salt
1 tablespoon finely chopped onion	Dash ground black pepper
1 teaspoon white wine vinegar	1 tablespoon butter or margarine
1/2 teaspoon sugar	4 6- to 7-inch corn tortillas or flour tortillas

1 In a small bowl stir together tomato, chile peppers, celery, onion, vinegar, sugar, and rosemary; set aside. In a medium mixing bowl beat together eggs, salt, and pepper with a wire whisk or rotary beater. Stir in tomato mixture.

2 In a large skillet melt butter over medium heat. Pour egg mixture into skillet. Cook without stirring until mixture begins to set on bottom and around edge. Using a large spoon or spatula, lift and fold partially cooked egg mixture so uncooked portion flows underneath. Continue cooking and lifting for 2 to 3 minutes or until eggs are cooked through but are still glossy and moist. Remove from heat.

3 Meanwhile, heat tortillas according to package directions. To serve, top each tortilla with some of the egg mixture.

NUTRITION FACTS PER SERVING: 211 cal., 11 g total fat (4 g sat. fat), 327 mg chol., 444 mg sodium, 16 g carbo., 2 g fiber, 11 g pro. DAILY VALUES: 24% vit. C, 10% calcium, 11% iron

Southwestern Breakfast Bake

Sometimes breakfast tastes great at suppertime. For a light dinner, serve this puffy egg-topped dish with a salad of mixed greens, tomato, chopped avocado, and onion.

PREP: 20 minutes BAKE: 45 minutes STAND: 15 minutes OVEN: 325° MAKES: 8 servings

1	15-ounce can black beans, rinsed and drained
³/₄	cup canned enchilada sauce
2	4¹/₂-ounce cans diced green chile peppers, drained
¹/₂	cup thinly sliced green onions (4)
2	cloves garlic, minced
	Several dashes bottled hot pepper sauce (optional)
1	cup shredded sharp cheddar cheese and/or shredded Monterey Jack cheese with jalapeño peppers (4 ounces)

3	egg whites
3	egg yolks
2	tablespoons all-purpose flour
¹/₄	teaspoon salt
¹/₂	cup milk
1	tablespoon snipped fresh cilantro
	Dairy sour cream (optional)
	Salsa (optional)
	Additional snipped fresh cilantro (optional)

1 Grease a 2-quart square baking dish. In the prepared dish combine black beans, enchilada sauce, green chile peppers, green onions, garlic, and, if desired, hot pepper sauce. Sprinkle with cheese.

2 In a medium mixing bowl beat egg whites with an electric mixer on medium speed until soft peaks form (tips curl); set aside. In a large mixing bowl combine egg yolks, flour, and salt. Beat egg yolk mixture with a wire whisk until combined (mixture will be stiff). Gradually whisk in milk until smooth. Fold egg whites and the 1 tablespoon snipped cilantro into yolk mixture. Carefully pour egg mixture over the bean mixture in baking dish.

3 Bake in a 325° oven about 45 minutes or until egg mixture appears set when gently shaken. Let stand for 15 minutes before serving. If desired, serve with sour cream, salsa, and additional snipped cilantro.

NUTRITION FACTS PER SERVING: 163 cal., 8 g total fat (4 g sat. fat), 96 mg chol., 488 mg sodium, 15 g carbo., 4 g fiber, 11 g pro. DAILY VALUES: 37% vit. A, 18% vit. C, 20% calcium, 11% iron

Turkey-Asparagus Brunch Bake

For relaxed late-morning entertaining, create a memorable menu featuring this recipe, fresh mixed fruit, juice, and Super-Big Cinnamon-Pecan Ring, on page 178. (See photo, page 198.)

PREP: 25 minutes BAKE: 23 minutes OVEN: 425° MAKES: 6 servings

1	pound fresh asparagus spears or one 10-ounce package frozen cut asparagus or cut broccoli
1	pound uncooked ground turkey
1	cup chopped onions (2 medium)
½	cup chopped red sweet pepper
3	eggs
2	cups milk

1	cup all-purpose flour
¼	cup grated Parmesan cheese
1	teaspoon lemon-pepper seasoning
½	teaspoon dried tarragon, basil, or thyme, crushed
1	cup shredded Swiss cheese (4 ounces)

1 Grease a 3-quart rectangular baking dish; set aside. If using fresh asparagus, wash and scrape off scales. Break off and discard woody bases of asparagus. Cut asparagus into 1½-inch pieces. In a covered medium saucepan cook asparagus in a small amount of boiling water about 4 minutes or until crisp-tender. (For frozen asparagus or broccoli, cook according to package directions.) Drain and set aside.

2 In a large skillet cook turkey, onions, and sweet pepper until vegetables are just tender and no pink remains in turkey. Remove from heat. Drain off fat. Arrange meat mixture in prepared baking dish; top with cooked asparagus.

3 In a large mixing bowl combine eggs, milk, flour, Parmesan cheese, lemon-pepper seasoning, and tarragon. Beat until smooth with a wire whisk or rotary beater. (Or combine ingredients in a blender container; cover and blend for 20 seconds.) * See below. Pour egg mixture evenly over layers in baking dish.

4 Bake, uncovered, in a 425° oven about 20 minutes or until a knife inserted near center comes out clean. Sprinkle with the Swiss cheese. Bake for 3 to 5 minutes more or until cheese is melted.

NUTRITION FACTS PER SERVING: 382 cal., 17 g total fat (8 g sat. fat), 193 mg chol., 440 mg sodium, 25 g carbo., 2 g fiber, 30 g pro. DAILY VALUES: 53% vit. C, 38% calcium, 15% iron

TO MAKE AHEAD: Prepare casserole as directed to the asterisk (*) in Step 3. Pour egg mixture into a bowl or pitcher; cover and chill. Cover and chill turkey and asparagus in the baking dish. To bake, stir egg mixture well and pour over turkey mixture. Bake, uncovered, in 425° oven about 30 minutes or until a knife inserted near the center comes out clean. Continue as directed.

Potato and Green Chile Brunch Bake

*If hosting guests for the weekend, avoid last-minute stress with this make-ahead recipe.
It's a wonderful Sunday send-off, allowing more time with your friends.*

PREP: 20 minutes BAKE: 25 minutes OVEN: 375° MAKES: 6 servings

3	cups refrigerated shredded hash brown potatoes
5	eggs
1	cup shredded Monterey Jack cheese with jalapeño peppers (4 ounces)
1/2	cup ricotta cheese or cream cheese, softened
3/4	cup milk, half-and-half, or light cream

1/8	teaspoon salt
1/8	teaspoon ground black pepper
2	tablespoons butter or margarine
1	tablespoon all-purpose flour
1	4 1/2-ounce can diced green chile peppers, drained

1 Grease a 2-quart square baking dish. In a medium bowl stir together potatoes, 1 of the eggs, and 1/2 cup of the Monterey Jack cheese. Spread mixture into bottom of prepared baking dish. Spread with a thin layer of ricotta cheese.

2 In a small mixing bowl beat together the remaining 4 eggs, 1/4 cup of the milk, the salt, and pepper with a wire whisk or rotary beater. In a medium skillet melt 1 tablespoon of the butter over medium heat. Pour egg mixture into skillet. Cook, without stirring, until mixture begins to set on bottom and around edge. Using a large spoon or spatula, lift and fold partially cooked egg mixture so the uncooked portion flows underneath. Continue cooking about 4 minutes or until eggs are cooked through but are still glossy and moist. Spoon eggs evenly over mixture in baking dish.

3 For sauce, in the same skillet melt the remaining 1 tablespoon butter. Stir flour into melted butter. Add the remaining 1/2 cup milk and the chile peppers. Cook and stir until thickened and bubbly. Stir in the remaining 1/2 cup Monterey Jack cheese until melted. Spoon sauce evenly over the eggs.

4 Bake, uncovered, in a 375° oven for 25 minutes.

NUTRITION FACTS PER SERVING: 289 cal., 16 g total fat (7 g sat. fat), 203 mg chol., 406 mg sodium, 22 g carbo., 2 g fiber, 16 g pro. DAILY VALUES: 22% vit. A, 143% vit. C, 23% calcium, 8% iron

TO MAKE AHEAD: Prepare casserole as directed; cover and chill up to 24 hours. Bake, covered, in a 375° oven for 25 minutes. Uncover and bake for 5 minutes more.

Cheese, Bacon, and Bread Bake

*The savory dill-accented bread shell holds a hearty mixture of ricotta cheese,
Swiss cheese, cream cheese, and crispy bacon. A marinated fresh
fruit compote makes a perfect companion.*

PREP: 30 minutes BAKE: 25 minutes OVEN: 400° MAKES: 8 servings

1½	cups all-purpose flour	½	cup shredded Swiss cheese (2 ounces)
1½	teaspoons baking powder	1	3-ounce package cream cheese, cut into small cubes
½	teaspoon baking soda		
½	teaspoon dried dillweed or ½ teaspoon dried thyme, crushed	3	tablespoons milk
		2	teaspoons Dijon-style mustard
½	teaspoon finely shredded lemon peel	2	tablespoons finely chopped green onion (1)
1	8-ounce carton dairy sour cream		
8	slices bacon	1	tablespoon snipped fresh parsley
½	cup ricotta cheese		

1 In a medium bowl stir together flour, baking powder, baking soda, dillweed, and lemon peel. Stir in sour cream. On a floured surface knead dough just until smooth. Cover and set aside.

2 In a 10-inch ovenproof skillet cook bacon until crisp. Drain bacon on paper towels, reserving 1 tablespoon drippings in skillet. Crumble bacon; set aside. Cool skillet slightly. Press dough onto the bottom and ½ inch up sides of skillet. Sprinkle with all but 2 tablespoons of the crumbled bacon.

3 In a medium bowl stir together ricotta cheese, Swiss cheese, cream cheese, milk, mustard, green onion, and parsley. Spread cheese mixture in skillet.

4 Bake in a 400° oven about 25 minutes or until bread is golden brown. Cool slightly. Sprinkle with reserved bacon. Cut into wedges to serve.

NUTRITION FACTS PER SERVING: 272 cal., 17 g total fat (10 g sat. fat), 44 mg chol., 365 mg sodium, 19 g carbo., 1 g fiber, 10 g pro. DAILY VALUES: 14% vit. A, 2% vit. C, 17% calcium, 8% iron

Baked Eggs with Cheese and Basil Sauce

Add the unexpected to morning entertaining by topping eggs with a creamy sauce flavored with basil. Pick or buy enough of the fresh herb to attractively garnish each serving.

PREP: 15 minutes BAKE: 18 minutes OVEN: 350° MAKES: 4 servings

	Nonstick cooking spray	1	cup milk
3	tablespoons butter or margarine	4	eggs
2	tablespoons all-purpose flour	¼	cup shredded mozzarella cheese (1 ounce)
¼	teaspoon salt		Snipped fresh basil (optional)
⅛	teaspoon ground black pepper		
3	tablespoons snipped fresh basil or ½ teaspoon dried basil, crushed		

1 Coat four 8- to 10-ounce round baking dishes or 6-ounce custard cups with cooking spray; set aside. For sauce, in a small saucepan melt butter over medium heat. Stir in flour, salt, pepper, and, if using, the dried basil. Add milk all at once. Cook and stir until thickened and bubbly. Cook and stir for 1 minute more. Remove from heat. If using, stir in the 3 tablespoons fresh basil.

2 To assemble, spoon about 2 tablespoons sauce into each prepared dish. Gently break an egg into center of each dish. Season with salt and pepper. Spoon remaining sauce over eggs.

3 Bake in a 350° oven for 18 to 20 minutes or until eggs are set. Sprinkle with mozzarella cheese. Let stand until cheese melts. If desired, garnish with additional snipped basil.

NUTRITION FACTS PER SERVING: 213 cal., 16 g total fat (8 g sat. fat), 244 mg chol., 406 mg sodium, 7 g carbo., 0 g fiber, 11 g pro. DAILY VALUES: 23% vit. A, 2% vit. C, 15% calcium, 6% iron

HERB SUBSTITUTIONS All out of fresh herbs? In a pinch, you can substitute dried herbs. To do so, use one-third the amount of dried herb for the amount of fresh herb called for in a recipe. For example, substitute 1 teaspoon dried herb for 1 tablespoon fresh herb.

Before adding a dried herb to a recipe, crush it between your finger and thumb to help release the herb's flavors.

If you use a dried herb, add it to the recipe at the beginning of cooking to develop its flavor. If you use a fresh herb, add it at the end because long cooking can destroy its flavor and color. The exception to this rule is fresh rosemary, which can withstand long cooking times.

Cheese and Mushroom Brunch Eggs

If you anticipate a bunch for brunch, this casserole is ideal. The eggs will stay warm until all your guests have helped themselves.

PREP: 30 minutes BAKE: 20 minutes STAND: 10 minutes OVEN: 350° MAKES: 6 servings

3	tablespoons butter or margarine		Nonstick cooking spray
2	tablespoons all-purpose flour	1½	cups sliced fresh mushrooms
1	cup milk	¼	cup thinly sliced green onions (2)
⅓	cup shredded process Swiss cheese (1½ ounces)	12	eggs, beaten
3	tablespoons grated Parmesan cheese	1	medium tomato, chopped
2	tablespoons dry white wine or milk*		

1 For sauce, in a medium saucepan melt 2 tablespoons of the butter over medium heat. Stir in flour. Cook for 1 minute. Add the 1 cup milk all at once. Cook and stir over medium heat until thickened and bubbly. Stir in Swiss cheese and Parmesan cheese. Cook and stir until cheeses melt; remove from heat. Stir in wine; set aside.

2 For mushroom mixture, coat an unheated large skillet with nonstick cooking spray. Preheat skillet over medium heat. Add mushrooms and green onions to hot skillet. Cook for 2 to 3 minutes or until mushrooms are tender. Transfer mushroom mixture to a small bowl; set aside.

3 In the same skillet melt the remaining 1 tablespoon butter over medium heat. Pour in eggs. Cook without stirring until eggs begin to set on the bottom and around edge. Using a large spoon or spatula, lift and fold the partially cooked egg mixture so the uncooked portion flows underneath. Continue cooking and lifting until eggs are cooked through but still glossy and moist. Transfer half of the scrambled eggs to an ungreased 2-quart square baking dish or an au gratin dish.

4 Spread half of the mushroom mixture over eggs in baking dish. Drizzle about half the sauce over mushroom mixture. Top with the remaining scrambled eggs, mushroom mixture, and sauce.

5 Bake, uncovered, in a 350° oven about 20 minutes or until heated through. Sprinkle with tomato. Let stand for 10 minutes before serving.

***Note:** If using milk instead of wine, stir ½ teaspoon dry mustard in with the 2 tablespoons milk.

NUTRITION FACTS PER SERVING: 283 cal., 20 g total fat (9 g sat. fat), 452 mg chol., 356 mg sodium, 7 g carbo., 1 g fiber, 18 g pro. DAILY VALUES: 9% vit. C, 20% calcium, 11% iron

Low-Fat Cheese and Mushroom Brunch Eggs: Prepare as directed, except use fat-free milk, reduced-fat Swiss cheese, and 2½ cups refrigerated or frozen egg product, thawed, instead of whole eggs.

Ranch Eggs

Your taste buds will get a wake-up call with this Mexican-style casserole. If hot and spicy doesn't suit you in the morning, serve this meatless main dish for supper.

PREP: 10 minutes BAKE: 21 minutes OVEN: 400° MAKES: 6 servings

	Nonstick cooking spray
1	large onion, halved and thinly sliced
1	14½-ounce can chunky chili-style tomato sauce
1	fresh jalapeño pepper, seeded and chopped*
3	tablespoons snipped fresh cilantro

6	eggs
¼	teaspoon salt
⅛	teaspoon ground black pepper
1	cup shredded Monterey Jack or cheddar cheese (4 ounces)
	Warm flour tortillas or toast

1 Coat a 2-quart rectangular baking dish with nonstick cooking spray. Separate onion into half-rings and place in prepared dish.

2 In a small bowl stir together tomato sauce, jalapeño pepper, and cilantro. Pour sauce mixture over onions in dish. Break eggs, one at a time, over tomato mixture. Sprinkle eggs with salt and black pepper.

3 Bake, uncovered, in a 400° oven for 20 to 25 minutes or until eggs are set. Sprinkle with cheese. Bake for 1 minute more. Serve with warmed flour tortillas or toast.

*****Note:** Because chile peppers contain volatile oils that can burn your skin and eyes, avoid direct contact with them as much as possible. When working with chile peppers, wear plastic or rubber gloves. If your bare hands do touch the chile peppers, wash your hands well with soap and water.

NUTRITION FACTS PER SERVING: 270 cal., 13 g total fat (6 g sat. fat), 230 mg chol., 736 mg sodium, 26 g carbo., 0 g fiber, 15 g pro. DAILY VALUES: 23% vit. A, 19% vit. C, 19% calcium, 16% iron

Baked Denver Strata

This layered breakfast takes brunch to a new taste level. Though named for the mile-high city, it brightens any morning, anywhere—even at sea level.

PREP: 25 minutes COOK: 35 minutes STAND: 20 minutes OVEN: 350° MAKES: 6 to 8 servings

6	English muffins, split and quartered	1/2	cup sliced pitted ripe olives
9	eggs	1/2	cup finely chopped green onions (4)
1	cup milk	1	7-ounce jar roasted red sweet peppers, drained and cut into strips
1	4 1/2-ounce can diced green chile peppers, drained	1 1/2	cups shredded provolone cheese (6 ounces)
1/4	teaspoon salt		
1/4	teaspoon ground black pepper	1/2	cup shredded cheddar cheese (2 ounces)
1	cup diced cooked ham		

1 Grease a 3-quart rectangular baking dish. Arrange English muffin quarters in a single layer in a baking dish.

2 In a large mixing bowl beat together eggs, milk, chile peppers, salt, and black pepper with a wire whisk or rotary beater. Pour egg mixture over muffin quarters; let stand for 10 minutes. Sprinkle with ham, olives, green onions, roasted sweet peppers, provolone cheese, and cheddar cheese.

3 Bake, uncovered, in a 350° oven for 35 to 40 minutes or until a knife inserted near the center comes out clean. Let stand for 10 minutes before serving.

NUTRITION FACTS PER SERVING: 463 cal., 23 g total fat (10 g sat. fat), 365 mg chol., 1,159 mg sodium, 33 g carbo., 1 g fiber, 30 g pro. DAILY VALUES: 40% vit. A, 134% vit. C, 42% calcium, 24% iron

Mediterranean Strata

The flavors of roasted red sweet peppers, green olives, and feta cheese give this dish a fresh new taste.

PREP: 20 minutes BAKE: 35 minutes STAND: 5 minutes OVEN: 350° MAKES: 8 servings

Nonstick cooking spray	½ cup chopped pitted green olives
3 cups cubed Italian bread	½ cup crumbled feta cheese (2 ounces)
2 large onions, thinly sliced	6 eggs, beaten
4 cloves garlic, minced	1 14-ounce can chicken broth
2 tablespoons olive oil	¼ cup dry white wine or chicken broth
½ of a 7-ounce jar roasted red sweet peppers, drained and chopped (½ cup)	¼ teaspoon ground black pepper

1 Coat a 10-inch quiche dish with cooking spray. Arrange bread cubes in dish; set aside.

2 In a large skillet cook onions and garlic in hot oil over medium heat about 10 minutes or until onions are golden brown, stirring frequently. Remove from heat. Stir in roasted sweet peppers and olives. Spoon mixture evenly over bread cubes in dish. Sprinkle with feta cheese.

3 In a large mixing bowl beat together eggs, chicken broth, wine, and black pepper with a wire whisk. Pour egg mixture over bread mixture in dish.

4 Bake, uncovered, in a 350° oven for 35 to 45 minutes or until a knife inserted near center comes out clean. Let stand for 5 to 10 minutes before serving.

NUTRITION FACTS PER SERVING: 173 cal., 11 g total fat (3 g sat. fat), 166 mg chol., 515 mg sodium, 11 g carbo., 1 g fiber, 8 g pro. DAILY VALUES: 46% vit. C, 6% calcium, 9% iron

Brunch Scrambled Eggs

Wake up boring scrambled eggs with color and a flavor boost from spinach, oregano, and cheeses, such as Colby and feta. (See photo, page 200.)

START TO FINISH: 20 minutes MAKES: 6 servings

1	10-ounce package frozen chopped spinach, thawed	¼	teaspoon salt
12	eggs	⅛	teaspoon ground black pepper
½	cup milk	2	tablespoons butter or margarine
½	teaspoon dried oregano or thyme, crushed, or 1½ teaspoons snipped fresh oregano or thyme	1	cup shredded Colby cheese or cheddar cheese (4 ounces)
		1	cup crumbled feta cheese (4 ounces)

1 Drain spinach well, pressing out excess liquid; set aside. In a large mixing bowl beat together eggs, milk, dried oregano (if using), salt, and pepper with a wire whisk or rotary beater.

2 In a large skillet melt butter over medium heat. Pour in egg mixture. Cook without stirring until mixture begins to set on bottom and around edge. Using a large spoon or spatula, lift and fold partially cooked eggs so uncooked portion flows underneath. Stir in spinach, cheese, and half of the feta cheese. Continue cooking and lifting for 2 to 3 minutes or until eggs are cooked through but are still glossy and moist.

3 To serve, transfer egg mixture to a serving bowl. Sprinkle with remaining feta cheese and, if using, the fresh oregano. Serve immediately.

NUTRITION FACTS PER SERVING: 330 cal., 25 g total fat (12 g sat. fat), 472 mg chol., 631 mg sodium, 5 g carbo., 1 g fiber, 22 g pro. DAILY VALUES: 19% vit. C, 35% calcium, 15% iron

Mushroom, Blue Cheese, and Walnut Scramble

The occasion doesn't need to be breakfast when serving this creamy scrambled egg dish. It's rich and wonderful enough to stand up to the best of lunches or dinners.

START TO FINISH: 25 minutes MAKES: 4 servings

6	eggs, beaten	1	teaspoon Worcestershire sauce
1	cup milk	1/3	cup crumbled blue cheese or shredded Swiss cheese (about 1½ ounces)
½	teaspoon salt		
¼	teaspoon ground black pepper		Toast points or toasted English muffin halves
2	tablespoons butter or margarine		
1	cup sliced fresh mushrooms	2	tablespoons finely chopped toasted walnuts
4	teaspoons all-purpose flour		
½	teaspoon dry mustard		

1 In a medium bowl stir together eggs, ¼ cup of the milk, ¼ teaspoon of the salt, and ⅛ teaspoon of the pepper. In a large skillet melt 1 tablespoon of the butter over medium heat. Pour in egg mixture. Cook without stirring until mixture begins to set on bottom and around edge. Using a large spoon or spatula, lift and fold partially cooked eggs so uncooked portion flows underneath. Continue cooking and lifting until cooked through but still glossy and moist. Remove eggs from skillet.

2 Add the remaining 1 tablespoon butter to a clean skillet. Add mushrooms; cook and stir until tender. Stir in flour, mustard, the remaining ¼ teaspoon salt, and remaining ⅛ teaspoon pepper. Stir in the remaining ¾ cup milk and the Worcestershire all at once. Cook and stir until thickened and bubbly. Cook and stir for 1 minute more. Set aside 1 tablespoon of the blue cheese. Add remaining blue cheese and the scrambled eggs to the sauce; heat through.

3 To serve, spoon eggs on top of toast points or toasted English muffin halves. Sprinkle reserved blue cheese and the walnuts on top of each serving.

NUTRITION FACTS PER SERVING: 341 cal., 22 g total fat (11 g sat. fat), 363 mg chol., 777 mg sodium, 20 g carbo., 1 g fiber, 17 g pro. DAILY VALUES: 2% vit. C, 20% calcium, 13% iron

Mexican-Style Egg Skillet

Would you like a spicy and satisfying way to start your day? With hearty Mexican sausage, eggs, and cheese perked up with chiles and onions, you can awaken your taste buds to a veritable fiesta of flavor. (See photo, page 200.)

START TO FINISH: 25 minutes MAKES: 4 servings

4 6-inch corn tortillas, cut into quarters	¼ cup thinly sliced green onions (2)
1 tablespoon cooking oil	1 fresh serrano chile pepper, seeded and finely chopped (optional)*
6 ounces chorizo or bulk hot Italian sausage	2 tablespoons snipped fresh cilantro
6 eggs, beaten	¼ cup bottled salsa
¼ teaspoon salt	
1 cup shredded Monterey Jack cheese with jalapeño peppers (4 ounces)	

1 In a large nonstick skillet fry half of the tortilla quarters in half of the oil about 2 minutes or until crisp, turning once. Drain on paper towels. Repeat with remaining tortilla quarters and oil; cool. In the same skillet cook chorizo over medium heat until brown. Remove from skillet; drain off fat.

2 In a large bowl stir together eggs, tortilla wedges, and salt. Add egg mixture to skillet. Cook, without stirring, over medium heat until mixture begins to set on bottom and around edge. Using a large spoon or spatula, lift and fold partially cooked eggs so uncooked portion flows underneath. Continue cooking for 1 to 1½ minutes or until eggs are partially set. Stir in chorizo, ¾ cup of the Monterey Jack cheese, the onions, and, if desired, serrano chile pepper. Continue to cook and lift until eggs are cooked through and cheese is melted. Sprinkle with the remaining ¼ cup cheese and the cilantro. Serve with salsa.

***Note:** Because chile peppers contain volatile oils that can burn your skin and eyes, avoid direct contact with them as much as possible. When working with chile peppers, wear plastic or rubber gloves. If your bare hands do touch the chile peppers, wash your hands well with soap and water.

NUTRITION FACTS PER SERVING: 503 cal., 36 g total fat (14 g sat. fat), 381 mg chol., 994 mg sodium, 15 g carbo., 2 g fiber, 28 g pro. DAILY VALUES: 6% vit. C, 30% calcium, 14% iron

Benedict-Style Eggs and Mushrooms

Traditional hollandaise sauce requires the cook to hover because it needs constant stirring over low heat to keep from curdling. This version—with low-fat yogurt and mayonnaise—is much easier to prepare, lower in fat, and versatile.

START TO FINISH: 25 minutes MAKES: 4 servings

4	cups shiitake or button mushrooms	⅛	teaspoon ground black pepper
2	tablespoons olive oil or butter	4	eggs
¼	teaspoon salt	1	recipe Easy Hollandaise Sauce

1 Remove stems from shiitake mushrooms; discard. Halve mushrooms. In a large skillet cook mushrooms in hot oil until tender. Sprinkle with salt and pepper.

2 Meanwhile, grease another large skillet. Add enough water to half-fill skillet. Bring to boiling; reduce heat. Break one of the eggs into a cup. Carefully slide egg into simmering water. Repeat with remaining eggs. Simmer, uncovered, for 3 to 5 minutes or until whites are completely set and yolks begin to thicken but are not hard.

3 To serve, arrange mushrooms on serving plates. Using a slotted spoon, remove eggs from water and place eggs on mushrooms. Drizzle with Easy Hollandaise Sauce.

Easy Hollandaise Sauce: In a small saucepan stir together ¼ cup plain low-fat yogurt, ¼ cup mayonnaise, 1 teaspoon lemon juice, and ½ teaspoon Dijon-style mustard. Cook and stir over low heat until warm; do not boil.

NUTRITION FACTS PER SERVING: 259 cal., 23 g total fat (4 g sat. fat), 222 mg chol., 302 mg sodium, 5 g carbo., 1 g fiber, 8 g pro. DAILY VALUES: 4% vit. C, 4% calcium, 12% iron

MUSHROOM SAVVY When it comes to cleaning and storing mushrooms, follow these helpful hints:
   The best way to clean fresh mushrooms is to wipe them with a clean, damp cloth. If you must rinse them, do it lightly, then dry them immediately—and gently—with paper towels. Never soak fresh mushrooms in water because it ruins their texture.
   As for storage, prepackaged mushrooms should stay in the package, but loose mushrooms or those in an open package should be stored in a paper bag or in a damp cloth bag in the refrigerator. This allows them to breathe so they stay firm longer. Storing mushrooms in a plastic bag causes them to deteriorate quickly.

Havarti-Mushroom Breakfast Rounds

*Mushrooms, cheese, and eggs top English muffin halves for these open-face,
breakfast-style sandwiches.*

PREP: 25 minutes BAKE: 10 minutes OVEN: 400° MAKES: 6 servings

3   English muffins, split and toasted

1½ cups sliced fresh mushrooms

½   cup finely chopped onion (1 medium)

1   tablespoon butter or margarine

2   eggs, slightly beaten

1½ cups shredded Havarti cheese or
    Swiss cheese (6 ounces)

¼   teaspoon seasoned salt

⅛   teaspoon ground black pepper

1 Arrange toasted English muffin halves, cut side up, on a baking sheet; set aside. In a large skillet cook mushrooms and onion in hot butter until tender. Using a slotted spoon, remove mushroom mixture from skillet. Drain in a colander. Arrange mushroom mixture on muffin halves.

2 In a small bowl stir together eggs, cheese, seasoned salt, and pepper. Spoon egg mixture over mushrooms on muffin halves.

3 Bake, uncovered, in a 400° oven for 10 to 12 minutes or until cheese is melted and bubbly. Serve immediately.

NUTRITION FACTS PER SERVING: 240 cal., 16 g total fat (2 g sat. fat), 111 mg chol., 391 mg sodium, 15 g carbo., 1 g fiber, 11 g pro. DAILY VALUES: 10% vit. A, 1% vit. C, 25% calcium, 6% iron

Spinach Cheese Puff

Resembling a soufflé—only less temperamental—this puff has the consistency of Southern-style spoon bread.

PREP: 30 minutes BAKE: 40 minutes OVEN: 375° MAKES: 6 to 8 servings

6	egg yolks
6	egg whites
2	tablespoons grated Parmesan cheese
1/4	cup finely chopped shallots (2 medium)
2	cloves garlic, minced
3	tablespoons butter or margarine
1/4	cup finely snipped dried tomatoes (not oil packed)
1/4	cup all-purpose flour
1/4	teaspoon salt

1/8	teaspoon ground red pepper
1	cup milk
1	cup shredded Swiss cheese or Gruyère cheese (4 ounces)
8	ounces fresh spinach, cooked, well drained, and finely chopped (3/4 cup)*, or one 10-ounce package frozen chopped spinach, thawed and well drained
1/4	cup finely chopped prosciutto
5	to 6 dried tomato slices (not oil packed)

1 Let egg yolks and egg whites stand at room temperature for 30 minutes. Grease bottom and sides of a 1½-quart soufflé dish. Sprinkle inside of the dish with 1 tablespoon of the Parmesan cheese; set aside.

2 In a medium saucepan cook shallots and garlic in hot butter for 1 minute. Stir in snipped dried tomatoes, flour, salt, and ground red pepper. Cook and stir for 1 minute. Add milk all at once. Cook and stir until thickened and bubbly. Remove from heat. Add cheese and the remaining 1 tablespoon Parmesan, a little at a time, stirring until melted.

3 In a small bowl beat egg yolks with a fork until combined. Slowly add about half of the cheese mixture to yolks, stirring constantly. Return yolk mixture to saucepan. Stir in spinach and prosciutto; set aside.

4 In a large mixing bowl beat egg whites with an electric mixer on medium to high speed until stiff peaks form (tips stand straight). Gently fold about one-third of the whites into spinach mixture to lighten; fold spinach mixture into remaining egg whites. Pour spinach mixture into prepared dish.

5 Bake, uncovered, in a 375° oven for 40 to 45 minutes or until puffed and a knife inserted near center comes out clean. Meanwhile, soak dried tomato slices in hot water for 5 minutes. Drain well on paper towels. Arrange tomato slices on top of puff and serve immediately.

*Note: To cook spinach, place fresh spinach leaves in a steamer basket over boiling water. Steam, covered, about 2 minutes or until wilted. Drain in a colander, pressing with a spoon to squeeze out liquid. Finely chop.

NUTRITION FACTS PER SERVING: 272 cal., 18 g total fat (10 g sat. fat), 252 mg chol., 477 mg sodium, 12 g carbo., 2 g fiber, 17 g pro. DAILY VALUES: 67% vit. A, 17% vit. C, 32% calcium, 14% iron

Herbed Ham and Vegetable Quiche

Refrigerated biscuits make a tender, easy crust for this colorful brunch headliner.
(See photo, page 200.)

PREP: 35 minutes BAKE: 25 minutes STAND: 10 minutes OVEN: 375° MAKES: 6 servings

2 cups thinly sliced zucchini and/or yellow summer squash (2 small)	¼ teaspoon garlic powder
1 cup chopped onions (2 medium)	⅛ teaspoon ground black pepper
½ cup sliced fresh mushrooms	2 eggs, beaten
½ cup chopped red sweet pepper	1 cup diced cooked ham
1 tablespoon butter or margarine	1 cup shredded mozzarella cheese (4 ounces)
¼ cup snipped fresh parsley or 1 tablespoon dried parsley	½ cup shredded fontina cheese (2 ounces)
2 tablespoons snipped fresh basil or 1 teaspoon dried basil, crushed	1 17.3-ounce package refrigerated large Southern-style biscuits (8)
1 teaspoon snipped fresh oregano or ¼ teaspoon dried oregano, crushed	Fresh basil leaves (optional)

1 Grease a 10-inch quiche dish; set aside. For filling, in a large skillet cook the zucchini and/or summer squash, onions, mushrooms, and sweet pepper in hot butter about 6 minutes or just until tender, stirring occasionally. Remove from heat. Stir in parsley, basil, oregano, garlic powder, and black pepper. Stir in eggs, ham, mozzarella cheese, and fontina cheese; set aside.

2 For crust, in prepared quiche dish arrange seven slightly flattened biscuits around edge, allowing dough to extend over side. Place remaining biscuit in bottom of dish. Pinch edges of biscuits to seal. Flatten slightly to form an even crust. Spread filling over crust.

3 Bake in a 375° oven about 25 minutes or until a knife inserted near center comes out clean. To prevent overbrowning, cover edge with foil for the last 5 to 10 minutes of baking. Let stand for 10 minutes before serving. Cut into wedges to serve. If desired, garnish with fresh basil leaves.

NUTRITION FACTS PER SERVING: 438 cal., 23 g total fat (9 g sat. fat), 110 mg chol., 1,290 mg sodium, 39 g carbo., 2 g fiber, 20 g pro. DAILY VALUES: 42% vit. C, 22% calcium, 18% iron

Pork-Spinach Pie

Pork sausage adds an extra zing of flavor to this hearty, quiche-style pie.

PREP: 15 minutes BAKE: 1 hour, 5 minutes STAND: 10 minutes OVEN: 400°/325° MAKES: 6 servings

½ of a 10-ounce package frozen chopped spinach, thawed

1 9-inch frozen unbaked deep-dish pastry shell

1 cup shredded Monterey Jack cheese or Swiss cheese (4 ounces)

8 ounces bulk pork sausage

½ cup herb-seasoned stuffing mix

3 eggs, beaten

1¼ cups milk

1 Drain spinach well, pressing out excess liquid; set aside. Place frozen pie shell in its pan on a baking sheet; do not prick. Bake in a 400° oven for 5 minutes. Remove from oven. Sprinkle cheese in bottom of partially baked pie shell; set aside. Reduce oven temperature to 325°.

2 Meanwhile, in a large skillet cook sausage until brown. Drain off fat. Stir stuffing mix and spinach into sausage in skillet. Spoon sausage mixture over cheese in pie shell. In a medium bowl stir together eggs and milk. Pour egg mixture over sausage mixture.

3 Bake, uncovered, in the 325° oven about 1 hour and 5 minutes or until a knife inserted near center comes out clean. Let stand for 10 minutes before serving. Cut into wedges to serve.

NUTRITION FACTS PER SERVING: 434 cal., 30 g total fat (12 g sat. fat), 148 mg chol., 628 mg sodium, 22 g carbo., 1 g fiber, 16 g pro. DAILY VALUES: 4% vit. C, 25% calcium, 10% iron

REAL COOKS DO MAKE QUICHE Although quiche in the United States can be traced back to the early 1940s, it wasn't until notable cooks such as Craig Claiborne and James Beard began promoting the savory custard pie in the late 1940s and 1950s that it began to grow in popularity. When Julia Child featured it on her television show in the mid-'60s, quiche became a household favorite. Julia encouraged her viewers to be creative with the seasonings and ingredients for the classic pie, and cooks have done just that ever since.

Basil-Tomato Tart

Whether you serve it for breakfast or brunch or as an appetizer at an afternoon get-together, be prepared. Your guests will ask you to share your recipe for this garden-fresh breakfast dish. (See photo, page 197.)

PREP: 40 minutes BAKE: 25 minutes OVEN: 450°/375° MAKES: 4 servings

½ of a 15-ounce package (1 crust) folded refrigerated unbaked piecrust

1½ cups shredded mozzarella cheese (6 ounces)

5 roma tomatoes (about 12 ounces)

1 cup loosely packed fresh basil (leaves only)

4 cloves garlic

⅓ cup mayonnaise or salad dressing

¼ cup grated Parmesan cheese

⅛ teaspoon ground white pepper

Snipped fresh basil (optional)

1 Unfold piecrust according to package directions. Place in a 9-inch quiche dish or glass pie plate. Flute edge. Line the unpricked pastry with a double thickness of foil. Bake in a 450° oven for 8 minutes. Remove foil. Bake for 4 to 5 minutes more or until pastry is set and dry. Remove from oven. Sprinkle with ½ cup of the mozzarella cheese. Place on a wire rack to cool slightly. Reduce oven temperature to 375°.

2 Meanwhile, cut tomatoes into ½-inch slices; drain on paper towels. Arrange tomato slices on melted cheese in pie shell. In a food processor bowl combine the 1 cup basil and the garlic; cover and process until coarsely chopped. Sprinkle mixture over tomatoes.

3 In a medium bowl stir together the remaining 1 cup mozzarella cheese, the mayonnaise, Parmesan cheese, and white pepper. Spoon cheese mixture over basil mixture, spreading to cover the top evenly.

4 Cover edge with foil. Bake in the 375° oven for 20 minutes. Uncover and bake for 5 to 10 minutes more or until top is golden brown and bubbly. Cut into wedges to serve. Serve warm. If desired, garnish with snipped basil.

NUTRITION FACTS PER SERVING: 532 cal., 38 g total fat (14 g sat. fat), 50 mg chol., 625 mg sodium, 33 g carbo., 2 g fiber, 15 g pro. DAILY VALUES: 32% vit. C, 39% calcium, 6% iron

Brunch Turnovers

These hearty ham-and-Swiss-stuffed triangles, which can be frozen up to three months, will satisfy brunch guests who desire more than a nibble of fruit and a dainty pastry. (See photo, page 194.)

PREP: 20 minutes BAKE: 25 minutes OVEN: 400° MAKES: 18 turnovers

1	17¼-ounce package frozen puff pastry (2 sheets)	⅔	cup finely chopped cooked ham (3 ounces)
2	tablespoons finely chopped onion	1	tablespoon snipped fresh parsley
1	tablespoon butter or margarine	½	teaspoon dried dillweed or 1 teaspoon snipped fresh dill
1	egg, beaten		Dash garlic powder
1	cup shredded Swiss cheese (4 ounces)		Dash ground black pepper

1 Let frozen puff pastry stand at room temperature about 1 hour or until thawed. In a small saucepan cook onion in hot butter until tender. For filling, in a medium bowl stir together egg, Swiss cheese, ham, parsley, dillweed, garlic powder, and pepper. Stir in onion mixture; set aside.

2 On a lightly floured surface roll each pastry sheet slightly to a 10½-inch square; cut into 3½-inch squares (18 total). Place 1 packed tablespoon of the filling just off center on each square. Moisten edges with water; fold in half diagonally. Seal edges by pressing with tines of a fork or fingers. Place turnovers 2 inches apart on an ungreased baking sheet.

3 Bake in a 400° oven about 25 minutes or until golden brown. Serve hot.

NUTRITION FACTS PER TURNOVER: 162 cal., 12 g total fat (1 g sat. fat), 21 mg chol., 195 mg sodium, 10 g carbo., 0 g fiber, 4 g pro. DAILY VALUES: 1% vit. C, 6% calcium, 1% iron

TO MAKE AHEAD: Prepare and bake turnovers; cool. Pack in an airtight freezer container; seal and freeze for up to 3 months. To serve, place frozen turnovers on baking sheet. Bake in a 375° oven about 15 minutes or until heated through.

Stuffed French Toast

Make breakfast an occasion. This medley of flavors—apricot, vanilla, walnuts, and nutmeg—is certainly not the plain French toast of yesteryear. (See photo, page 196.)

PREP: 20 minutes COOK: 4 minutes per batch MAKES: 10 to 12 slices

1	8-ounce package cream cheese, softened
1	12-ounce jar apricot preserves (about 1 cup)
1½	teaspoons vanilla
½	cup chopped walnuts
1	16-ounce loaf baguette-style French bread

4	eggs
1	cup whipping cream
½	teaspoon ground nutmeg
½	cup orange juice
	Fresh or frozen raspberries (optional)

1 In a small mixing bowl beat together cream cheese, 2 tablespoons of the apricot preserves, and 1 teaspoon of the vanilla with an electric mixer on medium speed until fluffy. Stir in walnuts; set aside.

2 Cut bread into ten to twelve 1½-inch slices. Cut a pocket in the top of each bread slice. Fill each pocket with about 1½ tablespoons of the cream cheese mixture.

3 In a medium mixing bowl beat together eggs, whipping cream, nutmeg, and the remaining ½ teaspoon vanilla with a wire whisk or rotary beater. Using tongs, dip filled bread slices in the egg mixture, being careful not to squeeze out filling. Cook on a lightly greased griddle over medium heat about 2 minutes on each side or until golden brown. Keep warm in a 300° oven while cooking remaining slices.

4 Meanwhile, in a small saucepan heat and stir the remaining apricot preserves and the orange juice over medium heat until preserves are melted. To serve, drizzle apricot mixture over hot French toast. If desired, top with raspberries.

NUTRITION FACTS PER SLICE: 452 cal., 24 g total fat (12 g sat. fat), 143 mg chol., 388 mg sodium, 49 g carbo., 2 g fiber, 10 g pro. DAILY VALUES: 15% vit. C, 9% calcium, 12% iron

Lower-Fat Stuffed French Toast: Prepare as directed, except use reduced-fat cream cheese (Neufchâtel); substitute 1 cup refrigerated or frozen egg product, thawed, for the whole eggs; and use fat-free milk instead of the whipping cream.

Oatmeal Waffles

Enjoy these hearty waffles with lots of fresh fruit for Sunday brunch.

PREP: 10 minutes BAKE: per waffle baker directions MAKES: twelve 4-inch waffles

1½	cups all-purpose flour	1½	cups milk
1	cup quick-cooking rolled oats	⅓	cup butter or margarine, melted
1	tablespoon baking powder	2	tablespoons brown sugar
½	teaspoon ground cinnamon		Powdered sugar (optional)
¼	teaspoon salt		Fresh fruit (optional)
2	eggs, slightly beaten		Vanilla yogurt (optional)

1 In a medium bowl stir together flour, oats, baking powder, cinnamon, and salt. Make a well in the center of flour mixture; set aside.

2 In a medium mixing bowl stir together eggs, milk, melted butter, and brown sugar with a wire whisk. Add egg mixture all at once to flour mixture. Stir until combined.

3 Pour about 1¼ cups of the batter onto grids of a preheated, lightly greased waffle baker. Close lid quickly; do not open during baking. Bake according to manufacturer's directions. When done, use a fork to lift waffle off grid. Repeat with remaining batter. If desired, sprinkle with powdered sugar and top with fruit and/or yogurt.

NUTRITION FACTS PER WAFFLE: 168 cal., 8 g total fat (4 g sat. fat), 52 mg chol., 231 mg sodium, 20 g carbo., 1 g fiber, 5 g pro. DAILY VALUES: 11% calcium, 7% iron

Baked Cranberry-Apple Pancake

The beauty of this crowd-serving pancake is it bakes in the oven,
so there's no tending the griddle.

PREP: 15 minutes BAKE: 15 minutes COOL: 5 minutes OVEN: 350° MAKES: 8 servings

2 tablespoons butter or margarine	4 teaspoons granulated sugar
¼ cup dried cranberries	½ teaspoon baking powder
1 small apple, peeled, cored, and chopped	½ teaspoon baking soda
¼ cup packed brown sugar	⅛ teaspoon salt
1 teaspoon finely shredded orange peel (set aside)	1 egg, beaten
¼ cup orange juice	½ cup buttermilk
¾ cup all-purpose flour	4 teaspoons cooking oil

1 Place butter in a 9-inch pie plate. Place pie plate in oven while preheating to 350°. Remove pie plate from oven when butter is just melted. Stir in dried cranberries and apple.

2 Meanwhile, in a small saucepan stir together brown sugar and orange juice. Bring to boiling; reduce heat to medium. Boil gently, uncovered, for 5 minutes. Pour brown sugar mixture over fruit in pie plate.

3 In a medium bowl stir together flour, granulated sugar, baking powder, baking soda, and salt. Make a well in center of flour mixture; set aside. In a small bowl stir together egg, buttermilk, oil, and reserved orange peel. Add egg mixture all at once to flour mixture. Stir just until combined. Pour batter evenly over fruit mixture in pie plate.

4 Bake, uncovered, in a 350° oven about 15 minutes or until top springs back when lightly touched. Cool in pie plate on a wire rack for 5 minutes. Carefully invert pancake onto a serving platter. Cut in wedges to serve. Serve warm.

NUTRITION FACTS PER SERVING: 151 cal., 6 g total fat (2 g sat. fat), 34 mg chol., 195 mg sodium, 22 g carbo., 1 g fiber, 3 g pro. DAILY VALUES: 8% vit. C, 4% calcium, 5% iron

Blueberry Cheesecake Flapjacks

Frozen berries will deepen the color of the syrup in these special breakfast or brunch treats.

PREP: 25 minutes COOK: 4 minutes per batch MAKES: 4 to 5 servings

1	8-ounce package cream cheese, softened	½	cup graham cracker crumbs
½	of an 8-ounce container frozen whipped dessert topping, thawed	1	tablespoon sugar
		1	teaspoon baking powder
1	cup pure maple syrup or maple-flavored syrup	½	teaspoon baking soda
		¼	teaspoon salt
1½	cups fresh or frozen blueberries, thawed	2	eggs, beaten
		1¼	cups buttermilk
1	cup all-purpose flour	¼	cup butter or margarine, melted

1 In a medium mixing bowl beat cream cheese with an electric mixer on medium speed for 30 seconds. Beat in whipped topping just until smooth. Cover and chill until serving time.

2 Meanwhile, for blueberry syrup, in a small saucepan stir together maple syrup and ½ cup of the blueberries. Heat just to boiling; remove from heat.

3 In a large bowl stir together flour, graham cracker crumbs, sugar, baking powder, baking soda, and salt. Make a well in center of flour mixture; set aside. In medium bowl stir together eggs, buttermilk, and melted butter. Add egg mixture all at once to flour mixture. Stir just until moistened. Gently stir in the remaining 1 cup blueberries.

4 Heat a lightly greased griddle or heavy skillet over medium heat until a few drops of water dance across the surface. For each flapjack, pour about ¼ cup batter onto the hot griddle. Cook over medium heat about 2 minutes on each side or until flapjacks are golden brown, turning to cook second sides when flapjacks have bubbly surfaces and edges are slightly dry.

5 For each serving, stack three or four flapjacks, spreading a little cream cheese mixture between each. Drizzle with blueberry syrup. Cover and store any remaining cream cheese mixture in the refrigerator for up to 1 week.

NUTRITION FACTS PER SERVING: 558 cal., 25 g total fat (15 g sat. fat), 161 mg chol., 751 mg sodium, 73 g carbo., 2 g fiber, 12 g pro. DAILY VALUES: 11% vit. C, 18% calcium, 20% iron

Jiffy Orange Pancakes

For lower fat and convenience, Test Kitchen home economists tried using milk in this pancake. The result was one tough flapjack. For a lighter, fluffier pancake, their recommendation is to use the half-and-half or light cream.

PREP: 10 minutes COOK: 2 minutes per batch OVEN: 300° MAKES: 4 to 5 servings

1	egg, beaten	1	cup packaged regular pancake mix (not complete mix)
1	cup half-and-half or light cream		
1	6-ounce can frozen orange juice concentrate, thawed (¾ cup)	½	cup sugar
		¼	cup butter or margarine, cut up

1 In a large bowl stir together egg, half-and-half, and ¼ cup of the orange juice concentrate. Add pancake mix. Stir just until combined but still slightly lumpy.

2 Heat a lightly greased griddle or heavy skillet over medium heat until a few drops of water dance across the surface. For each pancake, pour about 2 tablespoons of batter onto the hot griddle. Cook over medium heat for 1 to 2 minutes on each side or until pancakes are golden brown, turning to cook second sides when pancakes have bubbly surfaces and edges are slightly dry. Serve immediately, or place in a lightly covered ovenproof dish and keep warm in a 300° oven.

3 For sauce, in a small saucepan stir together sugar, butter, and the remaining ½ cup orange juice concentrate. Bring mixture to boiling, stirring occasionally. Serve warm sauce over pancakes.

NUTRITION FACTS PER SERVING: 480 cal., 21 g total fat (12 g sat. fat), 108 mg chol., 533 mg sodium, 67 g carbo., 1 g fiber, 8 g pro. DAILY VALUES: 134% vit. C, 19% calcium, 7% iron

---

PERFECT PANCAKES Pancakes are easy to make and require no tricky techniques. These pointers only make them better:

1 Begin by mixing all of the dry ingredients in a mixing bowl and stirring them until they're well combined. Beat eggs and other liquid ingredients in a separate bowl.

2 Great pancakes spring from a griddle or skillet that heats evenly and is lightly greased. Put a small amount of shortening on a pastry brush or paper towel and rub it across the griddle surface before heating. Or give the cold pan a quick spray with nonstick cooking spray. If your griddle or skillet has a nonstick surface, it may not be necessary to grease it.

3 Test the griddle for readiness by dripping a few drops of water on it. If the water dances over the surface, the griddle is ready.

4 Don't crowd your griddle; pancakes will cook better and look better if they don't run together.

5 Pancakes are ready to flip when the undersides are golden brown (use the edge of a thin spatula to check) and the top surfaces are covered evenly with tiny, unbroken bubbles.

6 Pancakes are best piping hot. Keep the first batch warm in a 300° oven while you cook the rest. Loosely cover with aluminum foil.

Sweet Cheese Blintzes

*Not in the mood for eggs? A delicate alternative is a tender, golden,
very thin pancake enclosing a sweet filling.*

PREP: 40 minutes COOK: 45 seconds per blintz MAKES: 10 to 12 blintzes

1	8-ounce carton mascarpone or cottage cheese
1	tablespoon honey
1	tablespoon milk
½	teaspoon finely shredded lemon peel or lemon verbena
¼	teaspoon anise seeds, crushed
¾	cup all-purpose flour
½	teaspoon baking powder
2	egg whites

¾	cup milk
1	egg yolk
2	teaspoons walnut oil or hazelnut oil
1½	teaspoons granulated sugar
½	teaspoon vanilla
	Nonstick cooking spray
1	cup green grapes, sliced
	Powdered sugar

1 For filling, in a small mixing bowl beat mascarpone cheese, honey, the
1 tablespoon milk, lemon peel, and anise seeds with an electric mixer on
medium speed until combined. Cover and set aside.

2 For blintzes, in a small bowl stir together flour and baking powder; set aside.
In another small mixing bowl beat egg whites with clean beaters of electric mixer
on medium speed until soft peaks form (tips curl). In a large mixing bowl beat
together the ¾ cup milk, egg yolk, walnut oil, granulated sugar, and vanilla until
well combined. Add flour mixture to milk mixture and beat just until mixture is
smooth. Fold in beaten egg whites (texture should be that of a milk shake).

3 Coat a nonstick griddle or skillet with nonstick cooking spray. Heat over
medium heat for 1 to 2 minutes. For each blintz, pour about 2 tablespoons
batter onto hot griddle. Quickly spread batter to a 4- to 5-inch circle. Cook blintz
pancake about 30 seconds or until light brown. Gently turn with a spatula; cook
second side for 15 seconds. Invert blintz onto a plate lined with paper towels.
Repeat with remaining batter to make 10 to 12 blintzes. (You may cook 3 or
4 blintzes at a time in a large skillet.) Place a dry paper towel between each
layer of blintzes. Cover and keep warm.

4 To serve, spoon 1 slightly rounded tablespoon of cheese mixture across
pancake just below center. Fold bottom of pancake over filling. Fold in sides; roll
up. Arrange blintzes, seam-side down, on dessert plates or in a serving bowl. Top
with grapes. Sprinkle with powdered sugar. Serve warm or at room temperature.

NUTRITION FACTS PER BLINTZ: 150 cal., 10 g total fat (5 g sat. fat), 43 mg chol., 40 mg sodium, 12 g carbo.,
0 g fiber, 6 g pro. DAILY VALUES: 2% vit. C, 3% calcium, 3% iron

Hot Barley Cereal

Mild in taste and rich in niacin, thiamine, selenium, and zinc,
barley makes a great grain for breakfast.

START TO FINISH: 15 minutes MAKES: 1 serving

½ cup cooked barley	1 tablespoon butter or margarine (optional)
⅓ cup milk	
1 tablespoon maple syrup or honey	

1 In a small saucepan stir together cooked barley and milk. Bring to boiling; reduce heat. Simmer, uncovered, for 10 minutes, stirring occasionally. Stir in maple syrup.

2 To serve, spoon hot cereal into a bowl. If desired, top with butter.

Basic Barley: In a saucepan bring 3 cups water to boiling. Stir in ¾ cup pearl barley. Return to boiling; reduce heat. Simmer, covered, about 45 minutes or until the barley is tender. Drain, if necessary. Makes about 3 cups cooked barley.

Quick-Cooking Barley: In a saucepan bring 2 cups water to boiling. Stir in 1¼ cups quick-cooking barley. Return to boiling; reduce heat. Simmer, covered, for 10 to 12 minutes or until tender. Drain, if necessary. Makes about 3 cups cooked barley.

NUTRITION FACTS PER SERVING: 189 cal., 2 g total fat (1 g sat. fat), 6 mg chol., 44 mg sodium, 39 g carbo., 3 g fiber, 4 g pro. DAILY VALUES: 1% vit. C, 12% calcium, 7% iron

PEARL OF A GRAIN The cultivation of barley dates back to ancient Mesopotamia, making it one of the oldest grains still grown. With a history this epic, you know these pearls of protein are good. Try barley in casseroles, salads, soups, and pilafs. For a cozy, nutritious cereal, stir a little maple syrup into some hot cooked barley.

Taffy Apple Doughnuts

Doughnut-on-a-stick? Absolutely! Not only are they fun to make and eat this way, but a skewer turns out to be the perfect handle for these sweet and sticky delights.

PREP: 15 minutes COOK: 3 minutes per batch MAKES: about 20 doughnuts

2	cups all-purpose flour	½	cup milk
⅓	cup granulated sugar	½	cup apple juice
1½	teaspoons baking powder	3	tablespoons butter or margarine, melted
1	teaspoon apple pie spice		Cooking oil for deep-fat frying
½	teaspoon salt	1	cup maple-flavored syrup
¼	teaspoon baking soda	¾	cup packed brown sugar
1	egg, beaten		Wooden skewers or sticks
1	cup chopped peeled apple	1½	cups finely chopped nuts

1 In a large bowl stir together flour, granulated sugar, baking powder, apple pie spice, salt, and baking soda. Make a well in center of flour mixture; set aside. In a small bowl stir together egg, apple, milk, apple juice, and melted butter. Add apple mixture all at once to flour mixture. Stir just until moistened.

2 In large saucepan or deep-fat fryer, heat 3 to 4 inches of oil to 365°. Drop batter by a well-rounded tablespoon into hot oil. Fry three or four doughnuts at a time, about 3 minutes or until brown, turning once. Using a slotted spoon or tongs, remove doughnuts and drain on paper towels. Repeat with remaining batter.

3 In a small saucepan stir together maple syrup and brown sugar. Bring just to boiling; remove from heat. Insert a wooden skewer into each doughnut. Dip each doughnut into syrup mixture; sprinkle with nuts. Cool on a wire rack.

NUTRITION FACTS PER DOUGHNUT: 264 cal., 14 g total fat (3 g sat. fat), 16 mg chol., 135 mg sodium, 35 g carbo., 1 g fiber, 3 g pro. DAILY VALUES: 3% vit. A, 1% vit. C, 6% calcium, 7% iron

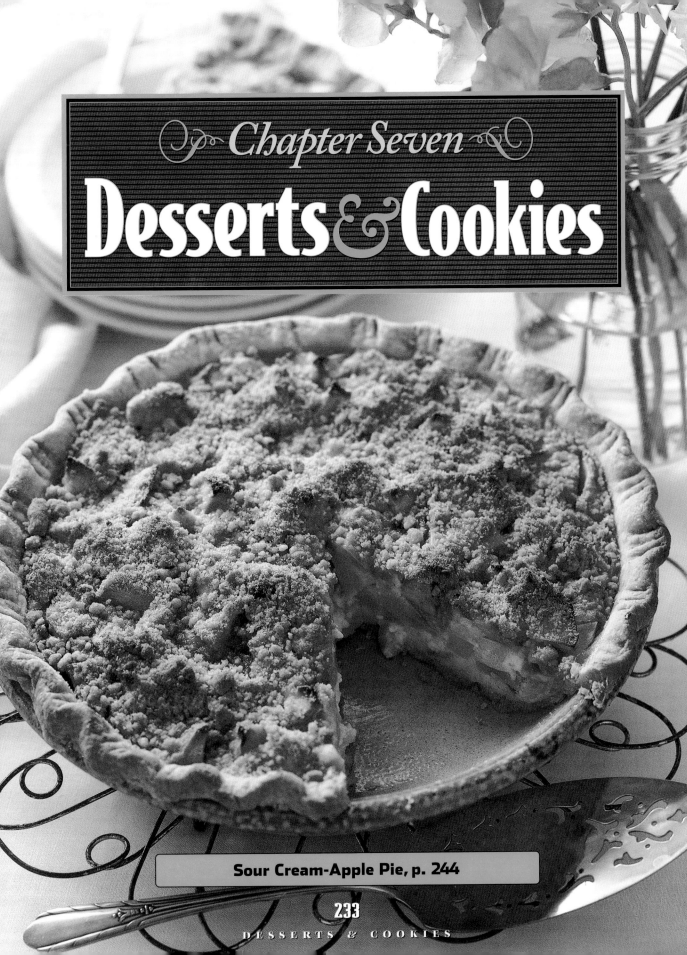

Chapter Seven
Desserts & Cookies

Sour Cream-Apple Pie, p. 244

Mocha Truffle Cookies, p. 276

Banana-Chocolate Bites, p. 268

Wintery Ice Cream Balls, p. 267

Top-of-the-World Brownies, p. 271

Cherry Cordial Brownie Torte, p. 253

Banana Split Trifles, p. 262

DESSERTS & COOKIES

▲ White Chocolate Fudge, p. 279

▲ Chocolate-Pecan Chess Pie, p. 241

▲ Blueberry-Citrus Cake, p. 249

▲ Brownie Meringues, p. 273

Chocolate-Pecan Chess Pie

This cross between a chess pie and a pecan pie—with some chocolate sprinkled in for good measure—is a Southern dessert dream. (See photo, page 240.)

PREP: 25 minutes BAKE: 52 minutes OVEN: 450°/350° MAKES: 10 servings

1	recipe Pastry for Single-Crust Pie	3	tablespoons butter or margarine, melted and cooled
1¼	cups sugar	1	teaspoon vanilla
4	teaspoons cornmeal	½	cup pecans, toasted and chopped
4	eggs	½	cup miniature semisweet chocolate pieces
⅓	cup half-and-half or light cream		

1 Prepare Pastry for Single-Crust Pie. On a lightly floured surface use your hands to slightly flatten dough. Roll dough from center to edges into a circle about 12 inches in diameter. Transfer pastry to a 9-inch pie plate. (Do not prick.) Trim pastry to ½ inch beyond edge of pie plate. Fold under extra pastry. Flute edges high. If desired, press the tines of a fork against fluted edges at evenly spaced intervals. Line pastry with a double thickness of foil. Bake in a 450° oven for 8 minutes. Remove foil; bake for 4 to 5 minutes more or until set and dry but not brown.

2 Meanwhile, for filling, in a small bowl stir together sugar and cornmeal; set aside. In a large mixing bowl beat eggs with an electric mixer on medium speed for 1 minute. Stir in the sugar mixture. Using a wooden spoon or rubber spatula, gradually stir in half-and-half, melted butter, and vanilla. Stir in pecans.

3 Place the partially baked pastry shell on the oven rack. Sprinkle chocolate pieces into bottom of pastry shell. Carefully pour filling into pastry shell.

4 To prevent overbrowning, cover edge of pie with foil (being careful not to let the foil touch the filling). Reduce oven temperature to 350°. Bake for 30 minutes. Remove foil. Bake for 10 to 15 minutes more or until center appears nearly set when shaken. Cool in pie plate on a wire rack. Refrigerate within 2 hours; cover for longer storage.

Pastry for Single-Crust Pie: In a medium bowl stir together 1¼ cups all-purpose flour and ¼ teaspoon salt. Using a pastry blender, cut in ⅓ cup shortening until pieces are the size of small peas. Using a total of 4 to 5 tablespoons cold water, sprinkle 1 tablespoon water over part of the mixture; gently toss with a fork. Push to side of bowl. Repeat until all is moistened. Form into a ball.

NUTRITION FACTS PER SERVING: 365 cal., 20 g total fat (4 g sat. fat), 90 mg chol., 123 mg sodium, 43 g carbo., 1 g fiber, 5 g pro. DAILY VALUES: 2% calcium, 8% iron

Apple-Berry Pie

A bit like a pie (though far easier to make) and a bit like a cobbler—that's the fun of this homey baked fruit dessert. Serve it slightly warm and top it with a scoop of vanilla ice cream or a spoonful of cream. Your guests will eat it with gusto!

PREP: 20 minutes BAKE: 40 minutes OVEN: 350° MAKES: 8 servings

1	pound baking apples, quartered and cored (3 medium)	½	cup all-purpose flour
1	cup cranberries	½	cup butter, melted
¼	cup walnuts	⅓	cup sugar
½	cup sugar	1½	teaspoons finely shredded orange peel
¼	cup raisins	½	teaspoon vanilla
1	tablespoon finely shredded orange peel	⅛	teaspoon salt
1	egg		Several drops almond extract

1 Generously butter a 9-inch pie plate; set aside. Place unpeeled apples in a food processor bowl. Cover and process until coarsely chopped. Remove from bowl. Repeat with the cranberries until coarsely chopped, then the walnuts. (Or coarsely chop ingredients by hand.)

2 In a medium bowl stir together apples, cranberries, walnuts, the ½ cup sugar, the raisins, and the 1 tablespoon orange peel. Spread mixture evenly in the bottom of the prepared pie plate; set aside.

3 For topping, in the food processor bowl or a small mixing bowl combine egg, flour, melted butter, the ⅓ cup sugar, the 1½ teaspoons orange peel, the vanilla, salt, and almond extract. Cover and process or beat with an electric mixer on medium speed until smooth. Spread batter evenly over fruit mixture.

4 Bake in a 350° oven about 40 minutes or until topping is brown and a wooden toothpick inserted near center comes out clean. Cool slightly in pie plate on a wire rack. Serve warm.

NUTRITION FACTS PER SERVING: 290 cal., 15 g total fat (8 g sat. fat), 57 mg chol., 159 mg sodium, 40 g carbo., 2 g fiber, 2 g pro. DAILY VALUES: 9% vit. C, 1% calcium, 4% iron

TO MAKE AHEAD: Bake pie as directed and cool completely. Cover with foil and chill for up to 24 hours. To reheat, bake, covered, in a 350° oven about 20 minutes or until warm.

Pumpkin Pecan Pie

The pleasant dilemma of Thanksgiving: to make pumpkin or pecan pie?
Enjoy both in one recipe, which translates to twice the taste, half the work.

PREP: 25 minutes BAKE: 50 minutes OVEN: 350° MAKES: 8 servings

3	eggs, slightly beaten	³/₄	teaspoon ground cinnamon
1	15-ounce can pumpkin	1	unbaked 9-inch piecrust
³/₄	cup sugar	1	cup chopped pecans
¹/₂	cup dark-colored corn syrup		Whipped cream (optional)
1	teaspoon vanilla		

1 In a medium bowl stir together eggs, pumpkin, sugar, corn syrup, vanilla, and cinnamon. Pour pumpkin mixture into piecrust. Sprinkle with pecans.

2 Bake in 350° oven for 50 to 55 minutes or until knife inserted off center comes out clean. Cool in pie plate on a wire rack. Refrigerate within 2 hours; cover for longer storage. If desired, serve with whipped cream.

NUTRITION FACTS PER SERVING: 408 cal., 20 g total fat (4 g sat. fat), 80 mg chol., 124 mg sodium, 54 g carbo., 3 g fiber, 6 g pro. DAILY VALUES: 4% vit. C, 4% calcium, 13% iron

Sour Cream-Apple Pie

The Pennsylvania Dutch, natives of central Pennsylvania who have German origin, prefer making this streusel-topped pie with Summer Duchess apples just before the apples turn red. (See photo, page 233.)

PREP: 20 minutes BAKE: 45 minutes OVEN: 400° MAKES: 8 to 10 servings

1	egg, slightly beaten		4	cups coarsely chopped, peeled tart apples
1	8-ounce carton dairy sour cream		1	unbaked 9-inch piecrust
¾	cup granulated sugar		½	cup all-purpose flour
2	tablespoons all-purpose flour		⅓	cup packed brown sugar
1	teaspoon vanilla		2	tablespoons butter or margarine
¼	teaspoon salt			

1 In a large bowl stir together egg, sour cream, granulated sugar, the 2 tablespoons flour, the vanilla, and salt. Stir in chopped apples. Pour mixture into the unbaked piecrust. Cover edge of piecrust with foil. Bake in a 400° oven for 25 minutes.

2 Meanwhile, in a small bowl stir together the ½ cup flour and the brown sugar. Using a pastry blender, cut in butter until crumbly. Remove foil from pie. Sprinkle brown sugar mixture over pie. Bake about 20 minutes more or until top is golden brown. Cool in pie plate on a wire rack. Refrigerate within 2 hours; cover for longer storage.

NUTRITION FACTS PER SERVING: 433 cal., 19 g total fat (8 g sat. fat), 47 mg chol., 204 mg sodium, 64 g carbo., 3 g fiber, 5 g pro. DAILY VALUES: 6% vit. C, 5% calcium, 9% iron

PIECRUST ON THE DOUBLE When cooks in days gone by wanted to make pies, they had no choice but to make pastry from scratch. Today you can make your favorite recipe for piecrust or purchase one of several easy-does-it options. In your supermarket refrigerated dairy case look for folded refrigerated piecrust. Each package contains two rounds—enough for two 9-inch single-crust pies or one 9-inch double-crust pie. In the freezer case you'll find frozen unbaked pie shells. For the recipes in this book, be sure to choose the deep-dish shells. In the baking aisle look for a piecrust mix.

Tiny Apricot Cheesecake Tarts

For understated after-dinner elegance, present an array of diminutive desserts with espresso. As a complement to the tarts, cut 1-inch rounds from purchased pound cake slices; top each with whipped cream, a fresh raspberry, and mint leaf.

PREP: 35 minutes CHILL: 2 to 4 hours STAND: 30 minutes MAKES: 15 tarts

3 ounces bittersweet or semisweet chocolate, cut up	2 tablespoons dairy sour cream
½ teaspoon shortening (no substitutes)	2 tablespoons powdered sugar
1 2.1-ounce package baked miniature phyllo shells (fifteen 1¾-inch shells)	2 teaspoons apricot brandy or apricot nectar
1 3-ounce package cream cheese, softened	2 to 3 dried apricots, cut into thin strips
	Bittersweet or semisweet chocolate, grated (optional)

1 In a small saucepan stir the cut-up chocolate and shortening over low heat until melted. Remove from heat. Brush the bottom and inside edges of each phyllo shell evenly with melted chocolate mixture. Chill phyllo shells about 20 minutes or until chocolate is set.

2 Meanwhile, in a small bowl stir together cream cheese, sour cream, and powdered sugar until smooth. Stir in apricot brandy. Spoon 1 rounded teaspoon of cream cheese mixture into each shell. Place a strip of dried apricot on top of each. Cover loosely and chill for 2 to 4 hours.

3 Let tarts stand at room temperature about 30 minutes before serving. If desired, sprinkle with grated chocolate.

NUTRITION FACTS PER TART: 82 cal., 5 g total fat (3 g sat. fat), 7 mg chol., 28 mg sodium, 7 g carbo., 0 g fiber, 1 g pro. DAILY VALUES: 3% vit. A, 1% calcium, 2% iron

Double-Chocolate Buttermilk Loaf

*Although this very rich loaf could be served as a sweet bread, it is more like a cake.
Serve it topped with whipped cream or crème fraîche.*

PREP: 25 minutes BAKE: 1 hour COOL: 1 hour OVEN: 350° MAKES: 1 loaf (16 servings)

1²/₃	cups all-purpose flour	1	cup sugar
²/₃	cup unsweetened cocoa powder	2	eggs
¹/₂	teaspoon baking powder	1	cup buttermilk
¹/₂	teaspoon baking soda	¹/₃	cup chopped pecans or walnuts
¹/₂	teaspoon salt	¹/₄	cup miniature semisweet chocolate pieces
¹/₂	cup butter, softened		

1 Grease bottom and ¹/₂ inch up the sides of an 8×4×2-inch loaf pan; set aside. In a medium bowl stir together flour, cocoa powder, baking powder, baking soda, and salt; set aside.

2 In a large mixing bowl beat butter with an electric mixer on medium speed for 30 seconds. Add sugar and beat until fluffy. Beat in eggs until combined. Alternately add flour mixture and buttermilk, beating just until combined after each addition. Stir in pecans. Spoon half of the batter into prepared pan. Sprinkle with chocolate pieces. Spoon on remaining batter.

3 Bake in a 350° oven for 60 to 65 minutes or until a wooden toothpick inserted near center comes out clean. Cool in pan on a wire rack for 10 minutes. Remove loaf from pan. Cool completely on a wire rack.

NUTRITION FACTS PER SERVING: 200 cal., 9 g total fat (4 g sat. fat), 43 mg chol., 199 mg sodium, 26 g carbo., 0 g fiber, 4 g pro. DAILY VALUES: 6% calcium, 8% iron

Sundae Pound Cake

Chocolate lovers: Try this cake and claim your passion! The cake itself is intense, but the rich, dark glaze drives this recipe over the edge to chocolate bliss.

PREP: 20 minutes BAKE: 50 minutes COOL: 1 hour OVEN: 325° MAKES: 12 servings

½	cup butter
3	eggs
⅔	cup dairy sour cream
½	of a 4-ounce bar sweet baking chocolate, cut up
2	tablespoons milk
1	tablespoon water
1⅓	cups all-purpose flour
¼	teaspoon baking powder

⅛	teaspoon baking soda
1¼	cups sugar
1	teaspoon vanilla
1	teaspoon finely shredded lemon peel
1	recipe Dark Chocolate Glaze
	Fresh strawberries (optional)
	Vanilla ice cream (optional)

1 Let butter, eggs, and sour cream stand at room temperature for 30 minutes. Grease and flour a 6-cup fluted tube pan or 9×5×3-inch loaf pan; set aside.

2 In a heavy small saucepan combine sweet baking chocolate, milk, and water, stirring over low heat until chocolate is melted and mixture is smooth. Remove from heat; cool slightly. In a small bowl stir together flour, baking powder, and baking soda; set aside.

3 In a large mixing bowl beat butter with an electric mixer on medium to high speed until softened. Gradually add sugar, beating until very light and fluffy. Add vanilla. Add eggs, one at a time, beating on low to medium speed for 1 minute after each addition. Alternately add flour mixture and sour cream, beating on low speed just until combined. Stir in peel. Spoon half of the batter into prepared pan, spreading evenly. Drizzle with chocolate mixture. Spoon on remaining batter, spreading evenly.

4 Bake in a 325° oven for 50 to 60 minutes or until a wooden toothpick inserted near center comes out clean. Cool in pan on a wire rack for 10 minutes. Remove cake from pan. Cool completely on a wire rack.

5 Spoon Dark Chocolate Glaze over cake. If desired, serve with fresh strawberries and vanilla ice cream.

Dark Chocolate Glaze: In a small saucepan combine 1 ounce unsweetened chocolate, 2 tablespoons butter, and 2 tablespoons milk, stirring over low heat until chocolate is melted. Remove from heat. Stir in 1 cup sifted powdered sugar and ½ teaspoon vanilla. Beat until smooth.

NUTRITION FACTS PER SERVING: 329 cal., 17 g total fat (10 g sat. fat), 85 mg chol., 143 mg sodium, 44 g carbo., 1 g fiber, 4 g pro. DAILY VALUES: 3% calcium, 7% iron

Grilled Cinnamon Pound Cake

Not intended just for meat or fish, the grill becomes a versatile tool when you need a quick and innovative dessert.

PREP: 20 minutes GRILL: 2 minutes MAKES: 6 servings

1	16-ounce carton frozen sliced strawberries in syrup, thawed and undrained	⅓	cup whipping cream, whipped
1	10¾-ounce frozen pound cake, thawed		Ground cinnamon
2	tablespoons butter, softened		Toasted slivered almonds
½	teaspoon ground cinnamon		

1 Place undrained strawberries in a blender container. Cover and blend until smooth. Chill until ready to serve.

2 Cut thin slices off each end of pound cake. Cut remaining cake into six thick slices. In a small bowl stir together butter and the ½ teaspoon cinnamon. Spread butter-cinnamon mixture over one side of each cake slice.

3 Grill cake slices, buttered side down, on the rack of an uncovered grill directly over medium coals for 1 to 2 minutes or until golden brown. Turn and grill 1 to 2 minutes more. (Or cook cake on a griddle over medium heat for 1 to 2 minutes per side.)

4 To serve, divide strawberries among six dessert dishes. Top each with a pound cake slice, buttered side up. Spoon on whipped cream and sprinkle with additional cinnamon. Sprinkle with almonds.

NUTRITION FACTS PER SERVING: 360 cal., 20 g total fat (12 g sat. fat), 84 mg chol., 223 mg sodium, 44 g carbo., 2 g fiber, 3 g pro. DAILY VALUES: 13% vit. A, 53% vit. C, 3% calcium, 7% iron

MEASURING UP Making desserts that look and taste their best is achieved by correctly and consistently measuring ingredients. Follow these hints to measure ingredients that are commonly used in dessert recipes:

Flour: Proper measuring of flour is critical. Too much flour can cause baked goods to be dry or sauces to become too thick. To measure flour, stir it in the bag or canister to lighten it. Gently spoon flour into a dry measuring cup or a measuring spoon, filling it to overflowing. Scrape a metal spatula across the edge of the measure to level the flour. With the exception of cake flour, sifting is not necessary.

Sugar: Spoon granulated or powdered sugar into a dry measuring cup to overflowing; level it using the method for flour. Press brown sugar firmly into a dry measure until it holds the shape of the cup, then turn out the brown sugar.

Shortening: Measure solid shortening by pressing it firmly into a dry measuring cup or spoon with a rubber scraper. Level the shortening with the straight edge of a knife.

Blueberry-Citrus Cake

Mildly sweet blueberries are colorful foils to lemon and orange flavors. Until it's time for their starring role, store the berries in a single layer, loosely covered. Use within a day or two of purchase. (See photo, page 240.)

PREP: 25 minutes BAKE: 35 minutes COOL: 1 hour OVEN: 350° MAKES: 12 servings

1	package lemon cake mix (for 2-layer cake)	3	eggs
1	tablespoon finely shredded orange peel (set aside)	1½	cups fresh or frozen blueberries
½	cup orange juice	1	tablespoon finely shredded lemon peel
½	cup water	1	recipe Citrus Frosting
⅓	cup cooking oil		Orange peel curls (optional)

1 Grease and lightly flour two 8×1½-inch or 9×1½-inch round baking pans; set aside. In a large mixing bowl combine cake mix, orange juice, water, oil, and eggs. Beat with an electric mixer on low speed for 30 seconds. Beat on medium speed for 2 minutes. By hand, gently fold in blueberries, lemon peel, and finely shredded orange peel. Divide batter equally between prepared pans, spreading evenly.

2 Bake in a 350° oven for 35 to 40 minutes or until a wooden toothpick inserted near centers comes out clean. Cool in pans on wire racks for 10 minutes. Remove cakes from pans. Cool thoroughly on wire racks. Fill and frost with Citrus Frosting. If desired, garnish with orange peel curls. Store frosted cake, covered, in refrigerator.

Citrus Frosting: Finely shred 2 tablespoons orange peel and 1 tablespoon lemon peel; set aside. In a medium mixing bowl beat one 3-ounce package softened cream cheese and ¼ cup softened butter with an electric mixer on low to medium speed until fluffy. Add 3 cups sifted powdered sugar and 2 tablespoons orange juice. Beat until combined. In a chilled small mixing bowl beat 1 cup whipping cream with chilled beaters of an electric mixer on medium speed until soft peaks form; add to cream cheese mixture. Add the orange peel and lemon peel. Beat on low speed until combined.

NUTRITION FACTS PER SERVING: 493 cal., 25 g total fat (11 g sat. fat), 98 mg chol., 345 mg sodium, 66 g carbo., 1 g fiber, 4 g pro. DAILY VALUES: 12% vit. C, 9% calcium, 5% iron

Coconut-Orange Cake

A flourish of frosting gives a cake a luscious look. To keep the serving plate free of frosting, place narrow strips of waxed paper around the edge of the plate; then position the cake on top. Once you have frosted the cake, pull out the strips.

PREP: 30 minutes BAKE: 30 minutes COOL: 1 hour OVEN: 350° MAKES: 12 servings

1 package white cake mix (for 2-layer cake)	½ cup flaked coconut
1 cup milk	1 package fluffy white frosting mix (for 2-layer cake)
2 egg whites	⅓ cup flaked coconut or large coconut flakes, toasted
½ of a 6-ounce can frozen orange juice concentrate, thawed (⅓ cup)	

1 Grease and flour two 9×1½-inch round baking pans; set aside. In a large mixing bowl combine cake mix, milk, egg whites, and orange juice concentrate. Beat with an electric mixer on medium speed for 2 minutes. By hand, fold in the ½ cup coconut. Divide batter equally between prepared pans, spreading evenly.

2 Bake in a 350° oven for 30 to 35 minutes or until a wooden toothpick inserted near centers comes out clean. Cool in pans on wire racks for 10 minutes. Remove cakes from pans. Cool thoroughly on wire racks.

3 Prepare frosting according to package directions. Fill and frost cake. Sprinkle toasted coconut on top of cake. Store frosted cake, covered, in refrigerator.

NUTRITION FACTS PER SERVING: 291 cal., 6 g total fat (3 g sat. fat), 2 mg chol., 361 mg sodium, 57 g carbo., 0 g fiber, 3 g pro. DAILY VALUES: 18% vit. C, 7% calcium, 5% iron

NOW OR LATER? How far in advance can you make a cake? Once made, should the cake be stored in the refrigerator? Can it be frozen? The answers depend on the cake. Here are some guidelines: Cakes filled or frosted with whipped cream should be assembled no more than two hours before serving to prevent them from getting soggy. If your cake filling or frosting contains whipped cream, cream cheese, yogurt, or eggs, store it in the refrigerator. As an alternative to a cake cover, invert a bowl over the cake. To freeze an unfrosted layer cake, place the cooled cake on a baking sheet and freeze just until firm. Place the frozen cake in a freezer bag or airtight freezer container and freeze for up to four months. Angel food, sponge, and chiffon cakes are best frozen unfrosted. Place them in a large freezer bag and freeze for up to three months. Don't store them any longer than that or the delicate sponge texture may deteriorate. Thaw at room temperature for several hours before serving.

Pineapple Upside-Down Cornmeal Cake

To loosen cake from its pan, run a metal spatula around the sides in a continuous rather than sawing motion.

PREP: 15 minutes BAKE: 30 minutes COOL: 5 minutes OVEN: 350° MAKES: 8 servings

1	8-ounce can pineapple slices	1/2	cup yellow cornmeal
2	tablespoons butter or margarine	1	teaspoon baking powder
2/3	cup packed brown sugar	1/4	teaspoon baking soda
1	tablespoon water	1/4	teaspoon salt
1/4	cup dried cranberries, tart red cherries, or blueberries	2	eggs, beaten
1/4	cup broken pecans, toasted	1/2	cup dairy sour cream
1½	cups all-purpose flour	1/4	cup cooking oil

1 Drain pineapple, reserving 3 tablespoons juice. Halve pineapple slices. Melt butter in a 9×1½-inch round baking pan. Stir in ⅓ cup of the brown sugar and the water. Arrange pineapple slices, dried fruit, and pecans over brown sugar mixture in pan.

2 In a large bowl stir together flour, cornmeal, the remaining ⅓ cup brown sugar, the baking powder, baking soda, and salt. Make a well in center of flour mixture; set aside. In a small bowl stir together eggs, sour cream, oil, and reserved pineapple juice. Add egg mixture all at once to flour mixture. Stir just until combined. Spoon batter over fruit in pan, spreading evenly.

3 Bake in a 350° oven for 30 to 35 minutes or until a wooden toothpick inserted near center comes out clean. Cool in pan on a wire rack for 5 minutes. Loosen sides; invert cake onto a plate. Serve warm.

NUTRITION FACTS PER SERVING: 371 cal., 17 g total fat (5 g sat. fat), 68 mg chol., 217 mg sodium, 51 g carbo., 2 g fiber, 5 g pro. DAILY VALUES: 6% vit. C, 7% calcium, 14% iron

Caramel-Apple Pudding Cake

If you go gaga for gooey desserts, what can beat pudding cake? Most any pudding cake is best served warm, and this one is no exception—especially with vanilla ice cream oozing into the sweet, rich sauce.

PREP: 25 minutes BAKE: 35 minutes OVEN: 350° MAKES: 12 servings

2 cups peeled, cored, and thinly sliced tart cooking apples	1/2 cup milk
3 tablespoons lemon juice	2 tablespoons butter, melted
1/2 teaspoon ground cinnamon	1 teaspoon vanilla
1/8 teaspoon ground nutmeg	1/2 cup chopped pecans or walnuts
1/4 cup raisins	3/4 cup caramel ice cream topping
1 cup all-purpose flour	1/2 cup water
3/4 cup packed brown sugar	1 tablespoon butter or margarine
1 teaspoon baking powder	Whipped cream or vanilla ice cream (optional)
1/4 teaspoon baking soda	

1 Grease a 2-quart square baking dish. Arrange apples in bottom of dish; sprinkle with lemon juice, cinnamon, and nutmeg. Top evenly with raisins.

2 In a medium bowl stir together flour, brown sugar, baking powder, and baking soda. Add milk, the 2 tablespoons melted butter, and vanilla; mix well. Stir in pecans. Spoon batter over apple mixture, spreading evenly. In a small saucepan stir together caramel topping, water, and the 1 tablespoon butter. Bring to boiling. Pour caramel mixture over batter.

3 Bake in a 350° oven about 35 minutes or until set in center. While cake is warm, cut into squares, inverting each piece onto a dessert plate. Spoon the caramel-apple mixture from bottom of pan over each serving. If desired, serve with whipped cream.

NUTRITION FACTS PER SERVING: 223 cal., 6 g total fat (1 g sat. fat), 1 mg chol., 173 mg sodium, 42 g carbo., 1 g fiber, 2 g pro. DAILY VALUES: 4% vit. C, 5% calcium, 6% iron

Cherry Cordial Brownie Torte

This impressive torte starts with a brownie mix. Mark it as a good dessert for the winter holidays, and use dried cranberries instead of cherries. (See photo, page 238.)

PREP: 20 minutes BAKE: 35 minutes COOL: 1 hour CHILL: 30 minutes OVEN: 350° MAKES: 12 to 16 servings

1	21½-ounce package brownie mix	¼	cup whipping cream
⅓	cup white baking pieces	½	cup snipped dried tart red cherries
1	3-ounce package cream cheese, softened	⅓	cup semisweet chocolate pieces
1	tablespoon powdered sugar	1	teaspoon shortening
¼	teaspoon almond extract		

1 Lightly grease a 9-inch springform pan; set aside. Prepare brownie mix according to package directions. Spoon batter into prepared pan, spreading evenly.

2 Bake in a 350° oven for 35 to 40 minutes or until a wooden toothpick inserted near center comes out clean. Cool in pan on a wire rack for 30 minutes. Remove sides of pan. Cool completely.

3 Meanwhile, in a small saucepan heat and stir white baking pieces over low heat until melted. Cool slightly. In a medium mixing bowl beat cream cheese, powdered sugar, and almond extract with an electric mixer on medium speed until combined. Stir in melted white baking pieces. In a small mixing bowl beat whipping cream until soft peaks form. Fold whipped cream and cherries into cream cheese mixture. Spread cream cheese mixture over cooled brownie. Loosely cover and chill at least 30 minutes before serving.

4 Just before serving, in a small saucepan heat and stir chocolate pieces and shortening over low heat until melted. Cut torte into wedges and place on serving plates. Drizzle chocolate mixture evenly over wedges.

NUTRITION FACTS PER SERVING: 426 cal., 23 g total fat (8 g sat. fat), 50 mg chol., 186 mg sodium, 54 g carbo., 2 g fiber, 4 g pro. DAILY VALUES: 1% vit. C, 2% calcium, 15% iron

WHAT ABOUT WHITE CHOCOLATE? White chocolate contains cocoa butter, sugar, and milk solids and has a mild flavor that's unlike the darker chocolate products listed on page 259. Other products sometimes confused with white chocolate include white baking bars, white baking pieces, white candy coating, and white confectionery bars. Although these products are often used interchangeably with white chocolate, they do not contain any cocoa butter and legally can't be labeled chocolate in the United States.

Cherry-Apple Bread Pudding

Bring a cool fall evening to a sweet ending with this specialty dessert.
Tangy, sweet yellow apples complement tart cherries.

PREP: 25 minutes BAKE: 45 minutes COOL: 30 minutes OVEN: 350° MAKES: 8 to 10 servings

9	slices firm-textured white bread	½	cup dried tart red cherries
3	tablespoons butter, softened	6	eggs, beaten
3	medium Golden Delicious apples, peeled, cored, and very thinly sliced	3	cups milk
		½	cup sugar
2	tablespoons lemon juice		

1 Lightly butter one side of bread slices; cut bread into quarters. Arrange half of the bread pieces, buttered side down, in an ungreased 3-quart rectangular baking dish. In a large bowl toss together apples and lemon juice. Sprinkle apples and dried cherries on top of bread in baking dish. Top with remaining bread, buttered side up.

2 In a large bowl stir together eggs, milk, and sugar. Pour egg mixture evenly over bread in dish. Press mixture down lightly with back of a large spoon to be sure that all bread is moistened.

3 Bake, uncovered, in a 350° oven for 45 to 50 minutes or until set and a knife inserted near center comes out clean. Cool on a wire rack for 30 minutes. Serve warm.

NUTRITION FACTS PER SERVING: 315 cal., 11 g total fat (5 g sat. fat), 178 mg chol., 270 mg sodium, 45 g carbo., 2 g fiber, 10 g pro. DAILY VALUES: 8% vit. C, 13% calcium, 9% iron

Banana-Pecan Streusel Bread Pudding

Bananas add more appeal to an old-fashioned dessert. In this version croissants substitute for bread, increasing the rich flavor. Top each serving with whipped cream, French vanilla ice cream, or butter brickle ice cream for the ultimate dessert.

PREP: 20 minutes BAKE: 40 minutes COOL: 30 minutes OVEN: 350° MAKES: 10 to 12 servings

2	large croissants, cut or torn into 1-inch pieces (5 ounces total)		2	teaspoons ground cinnamon
3	eggs, beaten		¼	to ½ teaspoon almond extract
1	12-ounce can evaporated milk (1½ cups)		¼	cup packed brown sugar
1⅓	cups mashed ripe bananas (4 medium)		2	tablespoons all-purpose flour
½	cup granulated sugar		1	tablespoon butter or margarine, melted
1	tablespoon vanilla		½	cup chopped pecans
				Whipped cream or ice cream (optional)

1 Lightly grease a 2-quart rectangular baking dish. Arrange croissant pieces in dish. In a large bowl stir together eggs, evaporated milk, bananas, granulated sugar, vanilla, 1 teaspoon of the cinnamon, and the almond extract. Pour egg mixture evenly over croissants. Press mixture down lightly with back of a large spoon to be sure that all croissant pieces are moistened.

2 For streusel topping, in a small bowl stir together brown sugar, flour, melted butter, and the remaining 1 teaspoon cinnamon. Stir in pecans. Sprinkle topping evenly over croissant mixture.

3 Bake, uncovered, in a 350° oven for 40 to 45 minutes or until a knife inserted near center comes out clean. Cool on a wire rack for 30 minutes. Serve warm. If desired, top with whipped cream or ice cream.

NUTRITION FACTS PER SERVING: 280 cal., 12 g total fat (6 g sat. fat), 96 mg chol., 141 mg sodium, 38 g carbo., 1 g fiber, 7 g pro. DAILY VALUES: 8% vit. C, 9% calcium, 8% iron

Rhubarb-Pineapple Crumble

Just-picked rosy rhubarb is tart. When sweetened and cooked, however, it tastes more like apricot, strawberry, and lemon.

PREP: 20 minutes STAND: 1 hour BAKE: 45 minutes OVEN: 350° MAKES: 6 to 8 servings

7 cups fresh or frozen rhubarb, cut into 1-inch pieces	²⁄₃ cup all-purpose flour
1 8-ounce can crushed pineapple (juice packed), drained	1 tablespoon granulated sugar
1¼ cups packed brown sugar	1 tablespoon chopped crystallized ginger
2 tablespoons cornstarch	Dash salt
2 teaspoons finely shredded lemon peel	¹⁄₃ cup butter
	Vanilla ice cream (optional)

1 Thaw rhubarb, if frozen. Drain well. In a large bowl stir together rhubarb, pineapple, and 1 cup of the brown sugar. Let stand for 1 hour. Drain mixture, reserving juices. If necessary, add water to reserved juices to equal ²⁄₃ cup liquid.

2 In a small saucepan stir together juices and cornstarch. Cook and stir over medium heat until thickened and bubbly. Remove from heat. Stir hot mixture and lemon peel into rhubarb mixture. Spoon into an ungreased 2-quart square baking dish; set aside.

3 For topping, in a small bowl stir together the flour, the remaining ¹⁄₄ cup brown sugar, the granulated sugar, ginger, and salt. Using a pastry blender, cut in butter until mixture resembles coarse crumbs. Spoon topping over fruit.

4 Bake, uncovered, in a 350° oven for 45 to 50 minutes or until light brown and bubbly. Serve warm. If desired, serve with ice cream.

NUTRITION FACTS PER SERVING: 391 cal., 11 g total fat (7 g sat. fat), 29 mg chol., 158 mg sodium, 73 g carbo., 3 g fiber, 3 g pro. DAILY VALUES: 27% vit. C, 17% calcium, 11% iron

Peach-Praline Cobbler

If you purchase firm peaches, place them in a small, clean paper bag; loosely close the bag and store it at room temperature. Check the fruit daily and remove peaches that are slightly soft when gently pressed.

PREP: 25 minutes BAKE: 25 minutes OVEN: 400° MAKES: 12 servings

8	cups sliced, peeled, fresh or frozen peaches, thawed	¼	cup butter or margarine, melted
1	cup granulated sugar	1½	cups chopped pecans
1	cup water	2	cups self-rising flour*
2	tablespoons cornstarch	2	teaspoons granulated sugar
1	teaspoon ground cinnamon	½	cup shortening
¾	cup packed brown sugar	¾	cup buttermilk
			Half-and-half or light cream (optional)

1 In a Dutch oven combine peaches, the 1 cup granulated sugar, the water, cornstarch, and cinnamon. Cook and stir until thickened and bubbly. Transfer peach mixture to an ungreased 3-quart rectangular baking dish.

2 Meanwhile, for filling, in small bowl stir together the brown sugar and melted butter. Add pecans; toss to mix. Set aside.

3 For biscuit dough, in a large bowl stir together the self-rising flour and the 2 teaspoons granulated sugar. Using a pastry blender, cut in shortening until mixture resembles coarse crumbs. Make a well in center of flour mixture. Add buttermilk all at once. Using a fork, stir just until dough clings together.

4 Turn out dough onto a lightly floured surface. Quickly knead dough by gently folding and pressing for 10 to 12 strokes or until nearly smooth. Roll to a 12×8-inch rectangle; spread with filling. Roll up, starting from one long side. Cut into twelve 1-inch slices. Place biscuit slices, cut sides down, on hot peach mixture.

5 Bake, uncovered, in a 400° oven for 25 to 30 minutes or until biscuits are golden brown. Serve warm. If desired, serve with half-and-half.

***Note:** To substitute for the 2 cups self-rising flour, use 2 cups all-purpose flour plus 2 teaspoons baking powder, ½ teaspoon baking soda, and ½ teaspoon salt.

NUTRITION FACTS PER SERVING: 453 cal., 22 g total fat (6 g sat. fat), 11 mg chol., 331 mg sodium, 63 g carbo., 4 g fiber, 5 g pro. DAILY VALUES: 54% vit. A, 284% vit. C, 12% calcium, 12% iron

Peach Melba Crisp

Summer-fresh flavors can be savored in the winter with this simple crisp that can be made using frozen fruit.

PREP: 10 minutes BAKE: 40 minutes OVEN: 350° MAKES: 6 servings

5 cups sliced, peeled ripe peaches or 5 cups frozen unsweetened peach slices, thawed but not drained	1½ cups plain granola
2½ teaspoons cornstarch	⅔ cup flaked or shredded coconut
1 10-ounce package frozen red raspberries in syrup, thawed but not drained	3 tablespoons butter, melted
	Vanilla or cinnamon-flavored ice cream (optional)

1 In an ungreased 2-quart square baking dish arrange peach slices. Sprinkle with cornstarch; toss gently to coat.

2 If desired, press the undrained raspberries through a sieve; discard seeds. Spoon the whole or sieved raspberries over peaches. Bake, uncovered, in a 350° oven for 20 minutes.

3 Meanwhile, in a medium bowl stir together granola, coconut, and melted butter. Stir peach mixture gently. Sprinkle granola mixture evenly over peaches. Bake for 20 to 25 minutes more or until topping is golden and sauce is bubbly. Serve warm. If desired, serve with ice cream.

NUTRITION FACTS PER SERVING: 462 cal., 16 g total fat (7 g sat. fat), 16 mg chol., 81 mg sodium, 80 g carbo., 10 g fiber, 5 g pro. DAILY VALUES: 39% vit. C, 5% calcium, 11% iron

Chocolate Casserole

Ever dream of having chocolate for dinner?
This recipe may tempt you to make the dream reality.

PREP: 15 minutes   BAKE: 35 minutes   OVEN: 350°   MAKES: 6 servings

½ cup all-purpose flour	¼ cup unsweetened cocoa powder
¾ cup sugar	¾ cup boiling water
¾ teaspoons baking powder	⅓ cup coarsely chopped honey-roasted peanuts
⅓ cup milk	
1 tablespoon cooking oil	2 tablespoons crumbled chocolate-flavored graham crackers (optional)
1 teaspoon vanilla	
¼ cup peanut butter	Whipped cream (optional)
⅓ cup semisweet chocolate pieces	

1 In a medium mixing bowl stir together flour, ¼ cup of the sugar, and baking powder. Add milk, cooking oil, and vanilla. Stir until smooth with a wire whisk. Stir in the peanut butter and semisweet chocolate pieces. Pour batter into an ungreased 1-quart casserole; set aside.

2 In the same bowl stir together the remaining ½ cup sugar and the cocoa. Gradually stir in boiling water. Pour mixture over batter in casserole.

3 Bake, uncovered, in a 350° oven for 35 to 40 minutes or until a wooden toothpick inserted into cake portion comes out clean. Remove from oven. Sprinkle with peanuts and, if desired, graham crackers. If desired, serve warm with whipped cream.

NUTRITION FACTS PER SERVING: 333 cal., 15 g total fat (3 g sat. fat), 1 mg chol., 170 mg sodium, 42 g carbo., 3 g fiber, 7 g pro. DAILY VALUES: 9% calcium, 9% iron

TYPES OF CHOCOLATE There are many types of chocolate to love. Here are the main types you'll find at the supermarket:

Unsweetened chocolate is pure chocolate and cocoa butter with no sugar added. It's used for baking and cooking rather than snacking.

Semisweet chocolate and **bittersweet chocolate** are at least 35 percent pure chocolate with added cocoa butter and sugar. They can be used interchangeably.

Sweet chocolate is at least 15 percent pure chocolate with added cocoa butter and sugar. Sweeter and milder than semisweet chocolate, it is used in cooking and baking.

Milk chocolate is at least 10 percent pure chocolate with added cocoa butter, sugar, and milk solids. It is creamier and milder than semisweet.

Unsweetened cocoa powder is pure chocolate with most of the cocoa butter removed. Dutch-process or European-style cocoa powder has been treated to neutralize acids, making it mellower in flavor.

Cherry Puff

Bake this versatile dessert in small individual casseroles or in a large casserole. Either choice results in a tart cherry sauce nestled under airy sponge cake.

PREP: 25 minutes BAKE: 35 minutes OVEN: 325° MAKES: 6 servings

1	16-ounce can pitted tart red cherries (water packed)
½	cup sugar
2	tablespoons quick-cooking tapioca
2	egg whites
¼	teaspoon cream of tartar

⅛	teaspoon salt
2	egg yolks
⅓	cup sugar
⅓	cup all-purpose flour

1 Drain cherries, reserving ½ cup liquid. Transfer cherries to a medium saucepan. Add reserved cherry liquid, the ½ cup sugar, and the tapioca. Cook and stir over medium heat until boiling; reduce heat. Simmer, uncovered, for 5 minutes, stirring constantly. Remove from heat; keep warm.

2 In a medium mixing bowl beat egg whites, cream of tartar, and salt with an electric mixer on medium speed until stiff peaks form (tips stand straight); set aside. In a small mixing bowl beat egg yolks for 2 to 3 minutes or until thick and lemon colored. Add the ⅓ cup sugar to egg yolks and beat for 1 minute more. Stir a small amount of egg white mixture into egg yolk mixture to lighten. Fold remaining egg yolk mixture into egg white mixture. Sprinkle flour over egg mixture; fold in.

3 Pour hot cherry mixture into an ungreased 1½-quart casserole or into six 6- to 8-ounce casseroles or custard cups. Pour batter over cherry mixture.

4 Bake, uncovered, in a 325° oven for 35 to 40 minutes for the 1½-quart casserole or about 30 minutes for the small casseroles or custard cups or until top springs back when lightly touched. Serve warm.

NUTRITION FACTS PER SERVING: 216 cal., 2 g total fat (1 g sat. fat), 71 mg chol., 72 mg sodium, 48 g carbo., 1 g fiber, 3 g pro. DAILY VALUES: 5% vit. C, 2% calcium, 4% iron

Mocha-Ladyfinger Parfaits

A super-simple takeoff on the classic Italian dessert tiramisu, these parfaits are sized just right, served in individual goblets. Not only do you save time by blending instant pudding mix into rich mascarpone cheese, but single servings are easy to make gorgeous.

PREP: 40 minutes CHILL: 10 hours MAKES: 12 parfaits

2 4-serving-size packages instant French vanilla pudding mix

1 8-ounce carton mascarpone cheese or one 8-ounce package cream cheese

1 cup whipping cream

²/₃ cup strong coffee, cooled

1 tablespoon coffee liqueur or hazelnut-flavored syrup (syrup used to flavor coffee)

4 ounces milk chocolate or semisweet chocolate

2 3-ounce packages ladyfingers (24 ladyfingers), cut crosswise into thirds

12 fresh strawberries (optional)

1 In a large mixing bowl prepare pudding mixes according to package directions (using 4 cups milk). Cover and chill for 2 hours.

2 Meanwhile, let cheese stand at room temperature for 30 minutes. In a small bowl stir cheese until smooth. Gradually stir 1 cup of the pudding into cheese to lighten it. Fold cheese mixture into remaining pudding. In a chilled small mixing bowl beat whipping cream with an electric mixer on medium speed or with a rotary beater just until soft peaks form. Fold whipped cream into pudding mixture; set aside.

3 In a small bowl stir together coffee and coffee liqueur; set aside. Shave enough curls from chocolate to sprinkle over tops of parfaits. Finely chop remaining chocolate.

4 To assemble, arrange half of the ladyfinger pieces in bottoms of 12 goblets or glasses. Drizzle half of the coffee mixture over ladyfingers in goblets. Spoon half of the pudding mixture on top and sprinkle with chopped chocolate. Repeat with remaining ladyfinger pieces, coffee mixture, and pudding. Top with shaved chocolate curls. Cover and chill about 8 hours or overnight. If desired, garnish each parfait with a fresh strawberry.

NUTRITION FACTS PER PARFAIT: 353 cal., 22 g total fat (13 g sat. fat), 109 mg chol., 310 mg sodium, 36 g carbo., 1 g fiber, 9 g pro. DAILY VALUES: 2% vit. C, 10% calcium, 5% iron

Banana Split Trifles

A duo of hot fudge topping and strawberry preserves makes these trifles yummy. Substitute any combination of ice cream toppings or preserves, such as caramel and marshmallow, butterscotch and chocolate, or fudge and raspberry. (See photo, page 239.)

START TO FINISH: 15 minutes MAKES: 4 trifles

2 to 3 cups tin roof sundae, chocolate chunk, or vanilla ice cream

4 soft-style oatmeal or chocolate chip cookies, about 3 inches in diameter, crumbled

²/₃ cup hot fudge ice cream topping and/or strawberry preserves

½ cup whipped cream

2 small bananas, halved lengthwise and sliced into 1- to 2-inch pieces

1 In a medium bowl use a wooden spoon to stir ice cream to soften. To assemble, in each of four 6- to 8-ounce glasses layer cookie crumbs, softened ice cream, and hot fudge topping, layering ingredients almost to top of glasses.

2 Top each trifle with whipped cream, banana slices, and more hot fudge topping and cookie crumbs. Serve immediately or cover and freeze for up to 1 hour.

NUTRITION FACTS PER TRIFLE: 524 cal., 23 g total fat (12 g sat. fat), 48 mg chol., 161 mg sodium, 73 g carbo., 3 g fiber, 6 g pro. DAILY VALUES: 14% vit. A, 21% vit. C, 15% calcium, 7% iron

fresh Strawberry fool

Inspect berries closely so you'll use only the best in this pure dessert. The recipe is so simple, the subtly delicious flavor of perfectly ripe berries sails right through.

START TO FINISH: 15 minutes MAKES: 4 servings

½ cup whipping cream

⅓ cup powdered sugar

½ teaspoon vanilla

1 8-ounce carton lemon yogurt

3 cups sliced fresh strawberries or 2 cups fresh blueberries

½ cup coarsely crumbled shortbread cookies (5 cookies)

1 In a chilled medium mixing bowl beat whipping cream, powdered sugar, and vanilla with chilled beaters of an electric mixer on medium speed or a chilled rotary beater until soft peaks form. By hand, fold in yogurt and half of the berries.

2 To assemble, in each of four 10-ounce glasses spoon some of the whipped cream mixture. Top each with some of the remaining berries, all of the remaining whipped cream mixture, and the remaining berries. Serve immediately or cover and chill for up to 2 hours. Sprinkle with crumbled cookies before serving.

NUTRITION FACTS PER SERVING: 272 cal., 15 g total fat (8 g sat. fat), 47 mg chol., 98 mg sodium, 32 g carbo., 3 g fiber, 4 g pro. DAILY VALUES: 103% vit. C, 14% calcium, 4% iron

BERRY PERFECT Buy fresh berries at the height of their season for best value. Peak supplies often bring lower prices.

Avoid berry containers with excess juice in the bottom, overly soft fruit, and other telltale signs of age, such as bruises, mold, and unhealthy color.

Refrigerate berries in a single layer, loosely covered, in a shallow dish so they won't crush. Rinse berries just prior to using, not before. Blot dry on paper towels if needed. Invert raspberries to drain.

Peanut Butter Parfaits

Remember this scrumptious caramel sauce next time you make banana splits.
Or try drizzling it over pound cake slices for an easy-to-fix dessert. Make the sauce up to
five days ahead; store it, covered, in the refrigerator.

PREP: 15 minutes CHILL: 2 hours MAKES: 12 parfaits

1 cup packed brown sugar	¼ cup peanut butter
⅓ cup milk	3 pints vanilla ice cream
¼ cup light-colored corn syrup	Crushed peanut brittle or peanuts (optional)
1 tablespoon butter or margarine	

1 For caramel sauce, in a medium saucepan combine brown sugar, milk, corn syrup, and butter. Cook and stir over medium heat until sugar dissolves and butter melts. Remove from heat. Add peanut butter to brown sugar mixture, beating with a rotary beater or wire whisk until smooth. Cover and chill about 2 hours or until cold.

2 To assemble, in each of 12 parfait glasses alternate layers of ice cream and caramel sauce, beginning and ending with ice cream. If desired, top with crushed peanut brittle.

NUTRITION FACTS PER PARFAIT: 310 cal., 16 g total fat (9 g sat. fat), 48 mg chol., 95 mg sodium, 41 g carbo., 0 g fiber, 4 g pro. DAILY VALUES: 1% vit. C, 11% calcium, 3% iron

Mango Blossoms

A mango is ripe when the skin is bright in color and the fruit yields very slightly to touch and has a strong floral aroma.

PREP: 30 minutes GRILL: 2 minutes cake/4 minutes mango MAKES: 8 servings

4	mangoes		¼	cup butter or margarine, melted
4	kiwifruits, peeled		3	tablespoons molasses or honey
½	of a 15-ounce purchased angel food cake			Vanilla ice cream (optional)

1 Using a sharp knife, cut mangoes lengthwise along the broad, flat sides, keeping the blade about ¼ inch from both sides of the seed. Score mango halves, making cuts through fruit just to peel in a crosshatch fashion. Set aside.

2 Carefully remove and discard the peel around the mango sections that have a seed, cutting away as much of the fruit as you can; discard seeds. In a food processor bowl or blender container place removed fruit portion. Cover and process or blend fruit pieces until smooth. Transfer pureed fruit to a small covered container or a clean squeeze bottle. Chill until ready to use.

3 Rinse food processor bowl or blender container. Place peeled kiwifruits in bowl or container. Cover and process or blend until smooth. If desired, strain kiwi puree through a sieve to remove seeds. Transfer to a small covered container or squeeze bottle. Chill until ready to use.

4 Using a long serrated knife, cut angel food cake in half horizontally (forming two narrow rings). Brush all sides of cake with half of the melted butter. Grill cake on the rack of an uncovered grill directly over medium coals for 2 to 3 minutes or until lightly browned, turning once. Cut cake into large, irregular-shape croutons.

5 Brush fruit side of reserved mango pieces with molasses and the remaining melted butter. Grill mangoes, cut side down, on the rack of an uncovered grill directly over medium coals for 4 to 6 minutes or until brown around edges and heated through.

6 To serve, in each of 8 chilled, shallow dessert bowls spoon or drizzle mango and kiwi sauces. Carefully bend peel back on each mango half, pushing inside up and out until mango cubes pop up and separate. Place each mango "blossom" on sauces; surround with several cake croutons and, if desired, vanilla ice cream.

NUTRITION FACTS PER SERVING: 215 cal., 4 g total fat (3 g sat. fat), 15 mg chol., 249 mg sodium, 45 g carbo., 2 g fiber, 3 g pro. DAILY VALUES: 119% vit. C, 6% calcium, 5% iron

fruit Bowl Sundaes

This sundae uses fruit instead of ice cream to satisfy your sweet tooth with a light, seasonal touch.

START TO FINISH: 15 minutes MAKES: 4 sundaes

⅓	cup whipping cream	2	medium bananas, sliced
2	tablespoons chocolate-flavored syrup	1	cup strawberries, sliced
2	chocolate-with-white-filling sandwich cookies, crushed	2	tablespoons shredded coconut, toasted

1 In a chilled medium mixing bowl beat whipping cream with chilled beaters of an electric mixer on medium speed until soft peaks form (tips curl). By hand, gradually fold chocolate syrup into whipped cream until smooth. Fold in cookie pieces.

2 To assemble, in each of four dessert dishes arrange bananas and strawberries. Spoon whipped cream mixture on top. Sprinkle with coconut. Serve immediately.

NUTRITION FACTS PER SERVING: 188 cal., 10 g total fat (6 g sat. fat), 27 mg chol., 45 mg sodium, 27 g carbo., 2 g fiber, 2 g pro. DAILY VALUES: 43% vit. C

Wintery Ice Cream Balls

Dessert made easy hits new heights with this two-ingredient recipe.
Use it to express a heap of good lovin' for your family. (See photo, page 236.)

PREP: 25 minutes FREEZE: 1 hour MAKES: 6 servings

2   cups flaked coconut

1   quart vanilla or cinnamon-flavored
     ice cream

1 Place coconut in a shallow dish. Use an ice cream scoop and a large melon baller to create ice cream balls of varying sizes. Roll ice cream balls in coconut, pressing firmly, until coated. Place coated ice cream balls on a cookie sheet. Return ice cream to freezer for 1 to 2 hours or until firm.

2 In a serving bowl arrange ice cream balls to resemble a mountain.

NUTRITION FACTS PER SERVING: 70 cal., 4 g total fat (3 g sat. fat), 9 mg chol., 18 mg sodium, 7 g carbo., 0 g fiber, 1 g pro. DAILY VALUES: 2% calcium

Banana-Chocolate Bites

Big surprises come in small packages. This recipe transforms ordinary refrigerated rolls into clever wraps for a popular flavor combo—chocolate and bananas. (See photo, page 235.)

PREP: 20 minutes **BAKE:** 11 minutes **COOL:** 10 minutes **OVEN:** 375° **MAKES:** 16 bites

1	8-ounce package refrigerated crescent rolls (8)
3	tablespoons chocolate-hazelnut spread
2	medium bananas, cut into 16 slices (about ¾-inch pieces)
4	teaspoons lemon juice
1	egg yolk
1	tablespoon water

1 Grease a baking sheet; set aside. Unroll crescent roll dough and separate into eight triangles. Cut each triangle in half lengthwise, forming 16 long, narrow triangles. Place about ½ teaspoon of chocolate-hazelnut spread on wide end of each triangle. Brush each banana slice with some of the lemon juice. Place a banana slice on top of spread. Roll dough around bananas. Place bites on prepared baking sheet.

2 In a small bowl beat together egg yolk and water. Brush egg yolk mixture onto dough of each bite.

3 Bake in a 375° oven for 11 to 15 minutes or until golden brown. Remove bites from baking sheet and cool on a wire rack for 10 minutes. Serve warm, or serve within 4 hours.

NUTRITION FACTS PER SERVING: 80 cal., 4 g total fat (1 g sat. fat), 13 mg chol., 118 mg sodium, 11 g carbo., 1 g fiber, 1 g pro. DAILY VALUES: 3% vit. C, 1% iron

Top Banana Bars

Why monkey with awkward cutting and messy cleanup? Line the pan with foil and grease it as you would the pan. After baking and cooling, transfer, using the foil, to a cutting board. Slice the bars without the pan getting in the way.

PREP: 15 minutes BAKE: 20 minutes COOL: 2 hours OVEN: 350° MAKES: 20 bars

½	cup all-purpose flour	½	cup packed brown sugar
½	cup whole wheat flour	⅓	cup milk
1	tablespoon toasted wheat germ	¼	cup cooking oil
1	teaspoon baking powder	½	teaspoon vanilla
½	teaspoon ground cinnamon	⅓	cup mashed ripe banana (1 medium)
⅛	teaspoon salt	⅓	cup mixed dried fruit bits
1	egg, beaten	1	recipe Vanilla Icing

1 Grease an 11×7×1½-inch baking pan; set aside. In a large bowl stir together all-purpose flour, whole wheat flour, wheat germ, baking powder, cinnamon, and salt; set aside.

2 In a medium bowl stir together egg, brown sugar, milk, oil, and vanilla. Stir in banana and fruit bits. Add banana mixture to flour mixture, stirring to combine. Pour batter into prepared pan, spreading evenly.

3 Bake in a 350° oven for 20 to 25 minutes or until a wooden toothpick inserted near center comes out clean. Cool on a wire rack for 2 hours. Drizzle Vanilla Icing over top. Cut into bars.

Vanilla Icing: In a small bowl stir together ⅓ cup sifted powdered sugar and ¼ teaspoon vanilla. Add milk (1 to 2 teaspoons) until of drizzling consistency.

NUTRITION FACTS PER BAR: 91 cal., 3 g total fat (1 g sat. fat), 11 mg chol., 27 mg sodium, 15 g carbo., 1 g fiber, 1 g pro. DAILY VALUES: 1% vit. C, 2% calcium, 3% iron

Cherry-Walnut Bars

This goodie offers a rich buttery crust and a pretty pink topping that looks festive anytime.

PREP: 25 minutes BAKE: 45 minutes COOL: 2 hours OVEN: 350° MAKES: 48 bars

2¼ cups all-purpose flour	¾ teaspoon vanilla
½ cup granulated sugar	1 6-ounce jar maraschino cherries, drained and chopped (reserving ¼ cup liquid)
1 cup butter, softened	
3 eggs	½ cup chopped walnuts
1½ cups packed brown sugar	2 cups sifted powdered sugar
¾ teaspoon baking powder	2 tablespoons butter or margarine, softened
¾ teaspoon salt	

1 Lightly grease a 13×9×2-inch baking pan; set aside. In a large bowl stir together flour and granulated sugar. Using a pastry blender, cut in the 1 cup butter until mixture resembles coarse crumbs. Press flour mixture into bottom of prepared pan. Bake in a 350° oven for 20 minutes.

2 Meanwhile, in a medium bowl stir together eggs, brown sugar, baking powder, salt, and vanilla. Add cherries and nuts; stir to combine. Spoon cherry mixture evenly over baked crust. Bake for 25 minutes more. Cool on a wire rack for 2 hours.

3 For icing, in a small bowl stir together powdered sugar, the 2 tablespoons butter, and enough of the reserved cherry liquid (3 to 4 tablespoons) to make icing of spreading consistency. Spread or pipe over top of bars. Cut into bars.

NUTRITION FACTS PER BAR: 129 cal., 6 g total fat (3 g sat. fat), 26 mg chol., 96 mg sodium, 19 g carbo., 0 g fiber, 1 g pro. DAILY VALUES: 1% calcium, 3% iron

BUTTER IS BETTER FOR BAKING Nothing beats the flavor and richness that butter adds to baked goods. For many of the recipes in this book, the Test Kitchen recommends using butter rather than margarine. What doesn't make a difference is whether you use salted or unsalted butter (although if you use unsalted butter, you may want to increase the amount of salt in the recipe).

Technically, anything on your supermarket shelf labeled margarine must be at least 80 percent vegetable oil or fat, which—if used in baking in place of butter—will provide satisfactory results. However, there are so many look-alike margarines on the market—and their labeling can be so tricky—it can be confusing as to which is a true margarine. Any margarinelike product that has less than 80 percent vegetable oil or fat contains additional water and milk solids and can make your baked goods soggy or rock hard. If you do elect to use a true margarine, your rolled cookie dough, for instance, will be softer than if you use butter. You may need to chill it in the freezer to make it workable. Also it's critical to use butter in baked goods that rely strictly on butter for flavor, such as genoise and pound cake. Shortbread should be made only with butter to retain its characteristic butter flavor, richness, and dense crumb. Streusel toppings, too, shouldn't be made with margarine because they don't crisp up as they do when they're made with butter.

Top-of-the-World Brownies

Store these fudgy brownies for up to three days. Place them in a tightly covered container to keep them from drying out. (See photo, page 237.)

PREP: 20 minutes BAKE: 1 hour COOL: 1 hour OVEN: 350° MAKES: 16 squares

¾ cup butter	1 cup all-purpose flour
3 ounces unsweetened chocolate, coarsely chopped	3 tablespoons unsweetened cocoa powder
2 cups sugar	½ cup coarsely chopped hazelnuts (filberts) or pecans
2 teaspoons vanilla	2 egg whites
3 eggs	

1 Line bottom and sides of an 8×8×2-inch baking pan with heavy foil; grease foil and set aside. In a medium saucepan heat and stir the butter and chopped chocolate over low heat just until melted. Remove from heat. Using a wooden spoon, stir in 1⅓ cups of the sugar and the vanilla. Cool about 5 minutes.

2 Add whole eggs, one at a time, to chocolate mixture in saucepan, beating after each just until combined. Stir in flour and 2 tablespoons of the cocoa powder. Pour batter into prepared pan, spreading evenly. Sprinkle with nuts; set aside.

3 In a small mixing bowl beat egg whites with an electric mixer on medium to high speed about 1 minute or until soft peaks form (tips curl). Gradually add the remaining ⅔ cup sugar, beating on high speed until stiff peaks form (tips stand straight) and sugar is almost dissolved. Reduce speed to low; beat in the remaining 1 tablespoon cocoa. Using a tablespoon, carefully spoon the meringue in 16 even mounds on top of the brownie batter, keeping about ½ inch of space between them.

4 Bake in a 350° oven about 1 hour or until a wooden toothpick inserted near center of brownie portion comes out clean. Cool in pan on a wire rack for at least 1 hour.

5 To serve, before cutting, lift whole brownie from pan using foil. Cut into 16 squares.

NUTRITION FACTS PER SQUARE: 269 cal., 15 g total fat (7 g sat. fat), 63 mg chol., 107 mg sodium, 34 g carbo., 1 g fiber, 4 g pro. DAILY VALUES: 2% calcium, 7% iron

Orange-Coconut Triangles

These treats have great appeal, whether served after supper or at a shower.
Cut into triangular pieces or bars.

PREP: 20 minutes BAKE: 38 minutes OVEN: 350° MAKES: 18 triangles

½	cup all-purpose flour	1½	teaspoons finely shredded orange peel
1	cup granulated sugar	3	tablespoons orange juice
¼	cup butter	¼	teaspoon baking powder
½	cup finely chopped pecans	1	cup shredded coconut
2	eggs		Sifted powdered sugar (optional)
2	tablespoons all-purpose flour		

1 For crust, in a medium bowl stir together the ½ cup flour and ¼ cup of the granulated sugar. Using a pastry blender, cut in butter until mixture resembles coarse crumbs. Stir in pecans. Press mixture into an ungreased 8×8×2-inch baking pan. Bake in a 350° oven for 18 to 20 minutes or just until golden.

2 Meanwhile, for filling, in a medium mixing bowl combine eggs, the remaining ¾ cup sugar, the 2 tablespoons flour, orange peel, orange juice, and baking powder. Beat with an electric mixer on medium speed until combined. Stir in coconut.

3 Pour filling mixture evenly over baked crust. Bake about 20 minutes more or until edges are lightly browned and center is set. Cool in pan on a wire rack.

4 Cut into 2½-inch squares, then cut each square in half to make triangles or bars. If desired, sprinkle with powdered sugar.

NUTRITION FACTS PER TRIANGLE: 128 cal., 7 g total fat (3 g sat. fat), 31 mg chol., 41 mg sodium, 16 g carbo., 1 g fiber, 2 g pro. DAILY VALUES: 3% vit. C, 1% calcium, 2% iron

Brownie Meringues

Letting egg whites stand at room temperature allows them to gain greater volume when beaten with sugar than if they were cold. (See photo, page 240.)

PREP: 15 minutes STAND: 30 minutes BAKE: 10 minutes per batch OVEN: 350° MAKES: 24 cookies

2 egg whites	1 cup semisweet chocolate pieces (6 ounces), melted and cooled
½ teaspoon vinegar	¾ cup chopped walnuts
½ teaspoon vanilla	½ cup semisweet chocolate pieces
Dash salt	1 teaspoon shortening
½ cup sugar	

1 Grease cookie sheets; set aside. For meringue, in a large mixing bowl place egg whites. Let egg whites stand at room temperature for 30 minutes. Add the vinegar, vanilla, and salt to egg whites in bowl. Beat with an electric mixer on medium speed until soft peaks form (tips curl). Add the sugar, 1 tablespoon at a time, beating on high speed about 4 minutes or until stiff peaks form (tips stand straight) and the sugar is almost dissolved. Fold in the melted chocolate and walnuts. Drop mixture from teaspoons onto prepared cookie sheets.

2 Bake in a 350° oven for 10 to 12 minutes or until edges are firm. Remove cookies from cookie sheets and cool on wire racks. In a small saucepan heat and stir the ½ cup semisweet chocolate pieces and the shortening over low heat until melted. Drizzle over cookies.

NUTRITION FACTS PER COOKIE: 95 cal., 5 g total fat (2 g sat. fat), 0 mg chol., 11 mg sodium, 8 g carbo., 2 g fiber, 1 g pro. DAILY VALUES: 1% iron

MELTING CHOCOLATE Melting chocolate can be tricky if you're not melting it with butter or shortening as some recipes call for. For recipes that don't include fat, use these guidelines.

1 Chocolate can be melted on the range top or in the microwave. To speed things along, chop or break up the chocolate before you begin.

2 To melt chocolate on the range top, use a heavy saucepan or double boiler. Make sure the utensils are dry, and avoid splashing any water into the pan. Even a little water will cause the chocolate to seize up and get grainy and lumpy. Place the saucepan over low heat or the double boiler over hot, but not boiling, water. Stir the chocolate often to keep it from burning.

3 To melt chocolate in the microwave, place 1 cup of chocolate pieces or 2 ounces of chocolate in a small microwave-safe bowl. Heat, uncovered, on 100% power (high) for 1½ to 2 minutes or until chocolate is soft enough to stir smooth.

frosted Butterscotch Cookies

If you're languishing in the dessert doldrums—baking batch after batch of bought brownie mix—renew your spirit with the sweet, mellow flavor of these cookies.

PREP: 20 minutes BAKE: 10 minutes per batch OVEN: 375° MAKES: about 60 cookies

2½	cups all-purpose flour		1	teaspoon vanilla
1	teaspoon baking soda		1	8-ounce carton dairy sour cream
½	teaspoon baking powder		⅔	cup chopped walnuts
½	teaspoon salt		1	recipe Browned Butter Frosting
1½	cups packed brown sugar			Chopped walnuts or walnut halves (optional)
½	cup shortening			
2	eggs			

1 Grease cookie sheets; set aside. In a medium bowl stir together flour, baking soda, baking powder, and salt; set aside.

2 In a large mixing bowl beat brown sugar and shortening with an electric mixer on medium speed until well mixed. Add eggs and vanilla; beat until combined. Add flour mixture and sour cream alternately to beaten mixture, beating after each addition. Stir in the ⅔ cup walnuts. Drop dough by rounded teaspoons 2 inches apart onto prepared cookie sheets.

3 Bake in a 375° oven for 10 to 12 minutes or until edges are light brown. Remove cookies from cookie sheet and cool on a wire rack. Spread cooled cookies with Browned Butter Frosting. If desired, top with additional chopped walnuts or walnut halves.

Browned Butter Frosting: In a medium saucepan heat and stir ½ cup butter (no substitutes) over medium-low heat until golden brown. (Do not scorch.) Remove from heat. Stir in 3½ cups sifted powdered sugar, 5 teaspoons boiling water, and 1½ teaspoons vanilla. Beat with an electric mixer on medium speed until frosting is easy to spread. Immediately spread on cooled cookies. If frosting begins to set, stir in a small amount of additional boiling water.

NUTRITION FACTS PER COOKIE: 111 cal., 5 g total fat (2 g sat. fat), 13 mg chol., 67 mg sodium, 16 g carbo., 0 g fiber, 1 g pro. DAILY VALUES: 2% calcium, 2% iron

Ultimate Chocolate Cookies

*If you love chocolate, create these cookies for a chocolate encounter
not only to remember but to repeat.*

PREP: 20 minutes BAKE: 8 minutes per batch OVEN: 350° MAKES: about 36 cookies

1	12-ounce package semisweet chocolate pieces (2 cups)	2	eggs
2	ounces unsweetened chocolate	⅔	cup sugar
2	tablespoons butter	1	teaspoon vanilla
¼	cup all-purpose flour	1	cup chopped nuts
¼	teaspoon baking powder	4	ounces semisweet chocolate, melted
	Dash salt		

1 Lightly grease cookie sheets; set aside. In a heavy medium saucepan combine 1 cup of the chocolate pieces, the unsweetened chocolate, and butter. Cook and stir over low heat until melted. Transfer chocolate mixture to a large bowl; cool slightly.

2 Meanwhile, in a small bowl stir together flour, baking powder, and salt; set aside. To the chocolate mixture add eggs, sugar, and vanilla. Using a wooden spoon, beat until combined. Add flour mixture; beat until combined. Stir in remaining chocolate pieces and the nuts. Drop dough by heaping teaspoons about 2 inches apart onto prepared cookie sheets.

3 Bake in a 350° oven for 8 to 10 minutes or until edges are firm and surface is dull and cracked. Cool cookies on cookie sheet for 1 minute. Remove cookies and cool completely on a wire rack. Drizzle melted chocolate over cooled cookies.

NUTRITION FACTS PER COOKIE: 118 cal., 8 g total fat (3 g sat. fat), 14 mg chol., 19 mg sodium, 13 g carbo., 1 g fiber, 2 g pro. DAILY VALUES: 1% calcium, 4% iron

STORING CHOCOLATE Keep chocolate in a tightly covered container or sealed plastic bag in a cool, dry place. If stored in a too-warm place (higher than 78 degrees), your chocolate may "bloom" or develop a harmless gray film. Keep cocoa powder in a tightly covered container in that same cool, dry place.

Mocha Truffle Cookies

These double-chocolate cookies have a soft trufflelike center, a crispy outside, and a delectable coffee flavor. For the ultimate indulgence, serve them with cups of rich hot chocolate or flavored coffee. (See photo, page 234.)

PREP: 20 minutes BAKE: 10 minutes per batch OVEN: 350° MAKES: 36 cookies

½	cup butter		2	teaspoons vanilla
1½	cups semisweet chocolate pieces		2	cups all-purpose flour
1	tablespoon instant coffee crystals		⅓	cup unsweetened cocoa powder
¾	cup granulated sugar		½	teaspoon baking powder
¾	cup packed brown sugar		¼	teaspoon salt
2	eggs			

1 Lightly grease cookie sheets; set aside. In a large saucepan heat and stir butter and ½ cup of the chocolate pieces over low heat until melted. Remove from heat. Stir in coffee crystals; cool 5 minutes. Stir in granulated sugar, brown sugar, eggs, and vanilla.

2 In a medium bowl stir together flour, cocoa powder, baking powder, and salt. Stir flour mixture into butter mixture. Stir in the remaining 1 cup chocolate pieces. Drop dough by rounded teaspoons 2 inches apart onto prepared cookie sheets.

3 Bake in a 350° oven about 10 minutes or until edges are firm. Cool cookies on cookie sheet for 1 minute. Remove cookies and cool completely on a wire rack.

NUTRITION FACTS PER COOKIE: 123 cal., 5 g total fat (3 g sat. fat), 19 mg chol., 55 mg sodium, 16 g carbo., 1 g fiber, 1 g pro. DAILY VALUES: 1% calcium, 4% iron

Peanut Butter Peanut Brittle

*It is worth your while to search out raw peanuts for this brittle;
they are less likely to burn when stirred into the hot syrup. Check out a
health food market if your supermarket doesn't carry them.*

START TO FINISH: 30 minutes MAKES: 3 pounds or 48 servings

2	cups peanut butter		2	tablespoons butter
1½	cups sugar		2	cups raw peanuts
1½	cups light-colored corn syrup		1	teaspoon baking soda, sifted
¼	cup water		1	teaspoon vanilla

1 In the top of a double boiler warm peanut butter over low heat. (Or warm peanut butter in a heatproof bowl set over a pan of warm water over low heat.) Meanwhile, butter two large baking sheets; set aside.

2 Butter sides of a heavy 3-quart saucepan. In the saucepan combine sugar, corn syrup, and water. Cook and stir over medium-high heat until mixture boils. Clip a candy thermometer to side of saucepan. Cook and stir over medium-high heat until thermometer registers 275°, soft-crack stage (about 15 minutes).

3 Reduce heat to medium. Add the 2 tablespoons butter, stirring until melted. Add peanuts. Cook and stir about 5 minutes more or until candy starts turning brown and thermometer registers 295°, hard-crack stage. Remove pan from heat. Remove thermometer from saucepan.

4 Quickly sprinkle baking soda over mixture, stirring constantly. Stir in vanilla. Gently stir in warm peanut butter until combined.

5 Immediately pour candy onto prepared baking sheets. Working quickly, spread as thin as possible with a spatula or stretch using two forks to lift and pull candy as it cools. When cool, break into serving-size pieces.

NUTRITION FACTS PER SERVING: 156 cal., 9 g total fat (2 g sat. fat), 1 mg chol., 91 mg sodium, 17 g carbo., 1 g fiber, 4 g pro. DAILY VALUES: 1% calcium, 5% iron

Microwave Candy-Bar Fudge

It is essential that you use butter, rather than margarine or a spread, in this delectable fudge. Margarine can adversely affect the outcome of some candies.

PREP: 15 minutes COOK: microwave 7¾ minutes CHILL: 1 hour MAKES: 64 pieces

½	cup butter	30	vanilla caramels, unwrapped (about 10 ounces)
⅓	cup unsweetened cocoa powder	1	tablespoon water
¼	cup packed brown sugar	2	cups unsalted peanuts
¼	cup milk	½	cup semisweet chocolate pieces
3½	cups sifted powdered sugar	½	cup milk chocolate pieces
1	teaspoon vanilla		

1 Line a 9×9×2-inch pan with foil, extending the foil over edges of pan. Butter the foil; set pan aside.

2 In a large microwave-safe bowl microwave the butter, uncovered, on 100% power (high) about 1 minute or until melted. Stir in cocoa powder, brown sugar, and milk. Microwave, uncovered, on high for 1 to 2 minutes or until mixture comes to a boil, stirring once. Stir again. Microwave for 30 seconds more. Stir in powdered sugar and vanilla. Spread fudge mixture into prepared pan.

3 In a medium microwave-safe bowl combine unwrapped caramels and water. Microwave, uncovered, on 50% power (medium) for 2½ to 3 minutes or until caramels are melted, stirring once. Stir in peanuts. Microwave on medium power for 45 to 60 seconds more or until softened. Gently but quickly spread caramel mixture over fudge layer.

4 In a 2-cup glass measure combine semisweet chocolate pieces and milk chocolate pieces. Microwave, uncovered, on 50% power (medium) for 2 to 3 minutes or until melted, stirring once. Spread melted chocolate over caramel layer. Cover and chill for 1 to 2 hours or until firm.

5 When fudge is firm, use foil to lift out of pan. Cut into squares. Serve fudge at room temperature. Store, covered, in the refrigerator.

NUTRITION FACTS PER PIECE: 98 cal., 5 g total fat (2 g sat. fat), 4 mg chol., 29 mg sodium, 12 g carbo., 0 g fiber, 2 g pro. DAILY VALUES: 2% calcium, 1% iron

White Chocolate Fudge

Looking for a special gift to give for a birthday or the holidays?
Make a batch of this light-colored fudge loaded with coconut and toasted almonds.
Anyone with a sweet tooth will be delighted. (See photo, page 240.)

START TO FINISH: 30 minutes MAKES: 2 pounds or 36 pieces

2 cups sugar	1 teaspoon vanilla
1 cup evaporated milk	½ cup flaked coconut
½ cup butter	½ cup chopped unblanched almonds, toasted
8 ounces white chocolate baking squares, cut up	Unblanched almonds, toasted and chopped (optional)
1 cup tiny marshmallows	

1 Line an 8×8×2-inch baking pan with foil, extending foil over edges of pan. Butter the foil; set pan aside.

2 Butter sides of a heavy 3-quart saucepan. In the saucepan combine the sugar, evaporated milk, and butter. Cook and stir over medium heat until mixture boils. Clip a candy thermometer to side of pan. Cook until thermometer registers 234°, soft-ball stage (about 15 minutes), stirring frequently. Remove from heat. Add white chocolate, marshmallows, and vanilla; beat until melted. Quickly stir in coconut and the ½ cup chopped almonds. Pour into prepared pan. If desired, sprinkle with additional chopped almonds. Score into squares while warm.

3 When fudge is firm, use foil to lift it out of pan. Cut into squares. Store tightly covered.

NUTRITION FACTS PER PIECE: 132 cal., 7 g total fat (4 g sat. fat), 10 mg chol., 43 mg sodium, 17 g carbo., 0 g fiber, 1 g pro. DAILY VALUES: 2% vit. C, 3% calcium, 1% iron

INDEX

Note: Pages in italics refer to photographs.

For more recipes, visit our Recipe Center at
www.bhg.com/bhg/recipe

METRIC INFORMATION

The charts on this page provide a guide for converting measurements from the U.S. customary system, which is used throughout this book, to the metric system.

Product Differences

Most of the ingredients called for in the recipes in this book are available in most countries. However, some are known by different names. Here are some common American ingredients and their possible counterparts:

- Sugar (white) is granulated, fine granulated, or castor sugar.
- Powdered sugar is icing sugar.
- All-purpose flour is enriched, bleached or unbleached white household flour. When self-rising flour is used in place of all-purpose flour in a recipe that calls for leavening, omit the leavening agent (baking soda or baking powder) and salt.
- Light-colored corn syrup is golden syrup.
- Cornstarch is cornflour.
- Baking soda is bicarbonate of soda.
- Vanilla or vanilla extract is vanilla essence.
- Green, red, or yellow sweet peppers are capsicums or bell peppers.
- Golden raisins are sultanas.

Volume and Weight

The United States traditionally uses cup measures for liquid and solid ingredients. The chart below shows the approximate imperial and metric equivalents. If you are accustomed to weighing solid ingredients, the following approximate equivalents will be helpful.

- 1 cup butter, castor sugar, or rice = 8 ounces = $1/2$ pound = 250 grams
- 1 cup flour = 4 ounces = $1/4$ pound = 125 grams
- 1 cup icing sugar = 5 ounces = 150 grams

Canadian and U.S. volume for a cup measure is 8 fluid ounces (237 ml), but the standard metric equivalent is 250 ml.

1 British imperial cup is 10 fluid ounces.

In Australia, 1 tablespoon equals 20 ml, and there are 4 teaspoons in the Australian tablespoon.

Spoon measures are used for smaller amounts of ingredients. Although the size of the tablespoon varies slightly in different countries, for practical purposes and for recipes in this book, a straight substitution is all that's necessary. Measurements made using cups or spoons always should be level unless stated otherwise.

Common Weight Range Replacements

Imperial / U.S.	Metric
$1/2$ ounce	15 g
1 ounce	25 g or 30 g
4 ounces ($1/4$ pound)	115 g or 125 g
8 ounces ($1/2$ pound)	225 g or 250 g
16 ounces (1 pound)	450 g or 500 g
$1 1/4$ pounds	625 g
$1 1/2$ pounds	750 g
2 pounds or $2 1/4$ pounds	1,000 g or 1 Kg

Oven Temperature Equivalents

Fahrenheit Setting	Celsius Setting*	Gas Setting
300°F	150°C	Gas Mark 2 (very low)
325°F	160°C	Gas Mark 3 (low)
350°F	180°C	Gas Mark 4 (moderate)
375°F	190°C	Gas Mark 5 (moderate)
400°F	200°C	Gas Mark 6 (hot)
425°F	220°C	Gas Mark 7 (hot)
450°F	230°C	Gas Mark 8 (very hot)
475°F	240°C	Gas Mark 9 (very hot)
500°F	260°C	Gas Mark 10 (extremely hot)
Broil	Broil	Grill

*Electric and gas ovens may be calibrated using celsius. However, for an electric oven, increase celsius setting 10 to 20 degrees when cooking above 160°C. For convection or forced air ovens (gas or electric) lower the temperature setting 25°F/10°C when cooking at all heat levels.

Baking Pan Sizes

Imperial / U.S.	Metric
9×1$1/2$-inch round cake pan	22- or 23×4-cm (1.5 L)
9×1$1/2$-inch pie plate	22- or 23×4-cm (1 L)
8×8×2-inch square cake pan	20×5-cm (2 L)
9×9×2-inch square cake pan	22- or 23×4.5-cm (2.5 L)
11×7×1$1/2$-inch baking pan	28×17×4-cm (2 L)
2-quart rectangular baking pan	30×19×4.5-cm (3 L)
13×9×2-inch baking pan	34×22×4.5-cm (3.5 L)
15×10×1-inch jelly roll pan	40×25×2-cm
9×5×3-inch loaf pan	23×13×8-cm (2 L)
2-quart casserole	2 L

U.S. / Standard Metric Equivalents

$1/8$ teaspoon = 0.5 ml	
$1/4$ teaspoon = 1 ml	
$1/2$ teaspoon = 2 ml	
1 teaspoon = 5 ml	
1 tablespoon = 15 ml	
2 tablespoons = 25 ml	
$1/4$ cup = 2 fluid ounces = 50 ml	
$1/3$ cup = 3 fluid ounces = 75 ml	
$1/2$ cup = 4 fluid ounces = 125 ml	
$2/3$ cup = 5 fluid ounces = 150 ml	
$3/4$ cup = 6 fluid ounces = 175 ml	
1 cup = 8 fluid ounces = 250 ml	
2 cups = 1 pint = 500 ml	
1 quart = 1 litre	